ESCAPE FROM PARADISE

ESCAPE FROM
PARADISE

Evil and Tragedy in Feminist Theology

KATHLEEN M. SANDS

FORTRESS PRESS
MINNEAPOLIS

ESCAPE FROM PARADISE
Evil and Tragedy in Feminist Theology

Credits continued on p. vi

Cover design: Nancy Eato
Cover graphic: Georgia O'Keeffe, *Pattern of Leaves*, c. 1923, used by permission of and © The Phillips Collection, Washington.
Interior design: Peregrine Graphics Services

Library of Congress Cataloging-in-Publication Data

Sands, Kathleen M., 1954–
    Escape from paradise : evil and tragedy in feminist theology / by
Kathleen M. Sands.
        p.   cm.
    Includes index.
    ISBN 0-8006-2636-2 (alk. paper)   2002394b
    1. Feminist theology—Controversial literature.   2. Good and evil.
3. Tragic, The.   4. Ruether, Rosemary Radford.   5. Christ, Carol P.
I. Title.
BT83.55.S26   1994
231'.8'082—dc20   94-9748
                                                                   CIP

The paper used in this publication meets the minimum requirements of American National Standard for Information Services—Permanence of Paper for Printed Library Materials, ANSI Z329.48-1984.   ∞™

Manufactured in the U.S.A.   AF 1-2636

98   97   96   95   94   1   2   3   4   5   6   7   8   9   10

For my mother and father
and for Peg, Jerry, and Jim

CONTENTS

PREFACE

NO ONE wants to be a proponent of tragedy, still less of evil. I find myself engaged with these fairly unpopular themes due to a combination of personal and social history and political and intellectual passions. My own life, like most, has afforded some strong encounters with what was traditionally called natural evil, as well as confrontations with what contemporary theology calls social evil or injustice. Natural evil is usually classed as tragic, meaning that its origins are no one's particular fault, its resolution within no one's power, and its incidence, while unfortunate, unrevealing about the character of the cosmos. As such, the tragic is often thought to lack moral or theological meaning. Social evil, in contrast, is nowadays seen as culpable, changeable, and systemic rather than random in its consequences. For that reason, social evil may seem to be of more theological interest and political relevance than the third and traditionally most individualistic category of evil, that of moral evil or sin.

In my own experience, however, evil has never been divided and dispatched so easily. Up close, the brutal deaths I have witnessed from disease or accident have not felt to me like empty meaninglessness, but like terrifying truths about the chaos and impersonality of life. When I fight injustices—for example, those suffered by lesbians and gay men—I am uneasily aware that there is no higher ground from which to adjudicate the differences between me and my opponents over what is "natural" or "just"; what I judge to be culpable evil, they assess as natural good. Moreover, having been on the wrong side of what I myself regard as justice, less by deliberation and choice than by the inherited presumptions of privilege, I know the fluidity of the boundary between what is and is not culpable, and how social freedom, unexercised, cramps and atrophies like an unused muscle. And although I understand that injustice

ix

calls for systemic analysis and response, I have seen also how one by one we ratify injustices for personal gain or refuse them at personal cost. I suspect that I am not alone in being so disturbed, and that for others as for me the disturbance is not only affective; it is also cognitive, moral, and spiritual information, hard but true, about the conditions under which we must construct some goodness and sense.

The historical dimension of the disturbance, as I see it, is related to our nation's slow loss of political and economic hegemony worldwide. Already, that is causing slippages in the once secure privileges of sex, class, and race. The loss of privilege, in turn, leads to reactionary offensives against those a rung or two lower in the social hierarchy who, in more affluent times, may have been treated with better will. One such prolonged offensive is the current campaign against "political correctness," which invokes ideals of freedom and equality to oppose precisely those policies that could actually promote practical increments in freedom and equality for marginalized peoples. Although some real gains have been made for nonelite people under those liberal banners, their amenability to reactionary usage ought to give us pause. Now, with the fall of the Soviet block, the supposed death of feminism, and the anticipated demise of multicultural education, we are said to be passing beyond a benighted moment of bias and irrationality into the clear light of objectivity and freedom which is our supposed intellectual and political heritage.

Whether these liberal ideals are used for reactionary or progressive purposes, they come from a long tradition of Western rationalism in which all contradictions can be resolved by appeal to an inclusive intelligibility. Their theological provenance is the privation theory in which evil, ontologically speaking, is not a something but a nothing. Evil, in other words, is only a lack: in classical Christianity, a lack of being; in modern secularism, a lack of knowledge, freedom, or the means to them. To make war against a lack, of course, is quixotic and irrational. If evil is only absence and wrong only misunderstanding, the ideal moral and intellectual postures are not advocacy or opposition but neutrality. Neutrality, if there were such a thing, could only leave the status quo intact, and so appeals most to the satisfied. Even when appropriated by those who want change, the privation-rationalist tradition requires sufficient faith in the status quo to believe that its faults can be corrected by more rigorous or consistent application of its fundamental methods and ideals. Those of us who are seriously dissatisfied, then, need to ask whether the ideals of freedom and equality, or more recently of inclusivity and diversity, are strong enough medicine for what ails us.

On the other hand, there is a long and related dualist tradition in which evil is openly and unapologetically blamed on an Other—for example, on a sexual or racial other, an opposing political system, a devil, or even matter itself. This too is amenable to usage across the ideological spectrum, from the racial ideology of white supremacy to the conspiracy theories of the North American Left. In view of the genuinely systemic character of many injustices, and because survival and joy are needed so urgently, dualism has real attractions. But here again, there is a caution, because dualism sees no good in its enemy and, precisely in hypostatizing evil, may become unable to change it. That caution is sinking in to nonelite people, many of whom are deciding that they would gladly give up the moralistic satisfactions of powerlessness and victimization for the sake of power and struggle in all their ambiguity.

My contemplation of the tragic, not as meaningless suffering but as the conflicted context where we must create what right and reason we can, is meant to contribute something toward a more illuminating ethical discourse. I am deeply aware of the dangers of doing this, since the language of tragedy has long been associated with complacency or despair and since the heuristic strategies I propose are liable to fly right through the crude filters afforded by the existing moral rhetorics. I feel the danger especially on behalf of my feminist loyalties, which require a moral language fierce enough to indict the ancient evil of patriarchy, yet intelligible enough to be heard across the multiple boundaries that divide women from each other. The questions I pose and the suggestions I offer in regard to feminist theological foundations are meant to enhance the vitality of religious feminism as it enters the postmodern age.

Writing this book has given me occasion to grasp some of the good reasons why so many academics write only about *dead* white men. Dead men don't change or talk back; no special sensitivity is due to their feelings and no special consideration for the exigencies of their lives. In writing about Rosemary Radford Ruether and Carol P. Christ, I have chosen women who, as people go, are not merely alive but exceptionally alive. That being the case, this book even more than most cannot stand as a monument but only adds another voice to a vital, ongoing conversation. Ten years from now, this book could not be written in the same way, particularly because feminist theology and thealogy will be much more global, multiracial, and multireligious enterprises. For the moment, what can be achieved is to open theological inquiry to questions of radical difference, and it is my hope that this text will crack that door a bit wider. My greatest hope, however, is that what I have written might foster respectful, challenging, and (I still dare to say) sisterly conversation among religious feminists on the question of evil. In this second and necessarily self-reflexive generation of twentieth-century religious feminism, the quality of academic discourse will depend very substantially on how constructively we criticize each other. If there is any criticism that is less than constructive here, the fault is, of course, not in my subjects, but in my own dialogical skills.

After sketching my own theory of evil and tragedy in an initial chapter, I review the career of evil in androcentric theology, on the conviction that, to respond more fruitfully to the theological problem of evil, feminists will need to diagnose it more closely. In a third and central chapter, I sketch an overview of evil in religious feminism, highlighting both challenges and continuities with evil in the malestream. Turning then to Carol Christ and Rosemary Ruether, I examine their respective positions on Goddess spirituality and patriarchal religion as illustrations of feminist efforts to make meaning of the most ancient suffering of women. The following chapters offer appreciative critiques of the theology of Ruether and the thealogy of Christ. Ruether's work, I argue, exemplifies certain moral and intellectual advantages of rationalism, while Christ's work offers the mystical and aesthetic gains of feminist romantic dualism. Both, however, are limited by certain continuities with the anti-tragic strains in the androcentric tradition, continuities that might be fruitfully pruned within the framework of their own intellectual commitments. In a final chapter, I reflect on four pieces of women's literature in order to suggest some of the theological gains that a tragic heuristic might yield.

Many people have assisted me with this project. Francine Cardman, S. Mark Heim, Flora Keshgegian, and Ellen Ross offered extensive support for my initial theological forays into evil. Margaret R. Miles, Judith Plaskow, Susan B. Thistlethwaite, and Emilie M. Townes provided cogent and constructive criticism of this manuscript, for which I am deeply grateful. Martin Andic, Richard Horsley, Jean Humez, Michael La Fargue, and other colleagues at the University of Massachusetts, Boston, have generously heard me out on some of the topics discussed here; I have benefited from their questions and insight. A number of friends have also read parts of this manuscript with great care and their support, both intellectual and emotional, has been my mainstay. I thank in particular Laura Briggs, Lisa Greber, Kathleen Henry, Mykel Johnson, Leona Leven, Deborah Schwartz, and Jessica Shubow. To all, my heartfelt thanks.

—*Kathleen M. Sands*

CHAPTER ONE

A MERMAID IN THE SHIP'S CABIN
TRAGIC CONSCIOUSNESS AS A
HEURISTIC FOUNDATION FOR THEOLOGY

> *When we did come home, Sylvie would certainly be*
> *home, too, enjoying the evening, for so she described*
> *her habit of sitting in the dark. Evening was her*
> *special time of day. She gave the word three syllables,*
> *and indeed I think she liked it so well for its tendency*
> *to smooth, to soften. She seemed to dislike the*
> *disequilibrium of counterpoising a roomful of light*
> *against a worldful of darkness. Sylvie in a house was*
> *more or less like a mermaid in a ship's cabin. She*
> *preferred it sunk in the very element it was meant to*
> *exclude. We had crickets in the pantry, squirrels in the*
> *eaves, sparrows in the attic. Lucille and I stepped*
> *through the door from sheer night to sheer night.*
> —*Marilynne Robinson*, Housekeeping[1]

NOW, IN the Evening of the Enlightenment, as the inflowing of the excluded tears modernity from its moorings, it may be time again to learn in darkness. From the rich and pregnant darkness of the present post-age, a long procession of the demonized, subjugated, and forgotten is emerging. What has been called "evil" fights back and demands a place; what has been called "bias" asserts itself as knowledge and presumes to teach. The earth itself protests the rapacious devolution that has destroyed irreplaceable life-forms and depleted vital resources.

Flooded with elements it was meant to exclude, theology too is catching its death. In post-time, there will be no clean or peaceful resurrection. What survives will be as disruptive as the beggars at the wedding banquet, as disturbing as the footprints of the past in this morning's snow,[2] as magical as the mermaid in the ship's cabin, drowned but still alive. In the shrinking light, the ultimate defeat of evil, irrationality, and death shows itself to have been a bad dream. Immersed in negativity, we may yet awaken to a better one.

The difficulty of speaking of tragedy in the language of the Christian theological tradition is a measure of the deadening distance that has grown up between theology and religious experience. It is also the mark of tragedy itself. Tragic speech is scarring speech, speech to be performed with ritual caution and fear. Tragic speech is about irrecoverable loss and irresolvable contradiction. But it is not about nothing. The wound is not nothing. It cannot be fixed or stopped from meaning. It goes on meaning, as the metaphor goes on meaning, as the blood goes on flowing. Here, in the central enigmas of life, even absence is not nothing; it can seduce and possess us.

The language of tragedy dispossesses us of the Logos of Theo, insofar as that Logos has served to fix meaning on an Absolute referent and to cover up the absence that is tragedy. Properly speaking, the language of that tradition cannot say what it is missing. But speaking improperly, we may slip between the elements and into the ship's cabin, where the God who was beyond question may be uncovered as absent.

* * *

Two patterns for the interpretation of evil can be identified within Western Christian theology, neither of which should be assumed to reflect the attitudes or practices of Christian women and nonelite Christian men. I will call the more predominant and official of these patterns "rationalism" and its shadow "dualism." The names are asymmetrical and nonoppositional because, in relation to the tragic, they describe complementary amnesic strategies. Rationalist interpretations of evil are moved by the passion to render reality as a single intelligible whole; dualist interpretations are moved by a hunger for a pure and unmixed good. True understanding and right action, intelligibility and innocence—these twin passions guard the gates of Christian paradise against incursions of the tragic.

In the classical Christian era, rationalist responses to evil grew from the Platonic view of being as good and evil as nonbeing. As a complete lack of goodness, which would also amount to complete unintelligibility, evil could not exist; quite literally, it had nothing for its ontological referent. The notions of superior and inferior forms of beings, however, did refer to something: the supposed natural inequality of created goods, expressed in the Neoplatonic metaphor of an organic chain in which degrees of goodness were at the same time degrees of being. Ontic privation established the possibility of moral evil or error, in which contingent beings strangely attempted to rebel against the inviolable order of being. Though capable of wreaking havoc on each other, contingent beings remained fundamentally oriented toward the good. For Christian rationalism, moral evil was, at least in principle, never beyond comprehension or rehabilitation. To make sense of evil was to make good of it, and to make good was to reestablish the hierarchical order proper to unequal things.

For the secular elites of modernity, the principle of intelligibility no longer needs religious or ontological justification. They place methodical Reason on the old throne of Being and make metaphysics surrender to epistemology as the warrant for certitude. Objectivity and universality become their justificatory discourse; dominative power is made to seem neutral insofar as it approaches universality, and good insofar as it passes for neutral. The very word *evil* is jettisoned, the ontological notion of nonbeing having become methodologically unintelligible. *Bias*, however, takes evil's nonposition and like evil serves to erase its subjects. Just as evil had been a false appearance with no autonomous raison d'être, so bias becomes a futile rebellion against Reason's rule. Rehabilitation is still enforced through the reestablishment of a propriety deemed inviolable, and the rationale for suppressing resistance is still the assumption that fundamental contradictions or conflicting orders do not really exist.[3]

In dualistic patterns of thought, reality is construed as a battlefield between good and evil. This *moral* division of reality has been the key to the ontological divisions that dualism also entails—for example, between spirit and matter, nature and civilization, or female and male. The moral *valuations* of ontological divisions may therefore be reversed without mitigating the dualistic structure of moral interpretation.[4] By distinguishing the true from the good and the rational from the real, dualism provides ideological frameworks for strategies of withdrawal, resistance, and destruction. Dualistic patterns of thought are at work whenever evil is apprehended as generating its own counterreality and counterintelligibility. For the dualist, evil does have a distinct raison d'être and cannot be comprehended in terms of the Good. Instead, one must "just say no." Change is effected by the dramatic reorientation of a determinative part—in the individual, by conversion of will, affect, or behavior; in society, by revolution or apocalypse; epistemically, by revelation or gnosis.

While enabling different responses to evil, these two patterns of thought remain, from the viewpoint of what they exclude, entirely interdependent. Under pressure, rationalism splits into dualism; at ease, dualism softens into rationalism. Always, one pattern shadows the other. Christian theological accounts of evil fancy themselves efforts to spurn the twin heresies of Pelagian rationalism and Manichaean dualism but in fact reel between them, tracing the circuit between metaphysical dualism and a single, absolutely transcendent Good. The Oneness of classical rationalism always depended on its Others, since despite the gradations of being, the categorical chasm between necessary Being and contingent beings could never be crossed. Western methodical Reason, too, needs the disparate intelligibilities it encounters worldwide; only by dominating these subaltern "reasons" can Reason's claim to superiority be secured. The circuit can be completed from the other side as well. The twoness of dualism, classical and modern, always remembered a single Good as the primal reality or anticipated its victory as the ultimate end. If for the dualist evil has a reality and intelligibility of its own, it is only a *counter*reality and *counter*intelligibility, unequal to the Good in power, worth, or sheer durability.

Each of these patterns of thought has much to commend it. At least for parts of the world, modern rationalism has produced authentic intellectual, political, and technical gains. Thinking well of things is often the least destructive strategy for making them well, and as distressing as the world is, our basic stance toward it must be one of affirmation. Dualism, too, has its compelling claims, which we feel when faced with entrenched hatred, violence, and injustice. All these forms of negativity, while initially rooted in responses that may have protected something good, can develop lives and logics of their own. Contemplating the awful histories of racism, class oppression, or misogyny, in regard to which nothing less than unequivocal condemnation is morally sufficient, the interpretation of evil as self-destructive appears intolerably tolerant. Both the moral repudiation of evil and its intellectual comprehension are praiseworthy responses in their appropriate contexts, and it is meaningful to distinguish between these responses. At the same time, there are also practical and theoretical reasons for noting, across the distinctions, a common reduction of the human good, which is richer than One and riskier than Two. Just as the navel is a sign of common humanity, so the wound of tragedy carries clues about the openings and vulnerabilities that define our moral lives.

Martha Nussbaum has made this argument in a persuasive way, against the anti-tragic position of the middle-period Plato.[5] Plato objected to tragic dramas for promoting the erroneous view that the human good can be undermined by *tuchē*, the chaotic force of circumstance. For Plato, the goal of moral education was just the opposite: to dispel the illusion of tragic conflict, lifting people beyond the world of corruption and change to contemplate the incorruptible, intelligible Good for which all human desires reach. Following Aristotle, Nussbaum countered that tragedies are crucial for moral education, precisely because distinctively human kinds of goodness are *not* invulnerable to circumstance. Since humans are relational and not fully self-sufficient, passionate and not simply rational, the effort to make ourselves morally invulnerable is paradoxically *de*humanizing. Human goodness, as Nussbaum observed with Pindar, is more like a plant than like a jewel. Living, complex, and delicate, humankind cannot partake of the more tenacious stability of the inorganic or the Ideal.

If rationalism and dualism are complementary responses to evil, tragedy chastens the latter as well. On the face of it, dualistic interpretations of evil bear a greater kinship to tragic sensibility: like the Greek tragedian, the dualist sees conflicts that are irresolvable and not merely apparent. But a hallmark of tragedy was the accusation of the deities, and here dualist patterns of thought are especially well-insulated. The Being who presides over degrees of being is at least responsible for permitting evil, but pure Goodness has no intercourse with its opposite. While rationalism discerns something to rehabilitate in what we call evil, dualism sees nothing at all to save in the rejected Other, and nothing to mourn when it is destroyed. No better than the One can the Two name the existential manyness of which tragedies speak so eloquently. Each, in its different circumstances, covers the absence and silences the grief that is tragedy.

Like the suppression of plurality, the negation of tragedy has had far more than intellectual consequences. The interpretation of evil influences what a people can and cannot desire, remember, and protest. It circumscribes methods of communal self-defense and self-critique; it marks enemies and sets policies for their reformation, suppression, or destruction. In Western Christianity, these consequences have been sharply felt by women, who have been symbolically associated with evil both as the demonic Other and as the rebellious inferior.[6] Patriarchal rationalism, which accords women a measure of goodness in their place, has some appeal to elite women, who may be allowed to imitate the purportedly higher values associated with maleness and thereby gain more direct access to male privilege. However, under any serious threat to patriarchal hegemony—for example, female reproductive freedom—rationalistic egalitarianism readily gives way to the demonization of women. Then, tenuously privileged women are forced to remember the demonization that is the normal status of women as beings who are wont to act with unnatural autonomy, who will not dance in the chain of being, or who cannot be "whitewashed" or neutralized. Even in rationalistic patriarchal minds, women are easily transmogrified from patronized inferiors to threatening monsters. Correlatively, patriarchal dualism cannot afford to forget the dependence of male life on the subjugated female and therefore must hold women in a state of abjection rather than eradicate us entirely.

*   *   *

> Is there no means to speak us fair, and yet tell the truth?
> It will not hide, when truth and good are torn asunder.[7]

Today, the emergence of women and nonelite men as theological subjects is exposing rationalistic and dualistic responses to evil as what Audre Lorde called "tools of the master." Such tools, she believed, could not "dismantle the master's house."[8] I am not so sure of that, but I am sure that they cannot build a shelter big enough for the rest of us. Theological responses to evil must be measured in relation to these emerging subjects, since it is in relation to the political crises of postmodernity that its intellectual crises gain their full theological significance.

In both dimensions, the postmodern problem of evil is more extreme than the sense of tragedy explicated by Nussbaum under the aegis of her liberal democratic politics.[9] Once society is apprehended as a network of diverse and often conflicting powers, tragic conflict becomes a routine function of social contradiction, not just an anomaly of social collapse. Once the social determination of knowledge is grasped not as a falsification but as a diversification of truth, there is no hiding the categorical difference between the true and the good. And once it is understood that what seemed like neutrality was actually a vote for the status quo, then we are forced more than ever to take sides, yet less equipped than ever to metaphysically indemnify the sides we take. In the postmodern moment, tragic conflicts do not just mark the borders of our lives but riddle them through and through. Now, nonelites within every border are breaking the illusion of self-evidence that so often surrounds hegemonic ethics and rationalties. What is passing, in postmodernity, is the time when people could credibly attribute to first principles, to ethics, or to God what *we* choose and what *we* do to each other in the rough and bloody theatre of history. Posted at the boundaries of this era is a warning that nowhere within it can we hope to encounter truth and goodness unaccompanied by the most profound questions about violence, conflict, and loss.

Speech is riddled with the same difficulty. All words establish what they name, but in the linguistic propriety of the Christian theological tradition, what evil and tragedy have established is a netherworld of prohibition. Evil, as Nonbeing or the utterly rejected Other, has served to institutionalize various forms of existence in the state of abjection. If the Good was necessary Being, evil was in effect *necessary Nonbeing* or *necessary Counterbeing* that stood in relation to the Good as the outside to the inside, the Other to the Self, dispossession to possession. The word *evil* itself marked the narrow passageway to the prohibited regions; as long as it could be spoken, the forbidden could not be entirely forgotten. So with the language of tragedy, which in the theological tradition could only refer to a worldview conquered by faith, and which for that reason had to be prohibited even more severely.

Today the embarrassed avoidance of the language of evil among liberal intellectuals signals the neutralization of Others as much as their inclusion and displays liberalism's reluctance to oppose injustice as much as its political optimism. When the tragic chorus is pushed off history's stage, irresolvable conflicts do not cease; they simply become invisible. When evil as a *heuristic* language is abandoned by progressives, then moral language loses its interrogative edge and begins to occlude inquiry and communication. Only if it were possible to live entirely without limits, prohibitions, and conflicts could we do without the language of evil, and only when limits, conflicts, and prohibitions are accepted without protest or regret do we forget the language of tragedy. These, unfortunately, have become the functions of the language of evil in theology today, where its avoidance usually signals the denial of limits and its usage draws an impermeable battle line. No longer opening even the smallest of passages between worlds, it sits like a stone in the mouth of a tomb, sealing off disturbance and blocking illumination.

It may be that Christian theology and modernity have together rendered the language of evil and tragedy so opaque that it will take other words to call forth the lost and vanquished. But since the negation of evil and tragedy, far from opening the needed inquiry, has served rather to obstruct it, there is no avoiding the words themselves. I use them, here and throughout, with ritual caution, conscious of how their history has problematized them. I use them as ways of letting in creative disturbance and lending voice to silenced questions. If these words are to be "right," they must be divested of their propriety, used not to fix certainty but to break it, not to stabilize meaning but to undock it from absolutes.

This divestment consists first of all in reconceptualizing the relationship between moral and ontological judgments. In the anti-tragic theological tradition, the former are simply ratifications of the latter, affirming what is ultimately real and negating what is ultimately unreal. When the possibility of tragic conflict is admitted, however, moral judgments are understood to add to ontological judgments an intention to affirm and nurture or to negate and destroy. Positive moral judgments are *ontologically creative* judgments, and negative moral judgments are *ontologically destructive*.

Evil, as I use the term, is a negative moral judgment, but it is predicated on a positive ontological judgment. To pronounce something evil is to establish its existence, even while that existence is protested, resisted, refused, or terminated. Evil is not that which destroys itself but the decision to destroy; not that which is unintelligible but that which we may understand and yet refuse; not that which lacks being but the willful destruction or suppression of being.

Much of what has been called "the mystery of evil" seems rather to be a mystification of ontological and evaluative judgments in their distinctiveness and in their interrelations. The postmodern moment has affected some demystification in this regard, but it has also suffused the heavens with its own kind of fog. Postmodernity problematizes or even reverses the classical Christian derivation of the moral from the ontic, hypothesizing instead that values, interests, and desires produce rather than reflect truth. That hypothesis also destabilizes the modern *episteme*, which had founded its claims to objective knowledge on the separability of truth and values. Moreover, postmodern thought shows that since interests, values, and desires are plural, truths can no longer be meaningfully regarded as One, a line of reasoning that sometimes issues in radical ontological relativism.

While I accept postmodern sensibilities about the creativity of desire and the plurality of truth, radical ontological relativism is not a position I want to espouse. I do not see all differences as the same, evaluatively speaking, and I do not conclude from the plurality of truth that there are no limits on what can be true. In fact, radical ontological relativism seems to me a vestige of the metaphysical dualism in which limitation applies only to the illusion of fixity called "nature," but not to language or sociality. It is a vestige, too, of the ancient conflation of the good and the true, only with a reversed order of derivation, so that it is desire which produces truth rather than the other way around.

Conceived more dialectically, all judgments—of truth as well as of value—might be imaged as part of a mirror dance between the human knower and the rest of the world. In such a dance, every movement on either side is at once a reflection and an innovation. Neither partner stands to the other as the original to the image, but each holds the other in moving relation. Ontological judgments, as I understand them, concern the structures of relationality, while moral judgments struggle and innovate in the space between relatives. The difference between these types of judgments, then, is not that the former are objective and the latter subjective, or that the former are universal and the latter particular. Both are bound to the conditions and limitations of consciousness as socially constructed, and both, like sociality, are bound within the parameters of the biosphere. But those ties are not so tight as to prevent innovation or error. Within constraint there is room to create and room to fail; for better and for worse, human judgment partakes of those possibilities.

What, then, is the difference between ontological and moral judgments? The difference, simply put, is *evil*—the negative moral judgments that set one's face against some part of life. *Tragedy*, as I understand it, is the inevitability of our involvement in evil, an inevitability that comes fully into focus only in a world unclouded by spiritual infinitism. In this world, where there is multiplicity but not infinity, where difference is beheld without the leveling horizon of eternity, there can be no delusion of sheer acceptance. In a radically plural and often conflicted world, we cannot be for everything and what we are against has a cost. Tragedy infects moral life with fault, and it troubles intellectual life with absurdity, since without negative moral judgments the plurality of truth would be benign and acceptable. Were there nothing in the world to protest or refuse, there would be no difference between saying that X exists and that X is good; even if one admitted a variety of truths or goods, one would not have to stand against any of them. In that case, tolerance might suffice for ethics and the will to inclusivity might suffice for knowledge. Today, however, those liberal strategies and their postmodern descendants are collapsing into their own logical circularity, unable to illuminate the depths of contemporary struggles over what is and shall be true. Those struggles are not of something against nothing, not of tolerance against intolerance or of bias against truth, but of power against power, truth against truth.

Moral judgments are rooted in the interests of real persons and communities; this much ontic basis we cannot do without. But ontic basis is not ontological justification, for if moral creativity is not *from nothing*, neither is moral negation *of nothing*. Growing from some part of what is, yet standing against other parts, negative moral judgments crack and riddle the world, exposing the places where regional intelligibilities cannot be made to agree or where various interests cannot be harmonized. Those are the places where the most profound ontological and moral questions—and the most profound theological questions—arise. For what is Truth if truths can conflict? And what is Good if goods are at odds?

By suppressing the tragic, the Christian theological tradition supplants these questions with the a priori assumption that truth and goodness, despite all contrary appearances, are ultimately one and the same. Theology is indeed "grounded" on this assumption and to this extent diminishes to faith-*stopping*-understanding; where God is invoked, there inquiry ends. But theology is not alone in its inability to think about evil. For the academy as a whole, thought clots where truths and values diverge, where epistemic paradigms cease to live peacefully side by side and begin to fight for each other's terrains. To stand over the cracks of intelligibility and there to think, to position oneself where values collide and there to discern—these, I believe, could be among the distinctive contributions of theology to the moral and intellectual quality of life. But to take up these tasks, we will have again to encounter the tragic.

Tragedies, as I define them, are stories or ways of telling stories that highlight elemental conflicts of truths, which I also call conflicts of powers. Elemental powers, in this definition, are the vital, integral dimensions of life in a particular context. They need not be permanent or eternal, and they are never beyond question. Tragedies illuminate the way in which such elemental conflicts afflict humanity with evil—that is, with negative moral judgments in which some elemental power must be opposed. In so doing, tragedies force their observers, both the inner ring or dramatic chorus and the outer ring or audience, to make their own judgments about the judgments of the tragic characters. Through confrontation with elemental conflict, the community can season its moral wisdom, sounding existential conflicts for their relative depths, discarding facile or immature solutions, and, right within the narrow horizon of the possible, identifying acts and attitudes that warrant praise or blame.

These definitions of tragedy and the tragic are intended more prescriptively than descriptively. While partly inspired by Greek tragedies, they are not an endorsement of those texts or a renewal of the ancient theological debate between Athens and Jerusalem. Nor would I nominate Greek tragedies for emerging feminist canons of women's sacred stories. To be sure, remarkable women are found in the Greek tragedies as remnants of Bronze Age mythology, contorted perhaps by the misogynist anxieties of the fifth-century poets. But when I refer to elemental conflicts of goods, I do not have in mind, say, the choice between the citizen's supposed duty to make war and the parental duty not to murder one's daughter! The significance of Greek tragedies lies neither in the specific stories they recount nor in the specific questions they raise, but in their rendering of religious myth as *heuristic drama* in which moral questions can be directed to elemental power. That significance is historical as well, since it was over against those dramas that Christian theology via Plato framed its own suppression of the tragic.[10]

In commending theological attention to the tragic, I am proposing a style of theology that is founded more on questions than on speculative or doctrinal claims. Tragedies foreclose the faith that forecloses questioning. Instead, they find every form of conflict and suffering *question-worthy* and *wonder-worthy*, especially those that present themselves as elemental and immovable. The Christian theological tradition, with its severe religious inhibitions about raising fundamental questions regarding elemental power, has been largely unable to grasp the educational and transformative functions of a tragic sensibility. Separated from its heuristic aims and aesthetic forms, tragedy is cast as a worldview rather than a world-questioning, and a pessimistic, complacent worldview at that. In contrast, of course, the superiority of Christian faith could appear self-evident. But tragedy in the fuller sense, as a judgment that generates questions and a question that generates judgments, has rarely been allowed to enter the theological scene.

Since not every conflict in our lives is of elemental magnitude, not every human story is tragic. In general, we ought not to expect every creative moral judgment to be equally destructive; there are plenty of moral roads-not-taken that can be nonetheless affirmed as choice-worthy, and plenty of elemental powers that are not incompatible. The same can be said of goods. Though some are both vital and incommensurable, many others exist in patterns of relationship that do permit commensuration. It is the possibility rather than the actuality of tragedy that must always be affirmed, just as what must always be negated is not transcendence as such but the illusion that circumstance can be transcended absolutely.

Tragic conflicts are not everywhere, but everywhere absolutes are absent. Not every human lifeboat is in a raging storm just now, but we are always, all of us, unmoored. Once we admit, for example, that food, shelter, jobs, health, and political self-determination are integral and indispensable to any good that deserves to be called human, then we must also admit that the human has always been an endangered species. Liberation theologies, in their focus on such concrete goods, sense the tragic implications of human physicality but are less attuned to the tragic dimensions of sociality. If society is torn by profound conflicts, and if character and consciousness are socially constructed, then human desire, affectivity, creativity, and intelligence are all subject to damage and defacement due to circumstances that, at least in the present, remain beyond our individual or even collective control. Not only are these distinct powers and goods separately vulnerable; so is our ability to weave them into some integral whole that does more good than harm. Not even the rudiments of morality—our powers to value, choose, and integrate goods—can root securely in the rocky peaks and precipices of history.

We see this tragic vulnerability best in what are called "extreme circumstances," for example in the morally repugnant choices people had to make in the Nazi death camps. William Styron's *Sophie's Choice* is a riveting fictional illustration.[11] What makes the story tragic is not only Sophie's horrible relinquishment of her daughter, but the way in which this forced and unimaginably cruel choice had the power to scar her spirit. Guilt was spread on Sophie like ashes, and that defilement was itself a murderous injustice against her. In principle her suicide was no more inevitable than was her social isolation. But people live *in practice*, not in principle, and in practice ordinary people make spirit-scarring choices every day. Abused women and children, in order to survive, may compromise their own dignity or offer their abuser other victims in their stead. In my city and many others, adolescent boys are routinely forced either to consider killing each other or to feel defenseless against the violence around them. Examples could be multiplied indefinitely. Tragedy speaks to extreme circumstances, but in practice extreme circumstances are not rare.

Religious stories are the stories with which a community makes a world and thereby marks the extremities of its circumstances—its origins and limits, its characteristic wounds and strengths. In a postmodern context, any such world is one among many, and its deities, no matter how imperialistically construed, are strictly local. Different worlds abut now in unprecedented ways, and worlds previously thought of as one fracture as subjugated knowledges stir. In the fractures and at the borders, the costs of a world become visible. We are reminded that to use resources, especially of the nonrenewable kind, is to deny them to others; to nurture any particular community as one's own is to deny that intensity of care to others; to stand for any concrete moral norms is to oppose moral claims that others find legitimate and compelling. We cannot live without borders and their costs, but we can expand what philosopher Philip Hallie calls the "spaces in the food web,"[12] by questioning the borders and extremities of our lives.

A conventional and often theological way of closing the question of tragedy is the argument that there is "more" good than evil in the world, as if good and evil were quantities that could be weighed on opposite sides of the same scale. Of course, this convention depends entirely upon perspective, since "more" or "less" appear differently, depending on how wide a sample is taken and on what is counted as good or evil. An optimistic calculus may appeal best to those who even now can count their profits and who can afford to discount losses which, for those who suffer them, are incalculable. No quantitative judgment could ever account for even a single domestic murder or political torture, though such events happen every day. Even one such common truth is enough to tear the moral universe, disclosing the difference between truth and goodness as categorical rather than coincidental. To speak that difference, to speak evil, is intellectually and morally repulsive. Tragic conflicts expose the limits of the principle of noncontradiction and they efface all innocence, human and divine. Tragic judgments are bewildering and defiling, and this, at the common extremities of life, is the cost of moral consciousness.

The tragic heuristic I propose is not a new universal or a new justificatory metanarrative, but a set of questions that may prove telling for those who must learn to live beyond the privileges and presumptions of modernity. Theology that attends to the tragic situates itself like a chorus on the heuristic edge of a community's narrative praxis. Part of the story and implicated in it, theology can transform religious narrative from justificatory theodicy to educational ritual. Since the conflicts that move stories are more than intellectual, a theology attentive to tragedy must be fertilized by the community's experience of power and piety, its art and expression, and its moral wisdom. Within a community and participating in its vital functions, however, the theologian's distinctive function is to raise critical questions. Subject both to the constraints of her story and to critical review by a wider audience, the theologian helps mediate the relationship between her world and others. Holding open a margin of questionability and transformation within religious stories, we can make the cracks and borders more telling, so that our and other stories might move forward in less tragic fashion.

The first demand of a tragic sensibility upon theology, then, is that we name the site of theological reflection as some particular community, embattled and complex as most communities are. To speak to a community, the theologian must herself be informed by the stories that shape the community's judgments and sensibilities. But the theologian should also raise questions about how our stories can deform us, how our particular sensibilities may render us insensitive or callous in regard to neighboring particularities. These questions need to be raised especially on behalf of the very nearest neighbors, the subjugated or marginated subgroups within what dominant people think of as a single community.

Voicing the questions of the silenced and marginalized, theology can also question the way the heroes of a religious story are conventionally identified. For example, women are rarely designated as heroes in canonical, conventional stories. Instead, as Catherine Keller has observed, they are fixed like Penelope as the still point from which male heroes wander and to which they must return.[13] When women do act as life-creating and life-negating agents, they become for men like Medusa or Medea, monsters rather than heroes. Attending to contradictions from the viewpoint of that sex which, as Luce Irigaray writes, is neither one nor two,[14] theology will have to reject male-defined individuality as the locus of heroism and instead focus jointly on separation and connection as the processes in which praiseworthy and blameworthy choices are made.

Tragedies involve at least three functions that play a part in any vital religious life and that therefore must play a part in any adequate theology—the mystical or illuminative, the aesthetic or expressive, and the moral or transformative. Attending to the tragic, theology would have to include each of these functions, while sharpening each with critical skill.

The mystical function of religious stories, when read with a sense of the tragic, represents a major challenge to Christian theism with its identification of power and goodness. Since Immanuel Kant, the speculative welding of power and goodness via theodicy has been largely abandoned. But that by itself does not place theology closer to religious experience; for Kant and his theological descendants, religion was reduced to moral will and its transcendental conditions. Profound religious experience cannot be had when the elemental powers of the real are apprehended only through the filter of moral idealism. In the bounded space of ritual, there must be an encounter with the energies that shape our lives for good and ill, so that we can draw on their powers and be illuminated as to their dangers.

Tragedies, however, do more than name and honor the deities; they also permit their indictment. If as postmoderns we are learning to think of our deities as our own creation, tragic consciousness stands as a reminder of how creativity itself gets out of our hands, how sociality is as much a condition of blindness and constraint as a promise of freedom and enlightenment. Like the divine, sociality is both within and beyond our control. The heuristic purpose of tragedy is to discern in the moment and for particular historical agents what is within our control and what is not, forming responsible judgments on the one side while holding compassion and desire open to what remains beyond.

Elemental power, as I have defined it, floods any hard and fast conceptual boundary between the "natural" and the "social." In a theology sensitive to the tragic, conceptual resolution is replaced with a demand for practical discernment, which directs us to look on every side for creativity within constraint. The bad news of the tragic is that we have no nature more incorruptible than our chameleon sociality, and that it is therefore no longer meaningful to construe evil as unnatural. But the good news is that we may begin to imagine all of life as partaking in consciousness, capable of suffering, generating creativity, holding memories, nurturing individuality, weaving connections—all in multiple and often contradictory ways.

In their aesthetic functions, religious stories appeal to the affective and expressive powers of a community. The aesthetic expression of conflict discloses patterns of integration that would never be evident to analytical reason alone. Art, as Alice Walker said of her mother, "makes a way out of no way."[15] Art stretches the cramped world, colors the black and white, and teaches even grief to sing. Although theologians need not be artists, nor need we be mystics, we must be personally connected to these vital functions, ourselves touched by the beauties and charged with the elemental powers of life in our communal context. Beyond that, a theology attentive to the tragic must also reflect on the affective disturbance we feel about the beauties that blossom in the sharp fissures of life. In *Beloved*, Toni Morrison's character Sethe remembers with horror the beauty of the sycamore trees in which black children hung.[16] There is a certain shame in bearing the beauty of such a violent world, and if beauty is not to numb us we need to keep that wound open. In a world where children hang, the only beauty we can have must come, like Sethe's, from growing into our scars. Theology needs to articulate both the scarring and the healing powers of the aesthetic, avoiding on the one hand an amoral aestheticism and on the other hand a moralistic disrespect for the autonomy of art as a differentiated function of community.

The moral or transformative functions of religious stories are those that integrate the vital functions of community life into a viable whole. It is moral sensitivity and moral judgment that distinguish tragedy from misfortune, just as it is beauty that sets the tragedy apart from the morality play. Tragedy raises radical questions to the Platonic and Kantian notions of the moral good as absolute and unconditional. Moral judgments, in a tragic context, are not apprehensions of an unconditional good; they are strategic, contextual judgments about how the diverse goods of life might best be integrated and unnecessary suffering minimized in a particular place and moment. Moral skill relies not only on understanding of the good; it also needs the insight and power that come from contact with the elementally real, and it needs the heart-stretching that comes from the creation and expression of beauty.

In the tragic heuristic I propose, moral judgment is wrenched beyond its conventional limits and dislodged from any secure metaphysical or transcendental grounds. It was for just this reason that Plato and, following him, Augustine, reacted to tragic dramas with such profound moral disgust. Tragedies often center on the awful enigma of nonculpable fault, which deflates the sails of morality and paralyzes movement until responsibility for evil is borne. Within the Christian theological tradition, original sin and fallenness are the vestiges of nonculpable fault. But their tragic character is sanitized and resolved by placing fallenness between an original paradise and a perfect ending, when the guilty conditions of human existence will be no more. In an age of ecological disaster and nuclearism, we have seen that the end can truly draw near, and that it comes as a threat rather than a promise. Now the moral task can only be that of making the world go on. In a world of suffering and radical conflict, making the world go on is not an innocent faith, but a *practice* of compassion. To honor the plurality of truth is a practice of intellectual compassion; to honor the plurality of values is a practice of moral compassion. Were it a faith, compassion might seem to save us from the guilt of negating and destroying, but as a practice within a tragic world, it does not. But in the negating and the destroying, compassion holds open a space of memory and of longing—not an infinite space, but larger than the local world and its presiding deities. Such a compassion is a wound, but such a wound is a lure to healing.

Immersed in living community and partaking critically of its vital functions, a theology sensitive to the tragic might speak in ways that cross more worlds. In the worlds where theology has grown so far, however, the tragic is still mostly hidden. Entering those worlds and searching for what is absent, we may discern the sites where a healing disturbance gathers to reemerge.

CHAPTER TWO

THE ONE AND THE OTHER
THE CAREER OF EVIL IN
ANDROCENTRIC THEOLOGY

> *But I asked further: "Who made me? Was it not my*
> *God, who is not only Good but Goodness itself? Who*
> *was it that set and ingrafted in me this root of*
> *bitterness, since I was wholly made by my most loving*
> *God? If the devil is the author, where does the devil*
> *come from? And if by his own perverse will he was*
> *turned from a good angel into a devil, what was the*
> *origin in him of the perverse will by which he became*
> *a devil, since by the all-good Creator he was made*
> *wholly angel?" By such thoughts I was cast down*
> *again and almost stifled; yet I was not brought down*
> *so far as the hell of that error, where no man confesses*
> *to you, the error which holds rather that you suffer evil*
> *than that man does it.*
>
> *—Augustine of Hippo*[1]

MORE THAN any other single figure, Augustine created the dominant
Christian way of telling the story of evil, and in his *Confessions* that story
was stamped in an enduringly androcentric form. Christian theology is
still entangled in the consequences of that, as in the rationalism and
dualism that were thoroughly intertwined in Augustine's life and thought.
The theological tradition, in its apologetic propriety, has typically credited
Augustine with synthesizing a middle position against the complementary
heresies of Pelagianism and Manichaeism. Within the parameters of his
own experience, Augustine's position was indeed philosophically deft
and introspectively profound. From the viewpoints of the improper and
the dispossessed, however, he represents both the insights of androcentric Western Christian theology and its characteristic blindness.

17

It was Neoplatonic rationalism that enabled Augustine to define sin as a perverse imitation of God, on the theory that only the good can be desired. His repudiation of Manichaean dualism was founded on this identification of sin as a disorientation of desire and his rejection of the view of evil as a distinct substance. Though sexual negativism continued to pervade the feeling and tone of his theology, Augustine was fully *intellectually* converted to the view of the body and the material world as good in their proper places. Contemplating God on analogy with the human mind, he grasped and rejected the implicit materialism of the dualistic view of spirit. Far from negating created beings, he concluded, Divine Being holds them in place. Augustine ordered these places hier- archically, on the premise that every existing thing has a measure of goodness that is equivalent to its measure of being. When things are kept in their appropriate places, desire moves upward through the chain of being to its divine source and goal. Sin, as the desire to violate this inviolable order, is fundamentally irrational and can result only in frus- tration and suffering.[2]

While Neoplatonic rationalism addressed Augustine's intellectual dis- satisfaction with Manichaean dualism, it did not address his moral dis- satisfaction with the real power that evil, in the form of sin, exerts over the human will. Sin, he concluded, must create its own perverse chain, in which the will is paralyzed rather than conducted toward God. "Be- cause my will was perverse it changed to habit, and habit not resisted became necessity."[3] Margaret R. Miles has effectively employed the con- temporary notion of addiction as an analogue for the sinful will as ex- perienced by Augustine.[4] While initially free and aiming at the good, sinful desire takes on an inner compulsion, and freedom contracts toward the vanishing point. Sin becomes its own worst punishment, miserably weld- ing desire to frustration and covering reason itself with a congenital cloak of ignorance.[5]

Augustine's moral dissatisfaction with rationalism and his intellectual dissatisfaction with dualism meant that he could never fully relinquish either. Of their unofficial cohabitation the twin doctrines of an original sin and a fallen world were born. The fact that evil, while ultimately nonexistent, appears in sin as an autonomous force indicated to Augustine the penultimacy of the world as we have it. This Nonbeing of evil is implicit in the anomie of the sinful will. Against the Manichees, Augustine argued that sin is not the preference for a single evil over a single Good, but an incoherent multiplicity of desire that left one virtually unable to will at all. His discussion of the bound will was meant to serve more as a description than an explanation of this alienation in which human beings are captured from birth.[6] Augustine did not blame the problem on the lower reaches of being; they remained good in their proper places. Yet in the fallen world, as he understood it, the intensity and plurality of the demands of these lower things could seduce the will to rebellion against the order of being. As alcohol is for the alcoholic, so the bodily and passional aspects of human being become for Augustine's sin-prone will. In his personal experience, the threat asserted itself most strongly in sexual compulsion, and to this threat Augustine responded with bewilderment and self-disgust. The same tones echo in his postconversion catalog of sensual delights; while affirmed theoretically as good in their proper places, even the tiniest and most unavoidable pleasures are relentlessly interrogated about their power to tempt the recovering will.[7]

In his account of history, too, the rationalistic and dualistic patterns within Augustine's thought each retained a vital role. Regarding the original and ultimate reality, the rationalist notion of Nonbeing could render a sufficient account of evil, at least for the saved. Paradise, reasoned Augustine, knew no evil more potent than privation; there was hierarchy but without force, bodiliness but no mortality, lack with no trace of suffering. After the fall, however, evil began to act as if it were an autonomous force. Lesser goods were congenitally infected with a lust for rebellion; natural hierarchy began to require coercive enforcement; bodiliness was wounded with mortality, disease, and insatiable libido.[8] The dualistic language of original sin and fall described this alienated situation, even while pointing to its penultimacy. Augustine's Platonic equation of the true and the good thus forced what became the dominant Christian myth about history: that life's great tensions and contradictions must be resolved by a final ending that will recapitulate and complete the paradisiacal beginning.

Augustine's disdain for tragic and comic dramas, with their quite contrary goals, was therefore not coincidental, nor were his related horrors of being pitied or derided by his readers.[9] His theory of sin, like the rationalistic and dualist interpretations of evil that generated it, was an effort to repudiate the tragicomic reality of elemental contradiction, an effort to fix life's moving questions by anchoring them speculatively to the story's anticipated end.

If the impotent male will was the subject of what was to become the Christian doctrine on evil, its object was women, who were associated with the lower and rebellious dimensions of being. Augustine did *not* blame women for male sexual crimes and compulsions; this paralleled exactly his decision not to blame the body for the disorders of the will. The common principle was that although the lower tends to rebel against the higher, the success of this unworthy rebellion can only be blamed on the higher. Nonetheless, the violent suppression of female autonomy could still be linked to the inviolable constraints of the natural hierarchy. For example, Augustine commended his mother for her patience with his violent and unfaithful father while repeating her criticism of less compliant women, who in Monica's view provoked their own beatings.[10] From the beginning of the Western Christian doctrine of evil to its anticipated End, the repudiation of tragic multiplicity has forced the elemental diversity of female being into a Procrustean bed in which no two equals can lie.

Protestant Moral Dualism and Secular Rationalism

So long as Christian society was intact, at least from the perspective of the literate elite, the world could be interpreted as providing a posteriori confirmation for the a priori equation of goodness and being. In the Middle Ages, the dualistic undertow of rationalism was most evident in the violent suppression of theological "misunderstanding," through the internal persecution of heretics and witches, the external campaigns against Islam, and the enigmatic punishment of Jews as both heretics and infidels. But it was not until the Protestant Reformation that dualistic interpretations of evil gained a central place in the theological mainstream. The justificatory mechanisms of Christian society, having lost their previously self-evidential character, now had to be asserted in a more positivistic and authoritarian manner. For the reformers this entailed a sustained criticism of the humanistic reason that had been used to buttress the ecclesial status quo. Stripping Reason of Sophia's ancient dignity, Martin Luther personified her as *wanton* woman, who—through the graced, masculine gaze—seemed whimsical, rebellious, and daft.[11] John Calvin was more respectful of reason's powers in regard to earthly things. But he insisted that reason, like every aspect of human nature, is corrupted by sin and, in the absence of divine illumination, utterly blind to spiritual matters. Though reason could comprehend many generalities, its discriminations fail when confronted with sin, which always occasions itself in the particular.[12]

For the reformers, the rehabilitation of reason depended on the integral salvation of the will. Analogously, divine goodness was to be conceived through divine sovereignty, rather than the other way around. Unlike Manichaean dualism, which affirmed divine goodness at the cost of divine omnipotence, the implicit dualism of the Reformation foiled all rationalistic and humanistic attempts to subject divine power to human standards, especially those of the Roman church. However, in discrediting the mediating force of reason, the reformers dismantled the elegant, ascending degrees of being that had run like a garden path through the dominant medieval view of nature. What was left, on the top and the bottom, were faith and reason, sin and grace, the saved and the reprobate, more starkly divided than ever before.

With the rise of a secular intelligentsia in the Enlightenment era, new forms of rationalism began to salvage and redefine Christian faith. Partly in response to sectarian conflict and wars of religion, Enlightenment thinkers beginning with Descartes proposed a notion of methodical reason as a means of establishing certainty, minimizing the need for faith and adjudicating otherwise intractable disputes. In terms of the problem of evil, the most significant feature of the Enlightenment era was the use of standardized methods of problem-resolution to mask the values and interests at work in knowledge. As dominative power was made to seem neutral and methodical neutrality made to seem good, the preferred mode of dealing with enemies became the denial of conflict; enemies were to be neutralized through inclusion. Just as the Christian society had once offered a posteriori evidence for the a priori identity of Being and Goodness, so the hegemony of European culture seemed to affirm the rationality of its methods. And just as the theory of evil as Nonbeing delegitimated the claims of the lower dimensions of the social hierarchy during the Middle Ages, so in the modern era the critique of bias would discredit subjugated knowledges by casting them as particular, subjective, and nonstandardizable.

It was the success of Enlightenment rationalism that necessitated the invention of "natural religion" and required the anthropocentric justification or proof of God. But the cost of rational certitude, then as now, was the extreme devaluation of the particular. God and religion, abstracted out of the range of falsification by the new sciences, were also prevented from obstructing the path along which new modern elites were advancing. Rationalistic Christianity was then enlisted in the rear guard, extolling the new virtue of optimism in the service of modern progress.

Theodicy, as formulated by Gottfried von Leibniz, replaced the reformers' submission to divine power with a rational explication of divine goodness that had Plato as its ancient forebear. Leibniz's self-sufficient and self-satisfied God, who could only be happy with the best possible world, permitted evil as part of a preordained harmony in which possibilities and necessities are arranged according to Eternal Verities, in bountiful variety and hierarchical order. Metaphysically speaking, evil is just the privation that places all finite beings at various distances from God. Physical evil is the result of sin and, like sin, is related to the inbuilt limits of finite being. For Leibniz, what people call evil was not unreal. But from the God's-eye view, which Leibniz was privileged to share, what we call evil is not actually bad.[13]

There were also attempts to accommodate to rationalism within some of the more sectarian theologies of the Enlightenment, beginning with the positive theologies of the late sixteenth and seventeenth centuries, which set out in humanistic style the authoritative sources or dogmas of the Christian faith. Then, acquiescing further to the justificatory mechanisms of modernity, fundamental theology arose to defend Christianity on firmer grounds. In the eighteenth century, natural religion provided those grounds; by the nineteenth century, fundamental theology turned from natural religion to German Idealism for epistemological certitude. The method was to separate the doctrinal content of Christian faith from its rational grounds, which were thought to be more certain. As Francis Schüssler Fiorenza has observed, fundamental theology was fated to lose its intellectual credibility once all knowledge, together with its supposed foundations, came to be understood as a social product.[14]

Kant occupies a pivotal position between modern rationalistic and dualistic responses to evil. His rejection of theodicy along with all speculative proofs of God,[15] his definition of morality in terms of the will, and his transposition of the question of evil from a speculative to a practical key—all these trace a dualistic trajectory. Still, this was mitigated by Kant's profound rationalism. His moral will remained a *rational will* and derived its unconditionality from the laws of reason. Beyond Augustine, Kant not only exonerated sensuous human nature for evil but also argued that despite habit and circumstance the will remains both obligated and free.[16]

The motives for Kant's treatment of evil were as anti-tragic as was Leibnizian rationalism. It was because Kant wanted to establish an absolute and unconditional moral good that he had to derive the goodness of the will solely from fidelity to the categorical imperative and to affect a principled indifference to concrete human goods. One ought to want to be *worthy* of happiness, he believed, but the moral will must not be defiled by the actual attempt to promote happiness. The disjunction between doing good and faring well was for him absolute and categorical; as *unconditional*, the moral good was definitionally immune to tragic circumstance.[17] In this theoretical context, a tragic worldview would involve a fundamental misunderstanding of the moral good.

Even in Kant, one can see how the positing of an absolute and unconditional Good inevitably implies metaphysical dualism. For example, he was forced to postulate an immortal soul, since without it the opportunities for moral progress were limited and the achievement of the unconditionally good will might be impossible. God, too, had to be postulated to support the hope for a final reconciliation of virtue and happiness. Most startlingly, radical evil had to be recognized as the counterpart to the absolute goodness of the moral will. Christianity, he argued, was philosophically right "to represent moral goodness as differing from moral evil not as heaven from *earth* but as heaven from *hell*."[18] The language, of course, was meant figuratively. But the effect, nonetheless, was to vitiate the mediating functions of nature and reason in moral life, leaving only a struggle between contrary and absolute principles. The definitional inability of life to support an unconditional good forced Kant off his earthly premises, just as the qualitative difference between necessary and contingent being had forced classical rationalism, under pressure, into dualistic reactions.

Although Romanticism includes an unwieldy variety of views, it generally favored dualistic patterns for the interpretation of evil. Beginning with Jean-Jacques Rousseau, the methodical reason on which Enlightenment thinkers had set their hopes was rejected as amoral and mechanical.[19] G. W. F. Hegel, with his relativization of reason as part of the historical development of Spirit, constitutes a category of his own. But he shared with the Romantics the sense that conflict, loss, and contradiction are more than apparent. As a result of Romanticism, evil became less a problem of speculative reason than of freedom, and its resolution was linked with the problematics of establishing freedom in the face of the conflicts to which the will and reason itself were subject.

Still, this renewed sense of contradiction did not imply a uniform rejection of theodicy. Rousseau supported Leibnizian optimism, though it was the social contract, not contemplation of a preordained harmony, that would lighten the burden of unhappiness. Hegel, making contradiction the grist for history's mill, paid unprecedented attention to negativity, yet feigned the most triumphal of resolutions—history itself as theodicy, culminating in the Prussian state and illuminated by his own philosophy.[20] Arthur Schopenhauer saw the connection between the need to defend the free will and the need to defend God; he rejected both. But he insisted that praise and blame be accorded only to human character, and he poured his purest vitriol on "the ministerial creature Hegel" and Hegel's grand theological scheme.[21] For all the Romantics, however, the a priori unity that reason, power, and goodness had formerly enjoyed as attributes of God was fractured in history, and this fracture was a foreshock of the fissures that were to end modernity.

Protestant liberal theology, as created by Friedrich Schleiermacher, took up the Kantian turn to the knowing subject as well as the Hegelian effort to overcome the dichotomy of Reason and Nature. On the basis of his "feeling of absolute dependence," Schleiermacher ventured a systematic harmonization of Christian faith and natural religion. Like Kant, he disliked metaphysical speculation; though the world is good, he believed, Leibniz had claimed too much. Schleiermacher interpreted evil in largely rationalistic terms: evil resulted from sin, which included social injustice, mixed with error. Natural evil, he argued, is something of a misnomer, since it is only to the eyes of sin that the limitations of life appear unacceptable. Sin itself was nothing more than an arrest of the God-consciousness. It was due, on the one hand, to the way the manifold desires of the "flesh" or "world-consciousness" resist the unified "God-consciousness," and on the other hand to the uneven development of insight and willpower. Defining both sin and grace as forms of *consciousness*, Schleiermacher could argue that sin was possible only in view of grace and that God, in the context of ordaining redemption, also ordains sin.[22]

Even in this consummately liberal theology, one feels the dualistic undertow that accompanies an absolutistic definition of the good. Despite his criticism of Augustine's sensual negativism, for example, Schleiermacher could state that in a sinless state the spirit and flesh would be one, "the flesh serving only as a living intermediary, a healthy organ, and never exhibiting anything not initiated and directed by the spirit."[23] Schleiermacher's suspicion was not directed against the body in particular; by "flesh" he meant "all the lower powers of the soul." The problem was not body versus soul, but the multiplicity of lower powers versus the higher unity of the spirit. Yet the empty instrumentality that Schleiermacher attributed to the lower powers in the ideal state betrays a notion of spirit fundamentally at odds with the diverse aims of worldly and historical life.

From Liberalism to Liberation

By the late twentieth century, methodical reason is buckling under the severe and sustained attacks initiated by Sigmund Freud, Karl Marx, and Friedrich Nietzsche. Significantly, each of these critiques involved a moral motivation. Freud condemned the irrational and excessive mechanisms by which civilization represses instinctual gratification and Marx the exploitative dynamics of economic and political power. Even Nietzsche's immoralism had what could be called moral motivations; for him it was not the sinful self that is powerless and *incurvatus in se* but the resentful anti-self of Christian morality. In each case reason itself was shown to be implicated in the unsavory dynamics of psychic, economic, and political power.[24]

The masters of suspicion decimated the unity that power, reason, and goodness had enjoyed within the sanctuary of Christian theism. As reason and power became more and more entangled with each other, their association with the good weakened. Power, in particular, became profoundly *morally* problematic. For many in our century, the indictment or rejection of God, which unveils the fissure between power and goodness, has become a virtual moral obligation, since only by acknowledging this fissure will humanity assume what responsibility it can. But Godlessness also signals the lack of consensus about normative methods, values, or authorities on the basis of which conflicting moral claims might be adjudicated. In the fracture of theism, morality itself grew less defensible, both as to its rationality and as to its efficacy.

No single feature has marked the theology of this century so deeply as the encounter with the radical evils washed up by the receding tide of modernity. Karl Barth wrote of discovering a bust of Schleiermacher in the post–World War II ruins of Bonn, and though he added that the bust "was rescued and somewhere restored to honor,"[25] in fact the honor of liberal theology was never to be wholly restored. Liberalism had not merely proven too weak a medicine for the century's moral illness; by overinoculating Euro-American culture against humility and caution, it had reintroduced the ancient infection in new and virulent forms. The terrible discovery of ourselves as the moral enemy, the remorse over specific historical atrocities, and the tendency to blunt this remorse by universalizing it into descriptions of the human condition as such—these have become the basic problematics of twentieth century Euro-American theology in the malestream.

Barth initiated the shift, characterizing modernity in its naïve humanism and progressivism as a manifestation of works-righteousness that incurs the wrath of God. The dualistic tone of Barth's objection to eighteenth-century optimism was evident in his complaint that "it does not so much eliminate as assimilate the shadowy side of human existence, i.e., its limitation by evil, sin and death, transforming it into a kind of margin to the sphere of light." In Leibniz and the other optimists, "reality is only half seen and therefore in the strict sense not seen at all. For it has two aspects." Leibniz was technically correct, Barth agreed, "in declaring the perfection of creation to be true and its imperfection illusory." But the optimists, in what Barth found to be a latent humanistic atheism, invoked divine goodness merely to ratify the satisfaction they already

took in the world and in themselves. He found more of worth in Schleiermacher's views, yet chastised Schleiermacher severely for reducing sin—
and, implicitly, even grace—to data of subjective experience. For Barth,
nothingness was the exclusionary side of a creation whose goodness,
too, was a matter of divine judgment, not a matter of self-evidence and
certainly not of self-sufficiency.[26]

Like the neo-orthodox or dialectical theologies that followed, Barth's
aim was not to reverse the modern turn from heaven to earth but rather
to set the best aspirations of modernity on humbler and more solid
ground. Reinhold Niebuhr and Paul Tillich each paid a degree of attention
to the tragic within these parameters. More recently, Edward Farley has
crafted a richly descriptive theological anthropology along the same
lines.[27] Each has articulated a Christian ethos that can account for the
severe constraints in which modern freedom and reason appeared in the
light of the world wars, Auschwitz, Hiroshima, and Nagasaki, without
taking recourse in an otherworldly flight. For the former purpose, they
invoke a moral dualism of sin and grace; for the latter reason, they reject
the metaphysical dualism of spirit and matter. While Niebuhr, Tillich, and
Farley each identify a *tragic dimension* to existence—in Farley's case,
most emphatically, a tragic structure—each decisively rejects a *tragic
view* of life as antithetical to a Christian view. Moreover, they associate
a tragic view of life with the metaphysical dualism they reject. To this
extent, their responses to evil depend on severing the irresolvable link
between moral and metaphysical dualism and on defining tragedy as a
dualistic rather than pluralistic view of the world.

For Tillich and Niebuhr, tragedy was associated more with human
greatness than with fragility, smacking of unself-conscious elitism as well
as of the sinful *hubris* tragedies deliberately rebuke. For Tillich, the tragic
grew from the genuine greatness of finite beings, who spontaneously
press against limitation and hence draw down upon themselves the sanc-
tions of law. Niebuhr identified two kinds of tragedy—the Promethean,
which is a function of creativity, and the Dionysiac, which is a function
of the unconscious passions. Both, in his view, expressed the tension
between life's vitality and its necessary laws. Farley understands the tragic
as the interdependence of the conditions that make for human frustration
and suffering with those that make for human well-being.[28] In his description of the tragic, one finds more emphasis on human fragility and
hence a firmer claim for the generality of the condition. To correct the
relative neglect of the tragic within Christian interpretations of good and
evil is a primary aim of his theological anthropology.

In spite of these differences, however, each of these Protestant theologians effects a simultaneous exaggeration and minimalization of the

tragic as understood by the Greek poets. The exaggeration is evident in the infinitism of the Christian account of desire through which tragedy becomes the inner riddle of human character rather than the result of specific and partially remediable conflicts. Tillich, for example, insisted that tragedy cannot be avoided by the avoidance of greatness, for that would also be tragic. Niebuhr noted the ethic of prudence implicit in the philosophy of Aeschylus, but found "more profound" the Aeschylean plot, in which humanity has not only a rational faculty but also "an imagination which surveys the heavens, aspires to the stars and breaks all the little systems of prudence which the mind constructs." Farley argues that human passions are tragically structured in that their horizon is the eternal; subjectivity, for example, could only be sated by an invulnerability that would contradict its own openness. These tensions, constitutive of the elemental passions as such, confer on life a "timbre of discontent."[29]

At the same time, the tragic paradox of unavoidable fault is minimized by the assertion that despite the tragic structure or dimension of existence, sin remains a matter of freedom and fault, not a matter of fate. Tillich, interpreting the tragic through his Platonic dualism of essence and existence, argued that tragedy belongs to the estrangement and ambiguity of existence but "does not belong to the essential nature of things." Moreover, his repudiation of the tragic view of life was authorized by way of the doctrine of *creatio ex nihilo*, which meant for him that finitude as such could not be construed as "doomed to destruction by its very greatness." Just as existence is dependent on essence (the true, good, and ideal), so, under the "dominance of the dimension of the spirit," finite greatness can be understood in its dependence on the holy, which is "beyond tragedy."

Niebuhr's book on tragedy is entirely devoted to defending Christianity's transcendence of tragedy. Sin, he contended, is possible because people are free, "and therefore man and not life bears responsibility for it." Sin ought to arouse pity rather than tragic admiration and to elicit repentant self-blame rather than the accusation of God or life. If Christ's innocent death shows that "sin is so much a part of life that sinlessness cannot maintain itself in it," Christ also "proves that sin is not a necessary and inherent characteristic of life"; that evil has no part in God or in "essential man." Farley, while arguing that the tragic plays a part in the origins and not merely the consequences of sin, fixes his theological anthropology on the differentiation between sin and tragedy. He understands this conceptual differentiation as a "seminal insight" of the Hebraic tradition and contrasts it with the tragic view in which evil is imputed to "the very existence and character of imperiled finitude." He accepts the tragic *structure* of life only to refuse a tragic *view* of life and to affirm in principle the possibility of a world without sin.[30]

In sum, each of these theologies treats sin as a paradox of inevitability and nonnecessity, where the inevitability reflects the tragic dimension or structure of finite existence and the nonnecessity reflects the penultimacy of finite existence. In other words, the nonnecessity of sin is a reflection of the contingency of the world's being and value in relation to the absolute being and value of God; precisely insofar as its God is beyond the world, Christianity is beyond tragedy. Idolatry, which remains the paradigm of sin for Tillich, Niebuhr, and Farley, outlines the human dilemma in anti-tragic terms, as deifying that which is not God, rather than in tragic terms as the conflicts of Goddesses/Gods—i.e., conflicts of the specific goods that warrant integration and the specific powers that exact honor in our lives. While tragedy presupposes and demands a partial freedom, the critique of sin as idolatry presupposes an unlimited freedom that, definitionally, cannot be actualized. And while Greek tragedy, as Niebuhr observed of Aristotle and Aeschylus, taught an ethic of justice and prudence in which goods and powers are weighed and assessed in relation to each other, the negation of tragedy generates an ethic of absolutism, in which finite goods and powers become equal in their relativity. A *generalized repentance* replaces or suppresses prudential judgment, which is the power of moral discernment *in the concrete and particular*. Desire, too, grows opaque when interpreted as a hunger not simply for the more and the better but for the infinite and the absolute. Humanity is expected to inflate itself to the point of explosion, when by God's grace we may be put back together again.

The rejection of tragedy is then implicit not only in the metaphysical dualism that these and most contemporary theologies refuse, but in the moral dualism that they endorse. For tragedy, in the ancient Greek view as well as in the postmodern view I am espousing, is not about duality but about plurality. Duality and plurality, in turn, are ways of thinking about the ideal, the real, and the relationship between them. If life is thought of as genuinely plural and conflicted, then moral judgment is not reducible to ontological judgment. If, on the other hand, the real and the ideal are the term of a single judgment that is at once ontological and moral,[31] then the world must either be totally sacralized or its being and worth construed as derivative. It is a commonplace for Protestant theologians to identify the first liability as the problem, while proposing the second liability, which relies on exactly the same logic, as the solution. Denaturalizing sin, they idealize nature, and nature idealized is not nature at all—just as an immortal body would no longer be a body, and an unambiguous existence would no longer be an actual existence.[32] Though the action on history's stage occurs under the aegis of the fall, this idealism remains history's eschatological backdrop. The demand that we stay in the world of ambiguity and exercise responsibility within it, a hallmark of Protestant ethical realism, is compromised by the eschatological expectation upon which that provisional acceptance of the world depends.

An anti-tragic eschatology is also very much at work in the political theology of Jürgen Moltmann. The Holocaust sits squarely in the center of his theological problematic, and this lends prominence to aims that ordinarily attach a sense of tragedy. He wants to keep alive the memory of the dead and to face the guilt that plays so large a part in the repression of the past. He intends to sharpen Christian sensitivity to suffering and to inspire the active struggle for justice on behalf of humanity as well as the endangered earth. He contends that Christian eschatological hope, far from undermining these sensibilities and commitments, is in fact vital for their sustenance. For Moltmann, "to think eschatologically means thinking something through to the end." Thinking thus, he construes theodicy as a process beginning with the resurrection of Jesus Christ, moving through the salvation of humanity and the earth, to the final conquest of death itself, when the dead will be raised and "every tear shall be dried." The ultimate goal of this process is not only soteriological but doxological—the justification and glorification of God.[33]

Moltmann's commitment to justice is active, passionate, and in this sense anything but otherworldly. Nonetheless, I would argue, the *absolutization* of the demand for the moral resolution is inseparable from the refusal of existence as such. To long for the death of death is to long for the death of life. Such a longing gains terrible force after Auschwitz, after American slavery, or after Hiroshima, when living can become a real and extreme difficulty for human beings who feel and remember, for survivors and victimizers as well as their descendants. To hear the wailing earth and yet make the world go on takes all the spiritual resources we have, perhaps more. From a practical point of view, it is wasteful to feign evil's resolution by "thinking it through to the end," when what is needed is illumination, creativity, discernment, and transformation in evil's midst. Looking for the end, faith in divine goodness suppresses the radical questioning of power, and the hope of beholding divine glory dampens the human creation of beauty.

It may be that only the privileged can afford this waste. When Moltmann describes Christ's love as "self-surrender" or as "vicarious suffering" in solidarity with the oppressed,[34] must he not have in mind those whose history has endowed them with a surfeit of self and whose suffering is a matter of freely relinquishing privilege? Such language it seems to me, does not speak—it *ought not to speak*—for those who are not so privileged. And even the privileged ought to raise critical questions about their own attraction to surrender, which like all mystical impulses can become an escape and a compulsion.

Black and liberation theologians have challenged the responses to evil within Protestant dialectical and political theology in several ways. Situated closer to the experience of oppression, they call for more emphatic and less equivocal political commitments. Centered in the struggles of the present more than in the irresolvable losses of the past, they refuse what José Míguez Bonino calls "the cult of powerlessness"[35] and demand of theology a realistic, proportionate, and historically sensitive response to the problems of force and violence. Unmasking the bias of rationalistic neutrality or universality, liberation theologians criticize Protestant ethical realism for its effective support of the status quo, and black theologians show how the purported abstractions of theology actually serve the interests of white supremacy.

For all their worldly passion, however, even these theologies of liberation may rest on a foundation of metaphysical dualism, which shows through when they contemplate the tragic limitations that hem in the struggle for liberation. James Cone, for example, has called freedom and death inseparable and has argued that "blackness or salvation (the two are synonymous) is the work of God, not a human work." Míguez has argued that the struggle for justice must be founded on "faith in the historical and eternal vindication of innocent suffering and committed love (and of those who personally bear them)" rather than in the expectation of a "visible victory."[36] Liberation hope, endangered by the toxicity of history, is again tempted by eternity. This temptation becomes even more compelling in the midst of liberation struggles in which, as Míguez notes, the laying down of lives for the oppressed sister and brother forms the immediate context of theological reflection. Here, hope is a matter of survival, and to this extent eschatological or apocalyptic language may seem empowering. Cone made this point, for example, in referring to the effect on slaves of lines such as "Nobody knows who I am, Till the judgment morning." The problem, however, is not with the language of the spiritual but with the language of theology, and it calls for the kind of bold reconceptualization that William R. Jones did in pursuing the question "Is God a white racist?" In view of black suffering, he argued, black theology should base itself either in secular humanism or in a humanocentric theism in which God is not coercive on anyone's behalf and God's power is only of the persuasive kind.[37]

In Roman Catholic theology, a parallel journey from liberal rationalism to liberationist dualism began with the belated acceptance of liberal thought at the time of the Second Vatican Council. The transcendental neo-Thomists, Karl Rahner outstanding among them, developed ingenious critical *rapprochements* between Roman Catholic doctrine and modern thought, mediated by a progressive and universalistic phenomenolgy of human being. Johannes B. Metz was the first to show the moral and political weaknesses of this new rationalism, using as an illustration the German fable about the rigged race between the hare and the hedgehog. By placing his wife, who looked exactly like him, at the finish line, the hedgehog faked a victory without actually running the race. So, Metz argued, transcendental neo-Thomism posited an eschatological victory that dodged the actual crises and struggles of history and that inadvertently represented the interests of the middle class.[38]

In a most poetic and persuasive way, Metz has shown that evil, like all theological questions, is fundamentally addressed to practical rather than speculative reason. Nonetheless, for him the problem of the Christian message remains in the bearers rather than in the message. Still assuming the universalism and transcendentalism of neo-Thomism, he has not interrogated the God explicated by Christian rationalism, but only insisted that the meaning of theological claims be unfolded in transformative political praxis. Once universalism and transcendentalism themselves lose their persuasive force, then this kind of political theology, like its liberal predecessors, is severely endangered.

In Roman Catholic theology, as in Protestant theology, responses to evil have taken on more dualistic tones under the pressure of struggles for liberation. In his meditation on the book of Job, Gustavo Gutiérrez has pointed out that for Latin Americans the question is less, "How are we to do theology after Auschwitz?" than, "How is theology to be done now, in the *presence* of innocent suffering?"[39] For Gutiérrez, Job's temptation was to speak ill of God; the outcome of Job's spiritual struggle, which Gutiérrez commends to theology, is to learn how to speak well and truly of God in the face of the suffering poor. He does not question theology's commitment to the defense of God, but he does repudiate the "doctrine of retribution" promulgated by the friends of Job, in which the justification of God hinges on the blaming of victims. In this sense, his meditation is an anti-theodicy, directed especially against theologians who, like the friends of Job, give sorry comfort. They would do better, Gutiérrez says, to place their hands over their mouths in the presence of the suffering poor, as does Job in the presence of God.[40]

Gutiérrez's refusal to justify injustice, together with his refusal to blame God, chisels a gap between his moral rejection of injustice and his mystical acceptance of evil as somehow within the will of God. This stance, he argues, is continuous with the spontaneous faith of the poor, which however requires "certain separations" to protect it from the alien ideologies that manipulate simple faith into hopeless resignation.[41] Gutiérrez's proposed separation is between contemplative and prophetic speech about God, which appears to parallel the theological relation of faith and works, and which thus accords to contemplative language the primacy of faith, grace, and revelation. A contemplative language must speak of the revealed gratuitousness of divine love, which evokes an "utterly disinterested" faith. At the level of contemplation it is revealed that "justice alone does not have the final say about how we are to speak of God." Just as the first stage of Job's journey led him into solidarity with all who suffer unjustly but without negating his individual suffering, so in the second stage Job's prophetic protest against injustice is placed within the larger framework of God's gratuitous love.[42]

It is moral concern that separates Gutiérrez's speech about God into two languages, but the common horizon of these languages remains a form of monotheistic rationalism. This horizon shows in his reference to God's self-imposed limitations within the realm of finite being, his view of evil as the chaotic residue of creation (which nonetheless remains under God's control) and his confidence in the ultimate triumph of the good, ensured by the resurrection.[43] What Gutiérrez tries to do, in Kantian fashion, is to handle evil with an epistemological dualism that no longer implies a metaphysical dualism. Though power and goodness are ultimately one, in the midst of history this oneness can only be known in revelation and grasped in faith. In the meantime, we must spend energy in the work of justice, rather than diverting it on metaphysical speculation that justifies injustice.

To explain less and struggle more is worthy advice to those of us whose profession borders perilously on the justification of evil. But does the combination of "utterly disinterested faith" and passionate political action make adequate use of the spiritual resources of the poor? Since the Enlightenment, as Harvey Cox has observed, the disparaging gaze of modern rationalism has been directed not only upward against ecclesial and monarchical authoritarianism, but downward at what were seen as the superstitions of ordinary people. Cox, like Mikhail Bahktin, has identified powerful resources of resistance and renewal in popular Christianity past and present, with its communitarian sensibilities, bawdy feasts, carnivals, and pilgrimages.[44] Anthropologists also discern in popular religion a wealth of practical and psychologically astute responses to evil, responses that may be indiscernible within the rationalistic and dualistic patterns of Western Christian thought.[45] In late medieval Europe as in the colonial Americas, the encounter between Christian elites and the common people had the effect of imposing a dualism on the practical plurality characteristic of indigenous religions. If people acknowledged the negative powers that touched their lives and employed ritual means to placate or negotiate with these powers, then from the viewpoint of elites they were deifying evil; what was not the Christian One must be the evil Other. This fatally rigid and unimaginative logic, which drove the European Inquisition and witch-hunts, was echoed in the demonization and suppression of the religions of the indigenous peoples of the Americas.

In the light of this history, theologians might take a new and more self-critical look at the responses to evil within our communities. Míguez, for example, argues that the mythical consciousness within popular religion in Latin America can undergo a "breakthrough" and begin to fuel an active, historical hope. But he anticipates this breakthrough only via the reinterpretation of biblical stories, rather than through the pre-Christian traditions that are so much a part of the people's Christianity.[46] Under the influence of modern European theology, he and others assume that evil must be entirely *denaturalized*, and that the problem with popular religion is its *naturalization* evils which are really social. But this modern view of nature, which assumed a clean division between a fixed, mechanical physical world and an arbitrary and changeable social order, has itself now been exposed as nothing more than a conventional ideal.

Liberation theologians are right to confront the religious resignation and despair that they find in much of the popular religion in Latin America. Such dispiritedness also afflicts many Christian women worldwide. Might it not be, however, that this dispiritedness comes less from pre-Christian forms of naturalism than from the supernaturalism of Christian elites? By splitting in two what had been a multiplicity of powers, and by consolidating into one what had been a multiplicity of goods, Christian elites may have sown rationalistic despair where practical hope had once grown. This is not to suggest that popular religion is not in need of critical reflection, or that theologians ought not to facilitate that kind of critique. It is to suggest, however, that the relation between theologians and popular religion ought to be a critical dialectic in which the responses to evil within popular culture, intellectually unsystematic though they may be, are searched as theological resources rather than cured as theological problems.

Postmodern Theology and the Tragic

A variety of theological positions are blossoming in the shade of the movements known as postmodernism. Different as these positions are, they share the sense that their time is one of radical plurality. In this respect, postmodern theologies presage a break with the rationalist-dualist pattern of Christian theology. Between the presaging and the knowing, however, a new confrontation with the tragic awaits.

In the meantime, the old patterns continue to retrace themselves within certain postmodern theologies. Dualist patterns are reiterated when the plurality of language and/or power results in consciously paradigm-dependent theologies. These can be further subdivided into theologies that understand plurality as a religious problem and those that relate to plurality as a moral and political challenge. The first subtype, exemplified by George Lindbeck's cultural-linguistic theory of religion, responds to plurality with a less apologetic and more sectarian theology.[47] The second subtype is exemplified by black and liberation theologies, and though these do not ordinarily classify themselves as postmodern, they in fact represent the political side of the crisis. Here the response to plurality is to make theology primarily accountable to the exigencies of liberation rather than to the closed circle of the church.

For each of these subtypes, the neutral ground of liberalism, if it was ever there in the first place, has been washed away. Theological positions are accessible within hermeneutical circles of enculturation or conversion, but not through progressive or universal means. Dualistic language guards the gates of entry inside and out, where "liberation" and "oppression" join the old company of sin and grace, reason and revelation, church and world. If the gain in these positions is their consciousness of what they are for and against, the loss is a decreased appreciation for the rejected Other and a decreased sensitivity to the tragic costs of moral and religious choice.

A rationalist type of postmodernism is exemplified in Mark C. Taylor's a/theology, which aims to cut loose from the binary oppositions on which he believes all previous theologies, including those of liberation, have been hamstrung. Erring and wandering, thoroughly unhinged from absolutes, a/theology enjoys the liberative levity of a radical nihilism that no longer hangs onto anything, especially itself.[48] In its errant freedom and its attention to culture as well as to ideas, Taylor's a/theology holds great promise. Its nihilism, too, as a relinquishment of metaphysical certainty, is a theological advance. But just as a fire cannot be made with a single stick, so a tragic heuristic does not come from metaphysical uncertainty alone but from the contradiction between metaphysical un-settlement and political-moral situatedness. Like the theologian, the a/theologian does not merely wander but sits, in a place that displaces someone else, in a present that rests on a particular past. Claiming to be nowhere may not be so different from claiming to be everywhere, and guarding God's grave not so unlike defending his life.[49] Without moral reflection, metaphysical nihilism remains a disappointed idealism; only with moral reflection can it light up the most vital questions.

The promise of postmodern theologies, then, hangs on the question of whether the intellectual and political dimensions of postmodernity can be brought into creative dialogue. There are portents of this already in *constructive* expressions of theological postmodernism, which attempt to reimagine community, spirituality, and ecology in terms that incor-porate a nonregressive critique of modernity. Popular religion, with its nuanced strategies for interpreting and transforming negativity, also of-fers vast resources and poses fertile questions for theology at the end of modernity. A third area of promise is Jewish-Christian dialogue, es-pecially on the question of evil, where Christians have much to learn from Jewish thinkers such as Marc Ellis who are confronting a Jewish history of victimization and guilt without recourse to utopic or eschato-logical escapes.[50]

After the Dream of Perfection

At century's end, one can see in mainstream Christian theology points of consensus with regard to the problem of evil, as well as the gaping holes through which a consciousness of tragedy threatens to seep. There is wide agreement that we are living at the end of liberal dreams of perfection, an end precipitated in no small part by the moral catastrophes of modernity itself. There is also wide but largely tacit abandonment of speculative reflection about evil, which is largely left to philosophers of religion who continue to redefine goodness and/or power until their apparent contradictions can be resolved.[51]

There are good reasons for the theological disinterest in rationalizing evil. As a discipline, theology does not forget the critique of reason first launched on religious grounds by the reformers and then on moral grounds by Marx, Freud, and Nietzsche. Nor does it forget the disarming of speculative theism by Kantian epistemology, or the more recent de-motion of epistemology itself to one more grand and dubious justificatory narrative. However, the fact that God is not defended does not mean that

God is questioned or accused. On the contrary, it appears to mean that God is safe as to the question of existence, which is deemed no longer worth asking. Meanwhile, what used to be called the divine "essence" is surreptitiously conjured to authorize particular visions of the good. This is so even for those postmodern theologies that claim to eschew all essentialist thinking; in their *via negativa*, such theologies are fully in line with the primary justificatory pattern of the Christian theological tradition, which masks the particularity of its choices by claiming a utopic or inclusive God's-eye view of the whole. Even liberation theologies, which own the particularity of their values and face the presence of countervailing powers, do not often allow questions of goodness and power to threaten the divine sanctuary. They ask, as a political question, how the good might be *made* politically powerful, but they do not raise theological questions about how goodness and power, in their differences and connections, tear and patch the cosmos within which our political lives are lived.

Certainly, there are compelling moral reasons for refusing to engage in the speculative *justification* of evil. But the measure of theology's alienation from the tragic is the assumption that to think about evil is either to "make good" of it or to render it utterly opaque. The rationalist strategy *has* done much good in response to evils that admit of progressive solutions, and the dualist strategy has done much good in response to evils that call for uncompromising refusal. In both strategies, however, theology defends an unequivocal good by erasing loss and negation, the one by denying the reality of the negated, the other by denying the entanglement of what is negated with what is affirmed.

Today it is harder to forget, harder to keep the dead and dying buried. In the angry, implacable ghosts of Auschwitz and Hiroshima, in the struggle among vital goods such as environmental and economic concerns, in the confrontation of irreconcilable definitions of moral responsibility, theology is again called to learn from tragedy. This call is linked with the question of the role of theology in those parts of the world whose time is postmodernity. In this context, when theology no longer has Christian society as its evidential basis, the discipline casts about for method as well as subject matter. Secretly or openly, God is still the subject matter of theology in the malestream, and protecting God its basic methodological commitment. Were God no longer to secure theology's good ending, perhaps the discipline might create for itself a future in the service of life's going on. Moving out of its stiff one-two step, theology might facilitate integral discourses about the risks and values of human existence amidst the elemental diversity of life.

CHAPTER THREE

ESCAPE FROM PARADISE
RESPONSES TO EVIL IN
RELIGIOUS FEMINISM

*One day, Eve noticed a young apple tree she and Adam
had planted, and saw that one of its branches stretched
over the garden wall. Spontaneously she tried to climb
it, and struggling to the top, swung herself over the
wall.*

*She did not wander long on the other side before she
met the one she had come to find, for Lilith was
waiting. At first sight of her, Eve remembered the tales
of Adam and was frightened, but Lilith understood and
greeted her kindly. "Who are you?" they asked each
other, "What is your story?" And they sat and spoke
together, of the past and then of the future. They taught
each other many things, and told each other stories,
and laughed together, and cried, over and over, till the
bond of sisterhood grew between them.*

*Meanwhile, back in the garden, Adam was puzzled
by Eve's comings and goings, and disturbed by what he
sensed to be her new attitude toward him. He talked to
God about it, and God was able to help out a little—but
he, too, was confused. Something had failed to go
according to plan. "I am who I am," thought God, "but
I must become who I will become."*

*And God and Adam were expectant and afraid the
day Eve and Lilith returned to the garden, bursting
with possibilities, ready to rebuild it together.*

—*Judith Plaskow*[1]

SINCE Judith Plaskow and her consciousness-raising group created this
revolutionary midrash on Genesis 1–3, the feminist study of religion has

37

become a busy concourse across and beyond the walls of the patriarchal paradise. Some, like Plaskow's heroines, have returned to rebuild the biblical garden. Others have broken with the domesticated Eve and eloped instead with Lilith, demon in the eyes of the garden God but priestess to an ancient Goddess.[2] For all, the bonds of sisterhood across difference have become more strained, and it is the privileged women of house and garden, not just "God" and "man," who hear a fierce demand for change from those they have excluded. For all, what is encountered beyond the false innocence of paradise is not merely the chimera of evil as defined by patriarchy, but the radical plurality of goods and powers that has become truth at the end of modernity.

Beginning with the New Testament's pastoral epistles, patriarchal Christianity has exegeted the Genesis stories of Creation and Fall to its own ends. As a result, women, body, and the extra-human world were knotted into what became, "naturally," the intractable problem of evil. For patriarchal theology, it could be said, woman-centered theology *is* the problem of evil, come alive and run rampant. For feminist theologians, though, evil as a theological problem is far more ambivalent. Women have the best of reasons for suspecting the language of sin, evil, suffering, and fault. Still, most women doing theology want to make powerful moral claims of their own against sexism and other structures of injustice. To make those claims, they have had not only to deconstruct evil as it has been established by androcentric theology, but also to reconstruct moral languages that can name sin or moral error in the most serious and authoritative ways.

Cutting the Gordian knot of evil, women scholars of religion are also retying it to bind different enemies. The cutting is under way when we disentangle evil from women, body, and nature and when we loosen the theistic equation between goodness and power. But women, like men, value power and exert it; women, too, choose and negate. We must look critically at the assumptions that bind us as we perform these basic moral and intellectual operations. Having scaled the walls of patriarchal paradise, we must learn to think good and evil in the wild and colored world from which the possibility of tragedy can never be expelled. In this world, it is not demon matter that must be contained but the dream of moral perfection and ontic surety that surrounds Adam and his God and for which Eve, Lilith, and their many sisters may still be homesick.

A historical root of the theological problem, I have suggested, are the notions of Original Sin and Fall elaborated by Augustine. Among feminists, Elaine Pagels has attacked this root most directly. Augustine's theory, she observes, implied that original human freedom could mar the natural world by bringing about death and could also efface the further possibilities of freedom itself. Pagels contends that this is "empirically absurd" and "utterly antithetical to scientific naturalism." While she emphasizes that the modern scientific view of nature would not have been relevant to Augustine or his opponents, she appreciates the view of the Pelagian Julian, who cast the natural and the voluntary as mutually exclusive.[3]

Pagels's analysis is insightful, particularly for highlighting the political stakes of these doctrinal disputes. But it is also emblematic of a tendency among some feminists to criticize ancient antinaturalism without noticing the links between that and ancient rationalism, and without sufficient reflection on their own modern rationalism and its dualistic shadow. For example, the Pelagian view, though recounted by Pagels as the more rational and empirical, seems to have rested on a metaphysical dualism in which rationality and freedom are undisturbed by the conditions of nature. I would argue that Augustine shared this premise insofar as he assumed that freedom could only be meaningful in the absence of such conditions. Moreover, Augustine's dualistic mistrust of the body and of sex went hand-in-hand with his rationalistic commitment to a hierarchical order. He saw death as unnatural, not because he despised the body, but because he believed the body a permanent part of human nature as divinely intended.[4] Similarly, Augustine and the theological tradition have been very far from repudiating either reason or freedom; on the contrary, reason and freedom have been believed in too absolutely. That was why freedom's very embodiment could feel like enslavement and why the existential frustrations of reason would seem to establish the necessity of revelation.

The Christian theological tradition, too, has wanted to affirm the body in its (read "her") proper place, avoiding what it saw as either the complete devaluation of the body or the disintegration of moral life by the inordinate demands uncontrolled bodies were likely to make. What could not be accepted—either by Augustine or by ensuing tradition—was the idea that the body and other spheres of life ought to be valued precisely as relatively autonomous goods that are often incompatible and each destined for dust. In terms of the tragic, Augustine and Julian struggled with the same problem, and so, perhaps, do their feminist heirs: If the good is presumed to be single or harmonious, whatever is fragile, conflicted, or incomplete cannot be truly good. For Augustine, this meant that desire itself grew monstrous and anomalous. For the Pelagians, it meant that nature was insulated from moral correction and beyond moral protest.

In general, religious feminists make a double move with respect to evil—on the one hand, exorcising the ideologies of evil and inferiority that have been attached to women and nonelite men, and on the other hand reattaching the notions of sins or evil to those same ideologies and the dominative interests they support. From the viewpoints of elites, the effect is a startling inversion of good and evil. But feminists do more than invert. They also think carefully about the social and political valences of moral discourse and transpose the genres in which that discourse has traditionally been cast—from the doctrinal to the symbolic and psychological, from the individual to the social, from the abstractly spiritual to the political. In altering both the genre of the question and the content of the answers, feminist scholars of religion have changed theological discourse on evil forever and for the better.

However, it is also true that feminists are reenacting versions of the ancient one-two step, choreographed in new ways. I discern three sets of responses to evil among religious feminists, and each of them bears the stamp of rationalism and dualism. This typology is meant as a heuristic device, not as an exhaustive description of particular groups of feminist scholars or of individual scholars within those groups. It is also meant to be appreciative rather than only critical. There were and are good motives for rationalism and dualism, such as the search for intelligibility, the hope that after loss and defeat life will get better, and the need to authorize a decisive No to injustice. But to work toward securing these goals in a shaky world is different from asserting, as an item of faith, that they are already secure in some final or ultimate sense. Feminist theologies, I believe, cannot assume and defend such a faith in the same way that God has been assumed and defended without inheriting the dogmatism and otherworldliness of androcentric theology. When terms such as "justice" and "nature" are employed not only to encode the *motives* for action but also as metaphysical *warrants* for action, then feminist theology as much as androcentric theology rests on foundations that cannot stay afloat in the postmodern world. Now "justice," too, is torn and controverted, as are "nature" and "woman." Elemental power floods every island where we might have hoped to think evil without being soaked in it.

One pattern of revision emerges mostly among white feminists attempting to find a positive heritage and future for women within Christianity or Judaism. In a later chapter, Rosemary Radford Ruether will serve as a detailed case study for this pattern. Ruether and similarly positioned scholars work with an eye to their religious traditions, but also with an eye to those feminist spiritualities that repudiate the biblical

God in favor of earth-centered and body-centered Goddesses. In order to undo the symbolic knot of women, body, and nature, they theologically vindicate the goodness of bodies and nature along with that of women. In order to preserve the transcendent dimension of the biblical deity, however, they also reject any unqualified identification of the divine with the given, immanently real. As a result, nature may become a *transcendent ideal*, apprehended more through belief or commitment than through any simple appeal to experience. Nature, including *human* nature, may then stand in for God as the metaphysical warrant for moral claims.

Rationalist trends predominate within this pattern; "nature" or "God" represents an absolutely transcendent and inclusive good that grounds a universal intelligibility. Male supremacy and other evils are classed as distortions or alienations beneath which believers can discern a truth and goodness common to all. The back door, however, is still open to dualism, because if evil is no part of what is ultimately true and real, then the world must be penultimate to the extent that injustice rules.

A second pattern can be interpreted among feminists, again mostly white, who have rejected Christianity or Judaism in favor of Goddess spiritualities. Carol Christ will be my case study for this pattern in a later chapter. In contrast to Jewish or Christian feminists, these postbiblical spiritualities wear their dualism on their sleeve. The world of patriarchy is seen as unrelievedly evil, and alienated, male-defined rationalities are denied moral authority over women, the earth, or other endangered goods. Instead, the grounds of moral authority are defined as "nature" and "women," which function as *immanent ideals*, immediately available in women's sensual, creative, and mystical experiences. This holism, though immanent, remains dualistic insofar as it can only be established by separating from the world of patriarchal division.

Still, like other Western dualisms, feminist dualism has a rationalistic underside. While the world of patriarchy is seen as evil, the language of moral evil is thought not to apply within the holistic sphere of nature or women. Negativity is still acknowledged but, separated from patriarchal structures and ideologies, it is counted not as evil but as the destructive side of a natural good. The language of evil, meanwhile, becomes a kind of border guard aimed outward against patriarchy and cordoning off a sacred sphere where women's mystical and aesthetic powers can be fostered.

In each of these patterns, nature—whether transcendent or immanent—is at once ideal and real, and that synergism of ideality and reality is the source of its moral authority. In the intellectual crisis of postmodernity, however, all ideals are being thoroughly *denaturalized*, especially that of nature itself. Rather than pointing beyond sociality to a truer and better reality, postmodern intellectuals suspect that "nature" is the most ideological of constructs, entirely bound to particular social positions and intelligible only in terms of them. Correlated with that intellectual crisis are the political crises borne by nonelite peoples. In the case of feminism, the result is that the concept *woman* is also being stripped of its claim to an ideal inclusivity. To vindicate "woman" and "nature," it will no longer suffice to invoke an Ideal beyond or beneath the real; it will only suffice actually to produce ways of living—in our bodies, on the earth, with each other—that are not ideal but are good enough for real women and men.

These intellectual and political crises are evoking a third set of responses to evil, especially among Christian scholars of religion who are women of color. Though too diverse to be called a single pattern, these theologies share certain features in how they frame and answer the problem of evil. They insist on treating evil as something to be changed rather than something to be understood or explained, so they measure responses to evil in terms of praxis, not in terms of theory alone. By itself, that is not a decisive dividing line between white and nonwhite Christian feminists. But the criteria of praxis take on special implications in light of the extremely complex and problematic relationship that nonwhite and non-Western women have to concepts such as *nature, women, good,* and *evil* as constructed by white Western culture and also by white feminists. Moreover, women of color and women of the two-thirds world may have relatively less investment in the symbolic and philosophical inheritance of white male thought on evil; instead of taking these as their starting points, they often prefer to begin with resources and problems specific to their own communities and histories.

For these reasons, Christian women of color are less likely to appeal to nature than to *justice* as the warrant for their ethical claims. Yet they also hope that justice can be made intelligible and morally compelling across differences of power and interest. Since their praxis is grounded in theistic or christocentric faith, their ideal of justice may occupy the theological place of God. Like God or like nature, justice may therefore be presumed and protected as a metaphysical first principle. Insofar as their ideal of justice is meant to function as a universal intelligibility, these theologies partake of the rationalist tradition on evil. But they modify liberal rationalism with a Marxist or socialist view of historical struggle. Dualistic tones may also show up among these diverse theologies; injustice may be seen as a function of autonomous, destructive, and even demonic interests. But again, this twoness presupposes an ultimate oneness; if injustice is cast as demonic, it is also expected to meet eschatological defeat.

By means of these interpretive strategies, substantial theological gains are being made for nonelite women. However, I will argue, the intellectual and political weaknesses of the Western tradition on evil are not resolved by the transposition from legitimating theory to transformative praxis as long as praxis still relies on a principle of absolute transcendence.

In Defense of the Transcendent God

Valerie Saiving's 1960 article "The Human Situation: A Feminine View," which inaugurated the current phase of feminist theology, broke the ground for the feminist interpretation of nature as a transcendent ideal.[5] The soteriology of male theologians was not bad or false for men, she argued; but it was exclusive, inadequate, and, for women, morally dysfunctional. For Saiving, sin was a universal condition, but a condition differentially inhibiting the full development of women and men as human beings. Behind her revisionist soteriology, then, lay an ideal of *human* nature as an inclusive good that could only be known obliquely, through the correction of sin. To that end, she urged theologians to attend to the distinctiveness of "feminine" experience and to address the typical sins of women.

From Saiving's rallying cry there arose a feminist theology still founded on a universal ideal of the human, which as such both included and transcended the particulars of women's experience. Moreover, as Judith Plaskow and others soon recognized, "feminine experience" as Saiving described it was itself yet another false universal.[6] That critique of "the feminine," however, did not necessarily lead to the abandonment of universals. For those committed to defending the transcendence of the feminist moral ideal, it issued in expanded critiques of patriarchy and its religions as *exclusive* or *partial* and in a more differentiated, inclusive analysis of oppression.

Letty Russell's liberation theology was an example of this strategy among Christian feminists. *Human* liberation, as she put it, was the goal on which all liberation struggles might hope to converge.[7] Taking inspiration from Rom. 8:22-23, she read the "groaning of creation" as the birthpangs of liberation. In this theology, justice is simply natural, but the natural is conceived as a liberative becoming rather than a static hierarchy. Coming into being, ontically, was for Russell the same as coming into goodness, politically and morally; if politics is struggle, so is creation. Artfully weaving liberal and Marxist ideas, Russell could affirm the goodness of nature as an eschatological ideal and could do so without compromising the transcendence of the biblical Creator.

Like Russell, a number of white feminists working within Christianity or Judaism built alliances with a variety of liberation movements, recognizing that the suffering of women is multiply determined by racial, ethnic, economic, and political factors.[8] As oppression became a complex and totalized notion, and as feminists grew less sanguine about the Bible and traditional theology, the problem of evil became for some a problem of theological method. Christian feminist Mary Hunt addressed this most directly.[9] Feminist theory, she argued, represents a "new phrasing of the question of theodicy." Hunt methodologically shifted the genre of that question, from the speculative or doctrinal to practical and political. But the rational value of inclusivity remained her theological norm, and she proposed to approach that norm by adding new viewpoints as they emerge in various struggles against oppression. In contrast to the transcendent values of justice and inclusivity, Hunt construed various oppressions as aspects of "cosmic evil." Her rationalism, however, is mitigated by the links she forges among theology, ethics, and ritual, which leave her method open to creative disturbance by the more-than-rational dimensions of spirituality.

As Plaskow and friends had predicted, God himself was to come unraveled as feminists deconstructed patriarchal evil. Carter Heyward developed a particularly profound feminist critique of traditional Christian theism. She argued that omnipotent or dominating power, far from epitomizing goodness, is the very paradigm of evil in the world.[10] But Heyward wanted to redeem God with a relational ontology, not abandon God in favor of a purely immanent goodness. By redefining the divine as "our-power-in-right-relation," Heyward re-created God as a good form of power—good in that it empowers the struggle for justice. Moreover, in her view this good power was not only the result of justice-making but also the source of justice.[11] The question of how to deploy this power in the midst of disempowering injustices became a question of praxis, not of speculation. Yet the privation theory seemed to survive behind Heyward's conception of evil as disempowering and of right relation as the structure of the world as divinely intended. Power and goodness, though decoupled in her picture of history, were recoupled in her concept of the divine, which therefore seemed to transcend history as the latter's ground and ideal.

A transcendent ideal of nature has also touched the interpretation of eros among feminists working in or on the boundaries of Christianity and Judaism. This trend in particular is not confined to white feminists; its proponents include Rita Nakashima Brock, Patricia Hunter, Judith Plaskow, and Carter Heyward.[12] Sex, so often demonized in traditional theologies, is vindicated by these theologians as an expression of eros. But eros, like nature and relationality, inflates into a transcendent ideal, not to be equated with or confined to women's actual sexual experiences. Instead, inspired by Audre Lorde's article "Uses of the Erotic,"[13] they set out not only to rehabilitate sex as a distinct good, but to elicit from eros a far-ranging feminist moral vision. Their eros, like Heyward's God, is a good kind of power, rooted in the relational character of created being. The fact that eros has a painful, disruptive side that cannot be blamed entirely on injustice is not denied, especially by Plaskow and Heyward. But that side too is hallowed among the rhythms of life, in the hope that erotic disruption may ultimately destabilize hierarchical rigidity. The implication, again, is that authentic "nature" can serve as a moral corrective to the inauthenticities of sociality. That analysis applies as well to rape, abuse, and misogynist pornography. These evils are not thought to obviate the goodness of eros, but are instead accounted for as its repression or distortion.

In the absence of reflection on tragedy, feminist theologies sensitive to postmodern trends may also remain within the orbit of rationalistic interpretations of evil. Rebecca Chopp's elegant work on feminism, God, and language is an example.[14] Drawing on deconstructionism and other contemporary approaches to language, Chopp opposes the monotheistic ordering of "the One against the other" with a view of the divine Word as the "perfectly open sign" and the "full inclusivity of discourse," to which women and other marginalized people are especially receptive. "Speaking freely" enhances specificity and difference among women as well as between women and men. Difference and even conflict can nurture a solidarity beneficial to all, Chopp argues, because the social-symbolic order of patriarchy does not work for anyone. It suppresses pleasure as well as suffering, and those at the center of power experience a psychic alienation that dimly mirrors the violence endured by those at the margins. Behind Chopp's theology of language, evidently, lies a privation theory of evil; difference is assumed to be essentially good, while injustice is thought of as the repression of difference.

These common appeals to a transcendent good should not obscure important differences among biblical feminists on the question of evil. Jewish feminists, clearly, are less tempted than are Christians to retreat to the perfect beginning or end that enwraps the view of history as fallen. In general, too, Jewish feminists place the appeal to a transcendent Good in the background of their proposals, while the history and practice of the Jewish community hold the foreground.[15] Among Christians, too, there are differences concerning whether and how to speak the language of fallenness, guilt, and fault. Some, like Rita Nakashima Brock, supplant that language with a discourse of suffering and healing while others find fallenness a meaningful way to speak of sin as social.[16]

But in general it can be said that religious feminists who rely on the transcendence of the biblical God have not been entirely alert to the rationalistic and anti-tragic patterns within their thought. Their critical scrutiny has focused instead on ancient metaphysical dualism, and they tacitly blame this metaphysical dualism for the hierarchical thinking of Western patriarchy. I have argued, however, that in Christian thought since Augustine dualistic patterns are bound up with rationalistic premises. Moreover, I have suggested that dualism and rationalism have been motivated not only by crude misogyny or antinaturalism (though there is plenty of that as well) but by laudable intellectual and moral aims that religious feminists may share. For example, by construing the Ideal as transcendent, the feminists just discussed have been able to affirm the goodness of women without foreclosing the possibility of self-critique by and among women. Their rationalist belief that all genuine goods are part of a transcendent and inclusive Good has shown its advantages as well, by mandating a search for the points where apparently conflicting interests may become congruent or where various liberation movements may form alliances. These and many other feminists rely on patterns that I call rationalistic in the belief that these ideas support strategies for change that are more progressive, more realistic, and less violent than other alternatives. Their rationalism, in other words, is not only an intellectual but a moral commitment.

But today, it seems to me, the chain to be broken is less that of ancient Being than that of modern Reason. Religious feminists are thinking like modern rationalists when they construe injustice as the coercive imposition of hierarchy on a natural world which would otherwise enjoy harmony and equality, or as the irrational constriction of reason and freedom, or as the repression of a natural eros. The modern ideal of neutrality, too, shows up when evil is reduced to an intolerance for difference. In practice, of course, feminists know that all differences (race, class, sex, culture, sexuality) are *not* the "same difference"; some call for acceptance and celebration and some for redress. The trick is to discern the moral difference among differences, but for this sheer rationalism can offer little guidance. For in rationalism, good is conceived in relation to evil as truth is conceived in relation to falsehood, and this formal distinction effaces the concrete criteria upon which real moral choices must be based.

Politically, an abstract, believed-in Goodness is dangerous because it can easily be made to substitute for real but limited solutions to social evils. That is why the language of modern rationalism can lend itself to the current reactionary campaign that names "political correctness" as its enemy. This campaign bases itself on the claim that, despite all appearances to the contrary, persons really are equal and that the methods of democratic capitalism really are objectively and universally valid. This believed-in equality and believed-in objectivity are then called upon to discredit the policies and values that would actually promote economic and political equality for the marginalized. In order to counter this reactionary trend, feminists need a more potent moral language than rationalism alone can provide.

Rationalism can also lend itself to an oversystematization of moral and political discourse. Good is oversystematized on the premise that all true goods must find their place within an inclusive and transcendent Good. Were that the case, it ought to have followed that the liberation of one oppressed group would tend to support the liberation of others. In feminist practice, however, those links have proven quite weak and their unhinging quite demoralizing. Assuredly, they can be forged and reforged, but only on the strength of subtle and differentiated analyses of oppressions based on race, ethnicity, sex, class, and sexuality, not on the assumption of a natural congruence of goods. Paralleling this oversystematization of the good, the privation theory may also lend itself, curiously, to an overly systematized view of evil. Since evil is not supposed to have intrinsic power, the world in which injustice rules may be assessed as a perverse counterreality under the sway of a cosmic, demonic force. This view may be especially compelling to Christian feminists, who inherit the idea of a fallen world.

When ideals are accorded a transcendent reality of their own, they lose their ability either to affirm experience persuasively or to criticize it effectively. That, it seems, has been the trajectory to date of the ideal of eros in Christian and Jewish feminist theologies. Insofar as eros is forced to include all true goods and to conflict with none, sex itself becomes a means to greater ends, not a (sometimes dangerous) pleasure that wants to be affirmed for its own sake. At the same time, bad forms of sex (e.g., rape) are classified as "not erotic" or even as "not sex," which means not only are they not *ideal* forms of sex but that they are not authentic expressions of human desire.[17]

Behind this and similar moral strategies lies the rationalist assumption that only the good can be desired, which in the erotic theologies may result in an assimilation of social injustice of every kind to psychosexual repression. There is a humane goal at work here: If oppression can be exhaustively traced to suffering—even to the suffering of its benefici-aries—then a given liberation movement may in the long run prove to be a gain-gain rather than a gain-lose proposition. This is an effective strategy for discovering congruences of interests where they exist. But it is not an effective response to the relative autonomy that gathers around conflicted social and economic interests. People, institutions, and states really do attach themselves to and fight to the death for privileges and powers that, from the viewpoints of their victims, are utterly unjust.

Intellectually, feminist rationalism is problematic for its vestigial spirit/ matter dualism, which makes it possible to imagine that sociality can and does become estranged from its physical bases, or that human beings become alienated from their "natural" goodness and interdependence. Such dissociations, I would argue, are impossible; bodies never become *un*related to minds, nor people to each other, nor culture to the ground beneath it—we just become *badly* related. Social forms do not only repress but also modify bodies, desires, sexualities; they do not falsify nature but instead generate disparate truths. The chaos of the world is therefore much more profound than if it were only a gap between the natural good and the estranged society. There are conflicts among com-pelling goods, conflicts among standards of goodness, conflicts among methods for achieving goods. The presumed paradise of unrepression, appealing at moments of relative powerlessness, offers little moral wis-dom about how to create and destroy in the process of gaining power and wielding it. As feminists reflect more on the ways women do and can exert power in the world, we need to search for this more-than-rational wisdom in the wilder world in which tragic conflicts also grow.

In Defense of the Immanent Good

For a time in the 1970s, the division between rationalist and dualist patterns for interpreting evil issued in a debate among some feminists over "essences."[18] Camps labelled "reformist" and "revolutionary" split over whether the biblical religions are essentially sexist, whether there are essential and morally significant differences between women and men, or whether the symbol *God* is essentially male and patriarchal. "Reformist" feminists, who were trying to find their way within Chris-tianity or Judaism, usually answered no. That response was partly stra-tegic, signalling an intention to fight for a nonsexist *future* in their traditions. For some, it was also deeply philosophical, resting on the soon-to-be-discredited conviction that "essence" as such was good—that is, that the better or ideal meaning of persons, traditions, and religious symbols is also in some sense their core historical or psychological meaning.

Postbiblical feminists, however, did not feel so compelled to equate the essential and the good. While the Christian feminists just discussed were "claiming the center," searching for "usable biblical traditions," and characterizing misogyny and sexism as "heretical" or "inauthentic," postbiblical feminists began calling themselves "heretics," "witches," and "bitches."[19] Taking patriarchal man at his word, postbiblical feminists concluded that women, bodies, and nature really are evil and subversive in relation to the moral and political status quo. They saw not one but two different and irreconcilable versions of the good and the true, only one of which could be chosen. Feminists within Judaism or Christianity felt themselves to understand their religion once its oppressiveness, however vast, could be interpreted as a distortion or incompletion of the religion's authentic meaning or promise. Postbiblical feminists, on the contrary, felt themselves to understand the puzzle of patriarchal religion when the pieces came together to disclose an inner intelligibility wholly opposed to female being.

Just as some Christian and Jewish feminists have been more critical of premodern thought patterns than of their own modern rationalism, so postbiblical feminism has had a keener eye for metaphysical dualism than for its own romantic dualism. In fact, postbiblical feminists typically see themselves as radically antidualistic, rejecting not only the split between spirit and matter but also the idea of a transcendent moral good. When they contrast women's spiritualities with patriarchy, it is not as good versus evil but as a primal, changing wholeness against the division, dismemberment, and rigidity of patriarchy. But this wholeness, while not "higher" than patriarchy, is nonetheless felt to be more basic and enduring. It cannot be penetrated by the dissecting categories of patriarchal ontology and morality and so is not defiled by them. As in ancient metaphysical dualism, the language of evil refers only to the rejected Other. "Evil" guards the borders of a spirituality belonging specifically to women, in which diverse forms of pleasure, beauty, and power can flourish free from moralistic male surveillance.

The Politics of Women's Spirituality was an early anthology of Goddess feminism, and Charlene Spretnak's introduction exemplified its characteristic responses to evil. Spretnak sketched a history, psychology, and theology predicated on the division between the alienated reality of

patriarchy and the holism of elemental female experience. Neuropsy-
chological research, she suggested, points to sex-differentiated psychic
proclivities: Male character, on average, is manipulative, analytical, and
dominative, while females tend to be communicative, integrative, and
connective. Historically, she followed Marija Gimbutas and Merlin Stone
in describing a pre-patriarchal era of female power and Goddess worship.
Theologically, she characterized patriarchal religions, including Christianity, Judaism, Islam, and much of Hinduism, as religions of alienation,
fear, guilt, and hierarchical order. For both women and men, psychic
wholeness could be restored by cultivating the consciousness that "all
is one" and "only the illusions of separateness divide us."[20]

While interpreting patriarchy as a destructive counterreality, Spretnak's analysis enabled a rationalist interpretation of evil within the universe of feminist holism. Patriarchy, she argued, needs to dissociate itself
from the experiences it calls "evil," but feminist and other holistic spiritualities integrate all experience as a source of learning. Just as traditional Christian rationalism presupposed a dualism between absolute and
contingent being, so Spretnak posed a tacit dualism between a harmonious nature and a patriarchal history in which the illusion of evil prevailed. Nature, though immanent, seemed to remain *ideal* and thus
inaccessible to the world of evil and division. For example, she argued
that a holistic ethic "would not allow coercion or domination, such as
forcing someone to birth or kill."[21] Her feminist critique of unjust forms
of force, in other words, was authorized by the ontological claim that
coercion and domination have no place in nature as such.

Postbiblical feminist freethinker Emily Culpepper has expressed a
sympathetic critique of Goddess feminism on somewhat similar grounds.
The problem, in her view, is that much postbiblical feminism still fancies
"the Goddess" in the familiar image of biblical monotheism and the tame,
homogeneous Good it represents.[22] For Culpepper, in contrast, Goddess
spirituality was a turn to radical polytheism and a complex view of life's
elemental powers. Beyond the benign maternity of the feminist Mother
Goddess, she has unearthed Goddesses, gorgons, and mermaids who,
like Kali, embrace anger, violence, and loss as well as comfort and nurturance. Yet for Culpepper not every negativity can enter this holism.
Christianity serves her only as "compost," its "core symbols" and "sub-
liminal structures" assessed as "inescapably hierarchical," "necrophilic
and sadomasochistic." Patriarchy and its symbolic world are to Culpepper
a global system of evil, with no inner complexity of the morally promising
kind. There is rationalism in her thealogy, too; she sees patriarchy as

ultimately void. And although she permits no dualism within her free-thinking spirituality, that freedom is won only when "we have withdrawn from patriarchy into another creation so profoundly that it has no substance."[23]

No postbiblical feminist has named the evil of patriarchy more boldly than has Mary Daly, and no feminist interpretation of evil is more radically dualistic. From the beginning of her journey beyond God the Father, Daly has identified feminism as a struggle between being and nonbeing. That sounds like the privation theory but it is not, since patriarchal nonbeing, for Daly, has never been a harmless nothingness. Rather, it is a murderous, systematic opposition to life and specifically to female being. Patriarchy is a reversal of being, a fabrication of lies, that must be seen and rejected in its totality. That was the point of the second passage in *Gyn/Ecology* in which Daly detailed the "sado-ritual syndrome" that enforces patriarchy across culture and history.

Buttressing this syndrome, Daly argued, is the patriarchal identification of women with evil. However, her response to this has not been to argue for the goodness of women, since the terms on which patriarchy defines goodness are utterly incompatible with female and all authentic life. Instead, she has sharpened and doubled the patriarchal language of evil into a labrys for amazonian battle against patriarchal morality. Her Self-identified woman is "positively revolting," naming herself "witch," "hag," "crone," and "harpie" and cultivating as virtues what for Christianity are deadly sins.[24]

Analyzing patriarchal religion as essential reversal and intentional deception, Daly's method beginning with *Beyond God the Father* was that of liberation, castration, and exorcism. But she has not aimed simply to reverse the reversals of patriarchy, since in her view dualistic thinking is an artifact of patriarchy. Moreover, she has always sensed that patriarchal dualism is morally and not just metaphysically based. The liberation of women, she has argued, promises a "mode of being and presence that is beyond patriarchy's definitions of good and evil," a "paradise beyond the boundaries of 'paradise.' "[25] Despite her playful and provocative reclaiming of the patriarchal language for evil, Daly has occasionally insisted quite seriously that the end of patriarchy should not be equated with the end of evil. She has even gone so far as to observe that "[r]epudiation of the scapegoat role and the myth of the Fall by the primordial scapegoats may be the dawn of real confrontation with the mystery of evil."[26]

In some respects, Daly's interpretation of evil is akin to Spretnak's. Speaking of patriarchy, her account of evil paints a dualism of cosmic-historic proportions; speaking of Self-identified women, evil as a serious problem fades away. But when it comes to patriarchy Daly is more moralist than rationalist. Rather than deflating the language of evil, she inflates it into a female gorgon who paralyzes efforts to "man-ipulate" women morally. Rather than attempting to build a bridge of intelligibility between feminism and patriarchy, she has tried to create a language that cannot be penetrated or possessed by "male-evolence." To this end, she transformed the language of evil into a kind of one-way mirror through which the world of patriarchal division can be clearly viewed but which reflects nothing about the biophilic wholeness of self-loving women.

In postbiblical feminism, as in some Christian and Jewish feminisms, reinterpretations of evil have also been spun around an idealized version of eros. The results are similar, but postbiblical feminists, for whom eros is an *immanent* ideal, have paid somewhat more attention to sexual experience itself as a channel for the sacred. Starhawk, a leading voice within feminist Wicca, has written of sexuality as expressing the moving force beneath all living forms. Western patriarchal culture has been wrong in its fear that sexual libido could overrun civilization, she contends, for sex has "its own regulatory principle, its own rhythm of expression and containment, arousal and satiety." Alienated consciousness, however, creates its own reality, a "culture of estrangement" in which sexual power becomes distorted into mastery and slavery, sadism and masochism. Authentic eros, which is for Starhawk experientially more whole, resonant, and true than is sex as power-over, can heal the alienated sexuality of patriarchy. In her immanentism, Starhawk resists the tendency of some religious feminists to make sex live up to a political agenda; in her view, the goal should be the other way around. The important question is not what we *should* feel or want sexually but rather, "What do I, at my root, at my core, desire?" The questioner, she hopes, can experience "that root of desire as the Goddess incarnate, as the source of power-from-within."[27]

Starhawk's treatment of eros is a good illustration of the theological advantages and perils of using nature as an immanent ideal. In her work, there is concrete, passionate affirmation of life, not just in principle but in and through sensual, affective, and social experience. Ethically, that leads to a preference for integration and balance over repression and fragmentation, at least in relation to those tensions that are counted as natural. However, like some Christian and Jewish feminists, Starhawk thinks of unjust social power as repressive rather than productive, and she too easily dismisses *bad* desire as *false* desire. That is especially dangerous when good desire is equated with what is psychologically or socially *powerful* for us. To judge something as good, I would argue, ought to be more than to experience it as powerful; moral judgment must involve a further, more reflective step.

In regard to sex, for example, we might reflect on Michel Foucault's thesis that "repression" itself functions as a cultural myth.[28] Under the spell of this myth, we are made to believe that certain sexual desires are being repressed, at the historical moment when these very desires are actually being produced and regulated. If Foucault's insight applies to the culture of estrangement, it also ought to be a caution for the anti-repressive culture Starhawk has proposed. When late capitalist culture claims to have bestowed a long-awaited sexual freedom on us, we ought to be as skeptical of that as when we are told which sexual expressions are or are not "natural." In our culture, even sex of the most utterly conformist kind can be made to seem an act of individuation and rebellion; in this way, sex can offer a compensatory substitute for other political and economic powers. Sex, I would agree, is among the elemental powers, but that does not make it a "natural" corrective to social "estrangement." Rather, sociality itself is elemental for humans, and that means that all our Goddesses and Gods, our values and our powers, are enmeshed in sociality and its attendant moral ambiguities.

Still, enmeshment in ambiguity ought not to paralyze feminists in terms of making moral judgment, and I appreciate the force of the moral judgment Goddess feminists level against male supremacy and its supporting ideologies. The violence and exploitation that women suffer as women are not simply due to social structures in the abstract, but to the entrenched and familiar privileges of maleness. Goddess spirituality (though not always excluding males) can offer opportunities for women to create spaces safe from male presumptions and assumptions, and within those spaces it can nurture women's bonds and women's cultures.

It has been my own experience that in feminist Goddess circles the aesthetic and mystical dimensions of religion are enjoying a special renewal, and I think this can be partly attributed to the ways in which evil is being reinterpreted. Because Goddess feminists tend to spare women the moralistic language they apply to patriarchy, they may foster within women-defined spheres more integral means of dealing with negativity. Moralism tends to dampen imagination and creativity; the women's spirituality movement, on the other hand, has inspired a wealth of images, music, and literature. For some women, Goddess feminism may also enhance the mystical aspects of religion, due to its conviction that certain kinds of negativity deserve to be honored as part of the sacred. When aging, decay, anger, and conflict, along with pleasure and harmony, are ritually evoked and celebrated, women are that much more able to tap into their strongest feelings and energies. In those transpersonal depths, many women find the wellsprings of the sacred. This has political dimensions, too: When we know what we feel, as Audre Lorde argued, we can discern what we want and unleash the energies to create it.[29]

The main shortcomings of the response to evil within Goddess feminism is its dualistic bifurcation of good and evil, so that where moral language is applied (that is, in reference to patriarchy) it becomes simplistically moral*istic* and where moralism is not applied, there is no adequate vehicle for self-critique. For example, it has often been complained that Goddess feminism lacks an adequate critique of racism and classism among women.[30] Hence, Goddess spiritualities of the kinds I have described have not had great appeal to women of color and economically poor women. When evil is understood only as the gorgon mask women present to patriarchy, we may fail to see harm in the familiar face of our own inherited privileges.

The fundamental intellectual problem here is an insufficiently critical use of the categories *nature* and *women*, which are idealized in order to serve as the ontological warrant for moral judgment. Even if we accept that some negativity should be accepted as part of "nature," we still need to discern what belongs to "nature" and what does not. For instance, in the current controversies about the causes of AIDS, not much light is shed by categorizing the disease as "natural" or "social" or even as both.[31] Whatever is classed as "natural" we must still try to cure, and whatever is classed as "social" still infects bodies. If "nature" is used as a code for the good or for acceptable negativity, that is only because everything that is adjudged bad or unacceptable has already been definitionally excluded. We are none the wiser as to the *grounds* for those moral judgments, but that is exactly where wisdom is needed. The same applies to *women*, which if used as a code for the human good will exclude all the human proclivities of which it disapproves, even if they happen to be found in females.

Goddess feminism challenges women to have the courage to make moral judgments that may be as fierce and unequivocal as the judgment against male supremacy, yet without the Archimedean point of absolute transcendence or moral innocence. As Daly has suggested, repelling the false naming of evil within patriarchy is only one side of the task; the other is to encounter evil in its authentic mystery. That mystery, in my estimation, is something to be wondered about; it is not the cognitive closure that comes from tracing evil to male nature or any other ontological something. To encounter that mystery is to think about what we are doing in thinking evil, on what authority and at what cost, to other women and other men.

In Defense of Justice

The two patterns of response to evil that I have just traced are partly determined by the question of whether to leave or to struggle within Christianity or Judaism. But a third set of responses to evil is afoot among religious feminists, and these arise especially among Christian women scholars who are not white or Euro-American and for whom the question of religious identity has a special complexity. Rather than choosing for or against Christianity as it has been androcentrically and eurocentrically defined, they want to affirm the legitimacy of their own, culturally indigenous forms of Christianity. For example, Kwok Pui-lan argues that "as Asian/Christians we are pagans/Christian at the same time," and she challenges white feminists to move beyond their "provincial" ways of marking religious boundaries. Ada María Isasi-Díaz and Yolanda Tarango point out that there are many pagan influences in the syncretistic spiritualities of Hispanic women in the United States. However, they argue that Christianity has always been syncretistic and that the self-identification of Hispanic women as Christian itself forms a part of Christianity's historical reality. Korean theologian Chung Hyun Kyung proposes that Asian women's theology foster a "survival-liberation centered syncretism," focused more on women's popular religiosity than on institutional religion.[32]

If religion is a different problem for nonelite women, so is the evil that religion reflects and produces. Woman, body, and nature are not only gendered symbols in the West; they also encode cultural norms about racial superiority and sexual normality. Cheryl Townsend Gilkes notices this when she coins the phrases "sexualized racism" and "racialized sexism" to name some of the complex oppressions affecting African American women. Nature, too, may be less readily idealized when one's culture or race as a whole has been demonized and romanticized. Susan Thistlethwaite observes that in the writings of some African American women nature is imaged as deeply conflicted and as partaking in the chaos of social life. It is also striking that an anthology of writings on feminist theology in perspectives of the two-thirds world took "our mothers' gardens" as its central image. Here, the nature that is of theological interest is a cultivated place rather than an unrealizable ideal or a refuge for wild and innocent female life. The gardens of the imperfect mothers are the meeting place of creativity and constraint, where their daughters find weeds and nourishment and get their own hands dirty.[33]

Nonwhite and non-Euro-American women scholars are especially aware that the battles of their people are not just against ideas and symbols but against social, military, and economic force. For that reason, they may stress the systemic and autonomous features of the oppressions they face, thus echoing dualistic approaches to evil. That represents a certain challenge to the tone if not to the basic premises of rationalist responses to evil, including those produced by white feminists, which may appear too abstract to support significant political change. As Salvadoran ecumenist Marta Benavides insists, women "need to be about struggles that are real and not just academic." On the other hand, there are frequent challenges to the dualistic systems of white feminists who seem to treat male nature or male privilege as a reductive explanation for evil. For example, Delores Williams argues that the concept of patriarchy "leaves out too much," in particular the responsibility of white women for the oppression of African American women. If the term is to be understood in a way that addresses the experience of African American women, she suggests, it will need revision in the context of discussion between womanists and feminists.[34]

A recent anthology of essays by womanist scholars, edited by Emilie Townes, is now enriching the theological discussion on evil and suffering.[35] As William Jones argued, theodicy is a special question for those who have suffered at the hands of a white concept of God.[36] The womanists in this volume agree with Jones's theological diagnosis of black suffering. However, their proposed cures have less to do with reconceptualizing God than with uncovering the resources for combatting injustice in African American women's lives. Jamie Phelps lists traditional forms of the theodicy question but herself chooses to put the question "in a less speculative and more historically concrete fashion," focusing on moral evil rather than "natural" evil and on social injustice rather than individual sin. Other essays approach the search for historical resources in a similar way. One example is Clarice Martin's essay on nineteenth-century political thinker Maria Stewart, in whom Martin finds a "theodic ideology" based on "a praxis of active, oppositional engagement against racial suffering and evil."[37]

According to these thinkers, the particular liabilities of dominant moral discourse for African American women include not only oppressive notions of evil, but also certain oppressive ideals of virtue, goodness, and beauty. Frances Wood argues that the African American woman, through the romanticization of her suffering, is made the "permissible victim" of black men as well as white society. Gilkes contends that African American women "by choice and by circumstance" violate the definitions of femininity and of beauty in American culture, and she exposes the wounds that this can inflict on self-esteem. Jacquelyn Grant objects to the "overspiritualization of servanthood" in the Christian tradition, which legitimates lives of servitude for black women.[38]

In order to exorcise these internalized ideologies and confront the entrenched social forces behind them, some womanists cast the problem of evil in dualistic terms. Rosita deAnn Mathews writes of systems as having "demons" and suggests that African American women may best retain their moral integrity by exercising "power from the periphery." Marcia Riggs notes that the black club women of the nineteenth century sometimes described their work as "a battle for the rights of humanity against the demons of prejudice and injustice." In Copeland's theological framework, evil is negation as well as privation, and the suffering it produces can lead to personal, social, and cultural gains or to "the borders of hopelessness and despair."[39]

Still, in Copeland's and several others' essays, these dualistic tones are accompanied by a confidence in the ultimacy of a justice upheld by God. The club women who fought the demons of prejudice also believed, according to Riggs, that "the world was ordered by God's justice and that justice for Black people was a command of God." Reflecting on a sermon of Zora Neale Hurston's, Katie Cannon argues that "the existence of Jesus as Redeemer is embraced prior to any rational consideration of the status of evil in the world." Emilie Townes's theological formulation also rests on a "resurrection faith" in the nonfinality of suffering. Drawing on Audre Lorde, she argues that suffering is "unscrutinized and unmetabolized pain," a passive reaction to the given. Suffering is "outrage" and injustice, signaling a failure to use freedom for purposes of liberation. For Townes, transformative pain is always possible, which implies that every person "is blessed with the ability to survive and struggle regardless of the circumstance and oppression."[40]

The womanist theology of Delores Williams places what I would call dualistic tones in its foreground. Faith in God is Williams's abiding background, but she avoids leaning on that background in any way that could foster passivity or could substitute believed-in answers for real answers. The evils under which African American women have suffered, she contends, can be characterized not simply as patriarchy but as "demonarchy." Using Hagar, slave of Sarah, as her key biblical model, Williams describes the injustice against African American women as "social-role surrogacy" and makes the case that white women have shared responsibility for that injustice. The defilement of black women's bodies and sexuality is closely related to surrogacy as Williams conceptualizes it, and through this defilement the spirit and self-esteem of black women have been deeply injured.[41]

The suffering of black women, as Williams notes, elicits a heartfelt "Why?" She argues that one causal factor is the symbology in which blackness represents evil or inferiority, while whiteness represents goodness or superiority. Religious factors are part of the problem; Williams therefore calls for the selective and critical use of Christian sources and, sometimes, for the substantial revision of eurocentric doctrines. For example, she argues that traditional doctrines of atonement, in which salvation comes through the defilement and death of an innocent victim, cannot be salvific for African American women. And she argues that the Bible, when read from the viewpoint of non-Hebrew slaves, shows a distinctly "nonliberative thread." Even the biblical God is not a guarantor of liberation, Williams suggests, for that God does not liberate Hagar. The deity Hagar meets in the wilderness is "a God of Seeing" (Gen. 16:13) who enables her to see the resources to survive and improve the quality of her life and that of her child. For Williams, though, these nonliberative moments seem not to count against God's goodness, since liberation is "sparked" by human initiative and human struggle. Still, behind these liberation hopes is a transcendent faith; Williams's book ends with the pointed observation that although black women have depended on themselves and on one another, their ultimate trust has always been placed in God.[42]

Though the sociocultural contexts of other women of color differ substantially from one another and from the womanists just discussed, similar theological patterns do appear in their responses to evil. Most often, the evils that are of theological concern are not "natural" or individual but social and systemic, calling for unequivocal denunciation and creative resistance. They include political domination and repression, exploitative capitalism, and cultural imperialism, as well as all the forms of violence and domination to which women are subjected as women.[43] The traditional sources of eurocentric theology are interpreted contextually and applied selectively, while the norm of theology is formulated to support directly the survival and liberation of nonelite peoples. Negatively, the goal is to defuse those religious applications that have supported structures of oppression. Positively, the goal is to mobilize those religious applications, whether Christian or not, that can empower survival and encourage liberation. Among the most frequently recurring Christian themes is that of theological equality of the sexes in the *imago Dei* and in Christ.[44] The fight for liberation is at once a struggle for full humanity and a revelation of the divine nature and plan. That confident sense of a struggle upheld by God may even be reflected in the optimistic language of apocalypticism. For example, a group of Asian women theologians pray that "our varied gifts and insights may be welded into one powerful tide to help overcome the forces of death and evil, and usher in the New Creation in Asia."[45]

Through these and other hermeneutic strategies, women of color and women of the two-thirds world are infusing Christianity with liberative meaning. Just as importantly, however, they are enlisting the cultural power and authority of Christianity for political ends. The key issue, it seems to me, is how to name and redirect that *religious* power in a way that does not deflate *political* power or obscure its innerworldly dynamics. The Asian women just quoted, for example, frame their apocalyptic hope as a prayer, an act of commitment—not as a dogmatic assertion, and not as a triumphalist expectation. I am struck too by how Shawn Copeland expresses her hopes for Harriet Jacobs, whose self-esteem was so injured by her forced sexual choices. "Can we not hope," asks Copeland, "that in the life of death, Harriet Jacobs has found 'god in [her]self and loves her/loves her fiercely?' "[46] It is a question, not a creed, and in the question is a lament as well as a hope, a promise to hold the past with honor and tenderness, however broken and unresolved that past may be.

Still, a profound theological dilemma arises here, between the commitment to transpose theology into a political, transformative key and the need to support that political agenda with the authority of religion and the surety of faith. In her introduction, for example, Emilie Townes observes that womanist thought "debunks the notion of universals and absolutes" in eurocentric discourse. Yet she also wants to claim for womanist ethics "a universal dimension and critique."[47] Jamie Phelps contends that racism and sexism are "not compatible with the Christian belief in the equality of all human beings," but she also details the historical fact that many white Christians had no religious misgivings about holding or trading slaves. Isasi-Díaz and Tarango buttress their argument that the spiritualities of Hispanic women have a right to be called Christian with the claim that the "core of the gospel message" is "justice and love." And a group of Asian women theologians authorize their revision of the Marian tradition with the claim that "the real meaning of the Virgin Birth is the end of the patriarchal order."[48] I fully support the moral and political values behind each of these statements, but I question the universalist and essentialist terms in which they are framed. How can we use theology to *change* what is true in this world without counting on another, higher world in which "what is" and "what ought to be" are eternally the same? What is the relationship between these theological truth claims made in the name of justice, and the historical sphere in which justice cannot be *asserted* as true but must be *made* true?

This dilemma is not at all unique to women of color. In my view, it is endemic to theology in the postmodern age. Now, the vitality of theology and of Christianity as a global religion hinges on how credibly contemporary ideas of justice can be applied to the interpretation of Christianity's past and the shaping of its future. However, when ideals of justice and equality are used to name the essence of Christianity or the direction of history, what is gained in moral suasion may be lost in political clarity. As J. B. Metz said of the hare and the hedgehog, we may fancy ourselves to have won the race, without having actually run it; for no one opposes "justice" in the abstract, but when we are dealing with differences of power and interest, it is not easy to forge a practical consensus about what comprises justice in the concrete. Along with African Americans, white Christian Americans in the 1990s may shake their heads at the hypocrisy of the slaveholding Christianity of the past; in so doing, whites can feel that they too are on the side of justice and that God is therefore not against them. But to work out in the *present* what it is necessary and possible and best to do about race relations is another, far more contentious matter. In order to foster real justice and equality in the present, I would argue, we should all beware the believed-in goodness of any God or Goddess who is invulnerable to the sufferings and chaos of history.

Tragic Sensibilities in Religious Feminism

These days, a sense of the tragic is seeping into religious feminism from every quarter. Wendy Farley's *Tragic Vision and Divine Compassion: A Contemporary Theodicy* is the most fully articulated reflection on tragedy in feminist theology to date.[49] Against the tradition of the Fall and against contemporary liberation theologies, Farley argues that suffering cannot be reduced to fault or even to injustice. In her thoughtful formulation, suffering results necessarily from the "tragic structure" of the finite world. Though not evil in itself, suffering regularly leads to radical dehumanization and to sin in its individual and corporate forms. Even our moral vulnerability to sin is built into the tragic structure of existence as Farley understands it. Nonetheless, she sees tragic dramas as testifying to the enduring possibility of resistance to evil. Theologically, Farley suggests a kinship between tragic resistance and compassion—a kind of love that is unself-centered, noncoercive, empowering, and universal in scope. In the phenomenology of compassion she discerns a justification of God: Compassion is the kind of power that it is logically possible for a loving

God to exert in a finite world. God thus remains both good and omnipotent; divine love must be tragically structured if creation is to be truly other than divine.

Farley observes that tragedies imply that life really is unjust. Yet she argues that in the hero's resistance "another layer of the world is peeled back" and we "glimpse something beyond the apparent finality of evil." Radical suffering, she writes, "can cripple the very humanity of its victims" and does so routinely. Yet the power of compassion, by her account, seems invulnerable to disfigurement. She images suffering as a "veil" and sin as "an iron curtain," but behind them is the "ultimacy of goodness" and mercy. In history and creation, she concedes, "evil *is* stronger than good."[50] Still, in adhering to the "nonfinality" of evil, she seems to point beyond history and creation to something more real and ultimate.

In its eloquence and sensitivity, Farley's work is as successful as a contemporary theodicy can be. But it seems to me that there is an inherent incongruity between tragedy, which indicts both the divine and the human, and theodicy, which aims to vindicate God. By linking tragedy more to finitude than to sociality, more to suffering than to fault, Farley notices the plurality and vulnerability of goods but does not absorb the shocking plurality of truth itself. So, while she remembers that even one event like the torture of Arthur Haley's Kunta in *Roots* "would mar and tear the very fabric of the created order," she still strains beyond this rent world to espy an ultimate identity of goodness and power. Greek tragedy, she observes correctly, was not nihilistic.[51] But, I would add, it was no single god and no single truth that saved the tragedians from nihilism, only concrete communities with their fractured but existentially ultimate worlds.

In identifying compassion as the outcome of a tragic sensibility, Farley names what I also take to be a chief theological gain of reflection on evil. But compassion itself, I would argue, is no one thing; as a feeling, it is a far from infinite energy, and as a moral orientation it selects no single course of action. I am uneasy with conceiving compassion simply as *empowerment*, because that implies that the things we judge evil are repressed forms of power rather than active and productive. I cannot call compassion universal if that allows us to retreat from the embattled world under the honorable banner of liberal inclusivity. And I cannot believe that compassion is entirely noncoercive, given the fields of political, economic, social, and legal force in which all activity, however compassionate, remains caught. In a postmodern world, compassion must allow itself to be broken by the multiplicity of truths and goods. In this context, when compassion as an item of metaphysical faith grows less credible, religious feminists can begin to explore together other meanings of compassion as a practice, choice, and disposition.

Tragedy is also beginning to present itself as a theological question in the work of feminists who are deeply committed to particular communities or involved in forming alliances across communities divided by historical injustice. In *Sex, Race and God*, Susan Thistlethwaite reflects theologically on the white racism that undermines alliances between white and African American women. In white women, she finds that racism is preserved within an intolerance of difference, which is expressed in a longing for moral innocence and undifferentiated unity, and in an inability to recognize their own anger and aggression. Faced with their responsibility for racism, Thistlethwaite points out, white women may become paralyzed with guilt or retreat into an idealized, harmonious nature to which women as a sex are thought to belong.

Rejecting this retreat from history to paradise, Thistlethwaite looks to Angela Davis and Toni Morrison for views of nature as conflicted and "deranged" by injustice. For Thistlethwaite justice can only be approached via the rough and forthright meeting of differences, which takes energy from "the raging chaos of the nature of things." Feminist theologians must work "after the Fall, after the knowledge of good and evil, not in the garden."[52] Like Karen McCarthy Brown, Thistlethwaite discovers that a tragic view of life can be energizing in that it countenances anger and aggression as among life's vital forces. Such a vision of life might assist white women in recognizing their own anger and aggression, which would then be less likely to "grab us from behind" in forms such as unacknowledged racism.[53]

Rather than synergizing this tragic vision with the intellectual questions of postmodernity, however, Thistlethwaite criticizes postmodern thought for potentially undermining the commitment to justice. While appreciating certain features of poststructuralism, she is uneasy with its relativism, which she fears will leave "no place to stand to absolutely condemn" evils such as "sexual violence against women, or even the sexual abuse of children." Taking her epistemological clues from Sojourner Truth, she instead proposes a community-based criterion of "truth-in-action"; truth is what effects movement toward justice in community.[54]

However, given that communities are internally conflicted and externally embattled, how can "truth-in-action" itself escape relativism? Here Thistlethwaite seems to lean on God, which she identifies with justice[55], as the firm ground on which communities can rise above the conflict of history and the derangement of nature. However, I have argued that justice, if constructed as both a moral ideal and an ontological warrant, is as endangered today as is God. It seems to me that what makes morality tragic today is also what makes it postmodern, namely the need to build moral commitments in the ruins of the Absolute.

For Sharon Welch, in contrast, tragic vision grew as the combined result of postmodern relativism and moral commitment to specific "communities of resistance and solidarity." For Welch truth is practical and not speculative.[56] With Michel Foucault, she thinks of power as productive rather than repressive of truth. She has therefore broken with the pattern of interpreting social injustice in terms of falsehood or repression, preferring instead to see liberation movements as what Foucault would call "insurrections of subjugated knowledges." In Welch's view, resisting knowledges do not fund their power through a bank of transcendent Truth; they are verified only in political actualization. Rejecting the God of classical theism, Welch defines the divine as "adverb" or "adjective," a *quality* of healing grace. It is a purely immanent ideal, not the *source* of relational power but simply relational power itself.[57]

Lacking absolute grounding of any kind, Welch's theology can neither avoid the risk of nihilism nor withdraw into the "cultured despair of the middle class."[58] In the face of tragedy and loss, especially the loss of innocence about the moral powers of humanity,[59] she risks commitment to the possible good. Like Thistlethwaite, she senses new energy in this theological approach. It is possible, she suggests, to "dance with life," to meet its conflict and constriction not only with resistance but also with mourning, rage, remembrance, celebration, *jouissance*.[60] Welch recognizes that in the postmodern era truth is breaking loose from goodness and instead becoming attached to the fractured, multiple discourses of power. Choosing a side, she identifies the divine with goodness as a moral *quality*, not with ontic structures or processes. The goodness for which she stands possesses its own kind of power, but that power is only one among many, just as the good of a particular community of accountability remains one of a plurality of goods.

But what is the status of other powers, especially those a feminist community might consider evil, such as racism, misogyny, or class privilege? If they are not less real than power-in-relation, what is gained by associating the latter with the divine? An aura of absolute authority still lingers around the ideals of "justice" that are framed under the auspices of biblical ethical monotheism. But that authority, I have argued, has its own intellectual and political liabilities. A parallel predicament applies to the plurality of goods, which are not perspicuously collected under any single moral quality. The religious and moral risk of tragic consciousness, I suggest, is to encounter elemental power/truth in its radical plurality, unmooring the good from any metaphysical anchor, so that it becomes an entirely human, entirely fragile creation.

In addition to the detailed reflections of Farley, Thistlethwaite, and Welch, there are many intimations of tragic sensibility in religious feminism. Partly, this is because the line between good and evil is now less likely to be placed between traditional religions and feminist spirituality. For example, Charlene Spretnak's *States of Grace* makes use of the "wisdom traditions" of mainstream world religions along with feminist spirituality and Native American ways.[61] At the same time, many feminists within or on the boundaries of Christianity or Judaism have explicitly rejected the ahistorical notion of a liberative "core" or essence within religious traditions.[62]

The tragic convention of questioning the divine is also making a resurgence among religious feminists. Catherine Madsen has put this most forcefully, arguing that "if God is God She is not nice," and that in view of the "inseparability of good and evil," feminists ought to give up the presumption of a benign divinity. Supporting Madsen's questions, Emily Culpepper argues against replacing theodicy with "theadicy" and shows how comfort can be found by "*living in the paradox*" of miracle and cruelty.[63] Jewish feminist Judith Plaskow faces the same issues from a monotheistic perspective. She argues that a truly inclusive monotheism must address evil as a part of God; she does not bother with justificatory theodicy but wonders honestly about "the irrationality and ambiguity of the sacred."[64]

When nature and the spirit world are less idealized, spirituality also becomes more susceptible to the creative disturbance of tragedy. Women's views of nature are undoubtedly as varied as are their experiences of life, but there may be a correlation between women's views of nature and their relative historical distances from indigenous traditions in which the world is an encompassing whole and "nature" is not a foil for patriarchy or fallen history. For instance, Karen McCarthy Brown finds a tragic but invigorating vision in the spirit world of Vodou, where conflict is "an inevitable, in fact, essential ingredient of life" and to understand something is "to know the dance that goes with it." Delores Williams describes the spirit of the black church and of womanist theology with similar metaphors. Like a jazz symphony, womanist theology may sound like discord to conventional ears; in fact, it *is* a "disruption of the harmony in both the black American and white American social, political and religious status quo."[65]

At heart, tragedy is the moral paradox that beings who want goodness cannot remain uncontaminated by evil, that even faultedness belongs to

the enigma of suffering. Katie Cannon articulated this paradox in a politically engaged way when she exposed the tacit race, sex, and class
provenances of the idea of an originally or absolutely free will; she
counterpoised a womanist "ethic of survival" to the classical Western
ethics that was predicated on these anti-tragic assumptions. Carter Heyward and Sally McFague, too, have each reflected explicitly on the tragic
and in the process have crafted compelling, socially activist redefinitions
of sin and evil.[66]

There is a depth of struggle in which we exist, women and men, before
and beyond our judgment and our acts, and here religious feminism stands
to be especially enlightened by responses to evil that are not confined
to the Western repository. Rita Nakashima Brock and Naomi Southard
write that Asian American women often describe community as founded
on a sense of unity in suffering and of God as present there as well.
These views of suffering link Christianity with Buddhist and Hindu themes
but, Brock and Southard contend, do not replicate "the martyrdom of
self-sacrifice associated with Christian masochism."[67]

As Chung Hyun Kyung says, "making meaning out of suffering is a
dangerous business."[68] I would add that it is a business women do every
day, and the closer theologians stay to those complex, organic processes,
the more *modes* of meaning we uncover for dealing with evil and suffering.
For example, Korean theologian Soon-Hwa Sun tells the stories of two
women who became deeply involved in the Korean workers' struggle. In
both cases, Sun notices, confrontation with ideologies of oppression
"strains the limits of women's faith even as faith becomes their means
for continuing struggle."[69] "Faith" here has more than one meaning, and
so does meaning itself. To find meaning and make meaning from the torn
fabric of suffering is something women do on many levels: We demand
social change and we search for intellectual coherence, but we also
release our feelings and let fly our tenacious creativity. Even absurdity
is included among the modes of meaning, and humor is among women's
most potent spiritual resources.[70] But a conceptual world with no room
for the tragic has no room for the comic either, since contradiction felt
as pleasure has been even more repugnant to Western moralism than
has been contradiction felt as pain. As religious feminism opens to the
tragic, we may rediscover the comic-religious along with the aesthetic-
and mystical-religious as theological resources.[71]

To Untangle the Suffering of Women

Welch, Thistlethwaite, Spretnak, and other feminists have good reason
for resisting the full theological implications of postmodern relativism

and/or tragic conflict. Feminism is fundamentally a set of moral and political commitments, and it is not clear how these commitments can be supported without the usual metaphysical warrants. Moreover, women scholars have different intellectual relationships to postmodernity depending on their historical relationships to modernity, whether as its beneficiaries or as members of communities that have as yet tasted little of "equality," "freedom," "progress," or "democracy." Although many Euro-American feminists have grown skeptical of these as ideologies of Western triumphalism and as emblems of the shrinking Enlightenment "subject," we do well not to impose a one-size-fits-all critique of liberalism on women scholars of religion. Sheila Greeve Davaney has rightly criticized the tacit ontological claims on which the theological programs of Rosemary Radford Ruether, Mary Daly, and Elisabeth Schüssler Fiorenza rest,[72] but if we are to force feminist work from its metaphysical islands, we must teach it to breathe in the deep waters of tragedy.

The forms of postmodernism most fashionable in academic circles today do not offer much of that kind of wisdom. There is talk about the political noninnocence of all cultural creation, but less about guilt; talk about the impossibility of neutrality but less about taking positions. Nor has the enthusiastic denaturalization of culture so far brought much new insight about how to fashion cultures that will replenish the earth. It is as if the critique of truth as plural excuses an abdication of intellectual commitment as such, or as if the critique of social injustice slips into a utopic evasion of sociality as such. Why would the death of the One leave only nihilistic truthlessness in its wake, unless Truth is still secretly assumed to be one and transcendent? Why would the critique of power aim at sociality as such rather than at social injustice, unless a human nature quarantined from the defiling effects of social power is still imagined?

The postmodernism of dominant people is still tempted by the universalism and transcendence that is its patrimony. Now as always, that is a false universalism and a false transcendence, disguising the actual political, moral, and aesthetic commitments on which intellectual work is shakily founded. Anti-tragic postmodernisms do indeed display what Frederick Jameson calls the "cultural logic of late capitalism."[73] They also display, feminists could add, the eviscerated logic of patriarchal spirituality, which could not survive the encounter with real multiplicity, embodiment, pleasure, and pain without collapsing into despair or fleeing from commitment. As Catherine Keller has observed, it is not coincidental that the postmodern critique of the self comes at just the historical moment when female and other subjugated selves are emerging into the fields of intellectual power.[74] For that and related reasons, she, Spretnak, Thistlethwaite, and others contend, feminists should adopt the insights of postmodernism selectively and critically, allowing themselves to be shaken loose from essentialism of every kind, but not giving in to new and universalistic forms of relativism.

The question of tragedy reemerges with such force in the postmodern situation because, precisely in the midst of radical plurality, we must make commitments and take sides. At this very point, postmodernity becomes a theological and ethical question; we must now justify our regional intelligibilities without reference to an absolute intelligibility, and we must quilt together the best integrity we can in a world that is not essentially whole. To do that, we need to demand as necessary and accept as sufficient a specific kind of theological warrant: the historical and political description of the contexts in which our theo-ethical claims can be made good and made true.

But women have an especially complicated relationship with the old metaphysical warrants that have so long been deployed to delegitimate female power and goodness. In response to this, I have shown, the basic moves of religious feminism have been to exorcise the patriarchal language of evil and to enlist ideals such as nature or justice in the service of women. Those procedures should not be abandoned, but additional methods are needed to handle the contradictions they generate. For the more complex the analysis of oppression becomes, the more women are also exposed as among its beneficiaries, whether by the privileges of class or race or sexuality. That does not mean that women are equally responsible with men for the injustices of history; equal responsibility would have to mean equal power, and power is unevenly distributed between women and men, as among men and among women. Women do have reason to fear the language of guilt, since elites are often eager to spread guilt more evenly than power has ever been. But only the utterly powerless are utterly innocent, and few women today want to claim that distinction. The web, valued by many feminists as an image of connection, is instructive here: Webs do connect women and their worlds, often more than they want, but in connecting may also capture and consume. The challenge is not for women to extricate themselves from the web, but to think and choose responsibly within it.

By applying a tragic heuristic, religious feminists can approach evil as a *question* for insight and judgment, not as a legitimating explanation. When evil is explained ontologically as a something, or explained away ontologically as a nothing, we reach a theological cul-de-sac, an end to further insight or strategies for change. That is the difficulty with the notion of patriarchy; though its descriptive adequacy as a name for social evil can be enhanced by inclusion of race, class, and other factors, its explanatory adequacy is impaired by the implication that evils of every kind are due to male interests or male nature. With regard to positive moral judgment as well, religious feminists might gain more insight from inquiring about plurality than from appealing to the ideal oneness of nature or justice. In a postmodern context, "nature," like "woman," can no longer be quarantined from the moral pollutions of social life. The social determination of consciousness can no longer be seen as a falsification of or alienation from a natural world that remains whole and intact beneath, nor can nature be meaningfully conceptualized as something outside sociality, either as the latter's raw material or as its Ideal. Sociality itself has to be thought of as a dimension of nature, and ideals of justice as a product of sociality, which alone can provide their confirmation.

Fundamentally, the issue at stake in feminist theological responses to evil is the purpose and method of theology in a postmodern age. Until now, theology has been a means of providing metaphysical authorization for particular visions of how the world ought to be. Women scholars are understandably tempted to seize that same legitimating procedure for feminist ends. But there are other ways to do theology, more suited to the present moment, like the method Chung Hyun Kyung compares to the Korean folk practice of *han-pu-ri*.[75] *Han*, Chung explains, is the "lump in the spirit" caused by built-up suffering and anger; even the dead may become ridden by a *han* that will not allow them to rest. *Han-pu-ri*, the "untanglement of *han*," can be achieved by "gentle" means such as dance and song, or by "militant means" such as organized political resistance. Only by naming the *han* and eliminating its causes wherever possible can the *han*-ridden be comforted.

Something like *han* rides women and the ghosts of women everywhere—for the brutality suffered at the hands of men and their institutions, for the exploitation and callousness that women, especially elites, have passed on to other women, even for the predatory, unmerciful faces of life. Our rightful rage, our secret remorse, and our human sorrows have been tightly bound and knotted under the long regime of patriarchal ideologies. To untangle that knot, feminist scholars of religion must themselves feel and name its contradictory truths, uncleansed and unidealized. This apprehension of complexity does not substitute for taking action; indeed, it may prove to support a more sustainable feminist politics.

In this tangled world, the religious reflection of women, like that of men, can draw more wisdom from the living functions and clashes of community than from pure Ideas or Ideals. The continuing power and persuasiveness of feminist theo(a)logy will depend much less on whether we have theoretical answers to evil than on whether we "know the dance" that goes with moral discernment in our places and moments. Dancing our many rhythms in the ruins of patriarchal paradise, women may meet in each Other the sylvan sister, scarred but strangely beautiful.

CHAPTER FOUR

LILITH AND EVE
SISTERS IN STRUGGLE

*I have traced the ideological patterns in Christian
thought which have served to justify violence and
oppression. . . .*

*The "headship" of men over women is seen as
reflected in the "headship" of God, imaged as a
patriarchal male, over creation and the church, imaged
as female. This "naturalizing" of social hierarchy also
is built on a spirit-matter, mind-body split. Racism,
classism, and human domination of non-human
nature are built on a similar model of head over body,
spirit over matter.*

—Rosemary Radford Ruether[1]

*With regard to life or death, there is no ultimate
justice, nor ultimate injustice, for there is no promise
that life will be other than it is. Knowledge that we are
but a small part of life and death and transformation
is the essential religious insight. The essential
religious response is to rejoice and to weep, to sing
and to dance, to tell stories and create rituals in praise
of an existence far more complicated, more intricate,
more enduring than we are.*

—Carol P. Christ[2]

Crying is a funny thing: what's it for?

—Doris Lessing[3]

FEMINIST THEOLOGY and thealogy, too, are funny things, and it will be my purpose in these chapters to meditate on what they might be for. What they are *from*, in any case, are the imponderable sufferings of women, which flood the earth and accuse heaven. For Rosemary Radford Ruether, women's passion for justice is itself heaven's defense, pouring down to lower the mighty and buoy the oppressed. For Carol P. Christ, heaven's God has been impeached and unseated, and it is the ancient rhythms of the living earth that rock in the weeping, loving, and dancing of women.

The style of their words matches these distinct responses to women's suffering. Ruether's usual tone is crisply analytical, her purview historical, her aims didactic and dialectical. Injustice is her guiding theological problem, and it has drawn her erudition and moral wisdom not only to the suffering of women but to a panoply of global issues. Her tone is analytical because she aims to demystify the ideologies of injustice, which misappropriate to social structures the stubborn exigencies of finitude itself. Her critical perception of *what ought not to be* casts into question every extant version of the "natural" and makes social renewal and change the primary means for recentering ourselves in life as divinely intended.

Christ's melodic writing mixes poetry and autobiography with history and argumentation. Her aim is not to wrest blessings from patriarchal Reason but to clear ground for the reemergence of a different intuition. Like Ruether she cares about justice and peace, but political struggle is not what comes to mind when she asks herself what is essentially *religious*. Religiously, she is persuaded by life's beauty and power, which she finds in the mixture of light and darkness,[4] birth, change, and death. The mixture heals, not by analytically separating finite necessity and moral fault but by artfully transforming sorrow into song. From nature's inscrutable acceptance Christ learns that even injustice is compost. In an interpretive pattern that is almost the inverse of Ruether's, she names both Western patriarchy's disgust with physicality and its denunciations of "sin" as refusals of life's mystery. While Ruether's skepticism is directed especially at the rhetoric of acceptance, it is the rhetoric of radical negation which Christ finds most dysfunctional.

Considering in one gaze the array of concerns present in each woman's work, we may be as loathe to choose between them as between bread and roses. Yet there is also some gap between the sensibilities of each thinker, some way in which her work says to the other "yes, but" rather

than "yes, and . . . !" These tensions, I will show, are more than simply
the result of the life-choices that have placed these and other Euro-
American religious feminists in distinct religious camps. They also mark
the fissures between intellectual patterns that fit together like puzzle
pieces, so that where one grows a bump, the other suffers a dent—pieces
that lie side by side unable to see that together they picture a world in
which tragedy, in the strong sense, cannot appear.

I am not proposing a one-size-fits-all feminist thealogy or theology; I
fully agree with Christ and Ruether that neopaganism and Christianity
are among the many authentic but imperfect religious options available
to feminists. I am arguing that every spiritual community optimally possesses functions that may be classified as mystical, aesthetic, and moral:
contact with and celebration of life's vital powers, an eye for beauty and
the skills to create and enhance it, an ability to mourn the losses, repent
the wrongs, and reform the injustices of the past. More controversially,
I am claiming that one or another of these functions are typically not
given their due within various feminist theo(a)logies. I am suggesting
that these inadequacies are partly due to certain long-standing anti-tragic
patterns of thought that have become so familiar in Christian theology
and its descendants as to be virtually unnoticeable. My own position is
no Archimedian point or Hegelian synthesis, but itself invites evaluation
even as it evaluates the characteristic strengths and weaknesses of the
other two positions.

So I set out on the bridge between Rosemary Radford Ruether and
Carol Christ—a bridge long flooded by their common desire to say that
sorrow cannot have been and cannot be life's first or final word for
women. Retreating from this flood to the higher ground of "nature," they
have both evaded the tragic vulnerability that clings to any truly integral
notion of the human good. Both misdiagnose the metaphysical dualism
of spirit and matter as patriarchal Christianity's illness, when in fact that
has been but the worst symptom of a more respectable disease: the
rationalism and moralism that refuse to make their home in a world of
absurdity and fault. Feminist theology and thealogy speak, as they should,
out of the absurdity and fault that are patriarchy's underside. But
our passion to make sense of that insanity and right those wrongs
becomes, at its extremities, susceptible to similar attacks from our own
excluded surd.

Construing the problem in twos, Christ and Ruether come offering
Ones: Christ with the memory of a primal whole in the pattern of feminist
romantic dualism, Ruether with the vision of an ideal but finite harmony
in the pattern of feminist rationalism. Today, I venture to suggest, it is

more helpful to think of patriarchal ideology as a reduction of multiplicity than as a splitting of oneness, and the reduction of multiplicity is not best addressed by the invocation of a unifying principle. In appealing to such principles, Christ and Ruether continue the long theological defense of God, which now becomes the defense of nature. This does not detract from the unique and substantial accomplishments of either thinker, which the next chapters will explore in some detail. It does limit their engagement with the elemental multiplicity of goods and powers, a multiplicity that now renders any One, including the attempted community of women, so intellectually and politically problematic.

The public dialogue between Ruether and Christ has consisted largely of disagreements over the relative feminist merits and demerits of biblical and Goddess-centered spiritualities. Sometimes they have questioned and criticized each other by name; at other times they have raised broad questions about the movement to which the other belongs. These disagreements touch on a wide range of issues, each of which is significant to feminist religious thought in its own right. Here, however, these disagreements are sketched only to highlight the distinct responses to evil or negativity on which the positions rest and to lift up a common need to resolve what cannot be fully resolved—the ancient suffering of women under patriarchy.

Evil as a Religious Problem: To Leave or Reclaim Christianity

Carol Christ, like many others, has gained from Ruether's critique of metaphysical dualism as the ideology of Western patriarchy. While still at Yale Divinity School, Christ wrote appreciatively of Ruether in this regard, mentioning as well Ruether's articulation of the link between the depredation of the earth under the Father God and the lost legacy of the Earth Goddess. This line of analysis, Christ would conclude, led away from the biblical God and back to the divinity of the natural world. She found similar implications in Ruether's dissection of Christian theological anti-Semitism, which she absorbed in the same period. Ruether had ably demonstrated that sexism and anti-Semitism are not mere anomalies in Christian thought but are deeply woven into its inner logic. When *Beyond God the Father* was published in 1973, Christ was ready to conclude with Mary Daly that Christianity was as irredeemably sexist as it was irredeemably anti-Semitic. By 1979 she aligned herself with the feminist "revolutionaries" who called "not only for a change in the understanding of the core symbolism of Western religion, but also for a change in the symbolism itself."[5]

For Ruether herself, however, her devastating critique of theology did not imply a wholesale rejection of Christianity. Utterly to condemn the Bible or biblical religions, she argued in 1979, is biased and unhistorical.[6] All important works of culture carry the imprint of patriarchal ideology, but they also contain critical insights and principles that can help to correct those ideological distortions. In the Bible Ruether discerned such a critical principle in the "prophetic-messianic" tradition, which measures the social and religious order from the standpoint of poor and oppressed people. Though not applied to women within the Bible itself, this critical pattern can be seized to voice women's demands for justice.

Ruether's approach to history and culture appeared to hinge on a theological principle: evil must be conceived as a problem internal to the lives of persons and traditions, not as an exterior wart on an otherwise perfect body. Ignoring this principle, she believed, led to bad ethics, naïve psychology, and poor historical scholarship. Neopagan feminists were constructing ancient Goddesses in the image of the nineteenth-century divine-feminine, but the historical provenance of their Goddesses was actually the Near Eastern Goddess-King cult. Moreover, Ruether observed, those Goddesses stood not for "nature" but for the forces of fertility and social life, which were jointly invoked to secure male kingship. On the basis of their modern Romanticism, Goddess feminists were effecting a "symbolic reversal" of male dominance; Ruether saw evidence of this in certain feminist separatist practices that portended that feminists themselves might become "megalomaniacal and lacking in self-criticism."

It was useful, Ruether felt, to correct patriarchal negativism about nature, women, and the body, but not by simplistically dividing history, religion, and humanity into feminist sheep and patriarchal goats. Her 1980 critique, which included Christ by name, centered on this question of how evil was being interpreted within Goddess feminism.[7] She was particularly disturbed by the suggestion in Daly's *Gyn/Ecology* that females are by nature morally superior to males. Some Goddess feminists, she suggested, seem to be identifying with the "suppressed animus" of patriarchy; no doubt she had in mind the self-identification of Christ, Daly, and others as "heretics," "witches," "hags," and the like. This rebellious identification with what patriarchy identified as evil, she feared, would inoculate women against genuine *self*-critique and "allow the evil [in women] to overwhelm and destroy our own souls." Likening the association of women and nature to the Nazi ideology of blood and soil, she even attacked separatist practices as "fascistic."

Ruether's moral alarm at Goddess feminism was evidenced by her provocative use of terms such as "fascist" and "Nazi," which function in the late twentieth century as the devil even rationalists can believe in. But the terms say something important, if not about postbiblical feminism, at least about Ruether's understanding of evil. Evil, for her, is not an ontological "something," nor is good an *immanent* "something." Her point was that evil must not be entirely projected onto an Other, since this legitimates the oppression of that Other and also leaves one's own group accountable to no higher good. This, to Ruether's mind, was the central error of patriarchal theology, and Goddess feminism was repeating it by absolutizing the immanent goods of women and nature.

Implicit in this analysis, however, was the paradox of Ruether's own view of evil and the reason for her moral alarm. In the tradition of Christian rationalism, she conceived evil as nothing more than illusion and falsehood. The intellectual problem of evil then becomes how to account for the fact that this falsehood and illusion take on a power that is real and systematic. The answer becomes a familiar one in Christian theology: insofar as the world is a place where evil exerts power, the world must be conceived of as estranged from Being. What is called good, natural, and necessary in the here and now must therefore be subjected to a transcendent proviso, lest the real but relative goods of the world begin to count themselves absolute. Evils, for Ruether, are only idols—false and ultimately impotent powers. But idols, believed in, become demons; in fact, she has often used the language of demons, powers, and principalities to characterize patriarchy and other unjust social structures.[8] Refusing to believe in idols, while acknowledging their power, she assumed that belief in a transcendent goodness is vital for a healthy moral consciousness and could not imagine how such a consciousness could be sustained when the divine is reduced to pure immanence. Moreover, she believed that the dynamics of social evil call for rational analysis and realistic politics, and she found little of either in the ritualism and intuitionism of the Goddess movement. Worst of all, it seemed to her, Goddess feminism tended to project evil entirely onto males, leaving behind the megalomaniacal illusion of innocent female power—an illusion that then exhibits the fearsome power of an unconscious motive.

Ruether's own affirmation of women, nature, and body was based on a concept of transcendence that inadvertently inferiorized the immanent deity of Goddess feminism. Ruether's God is reflected in nature, since nature is divinely created. But for Ruether, as we shall see, nature-as-divinely-created is not exactly what we have in this world. As she wrote in 1980, sin and injustice have defaced human character and even the cosmos itself, so that "the original harmony of humanity with nature and God" exists only "but as a lost paradise and future hope, which we taste now and again in the midst of our broken existence." Natural goodness, she cautioned, cannot be restored by magical or ritual action ("a romp on the beach or a chant around the campfire") or by escape "into an unfallen paradise of 'nature.' " For women, as for men, paradise *is* truly lost and can be reimagined only in the context of "ethical struggle" toward an Ideal that remains transcendent. The doctrines of "sin, fallenness, transcendence and future," stumbling blocks for Goddess feminists, became the cornerstones of Ruether's Christian feminism. Interpreting sexism as "a primal expression of human fallenness," she argued, this "biblical pattern" can be grasped "with new power and meaning."[9]

Christ was startled by the vehemence of Ruether's critique of the Goddess movement and attempted to respond point by point.[10] Against Ruether's charges of religious exclusivism, she pointed to her own support for religious diversity among feminists and observed that religious choices are complex matters of individual judgment. Nonetheless, she defended her personal rejection of the biblical God and traditions, the "essential core" of which she adjudged sexist rather than liberating. The God of the prophets took the side of the rural poor, Christ noted, but he also denounced their "idolatry"; he liberated the chosen people, but by making holy war on their enemies.

In fact, the issue of religious exclusivism has been somewhat misplaced on both sides of this dialogue. Christ has never impugned the integrity of women who remain loyal to Judaism or Christianity, but she has made a judgment, at once personal and philosophical, that the liberative elements of these traditions cannot be extricated from their patriarchal contexts. Ruether has never impugned the integrity of a religious choice for Goddess feminism. But she has insisted on the ambiguity of all traditions and asked how, in the absence of the moral language provided by biblical religions, Goddess feminists will deal honestly with the dangers of paganism, old and new. Accusations of religious intolerance have hidden the deeper and more theo(a)logical issue, which is how and whether the divine can be conceived in a way that does not automatically inferiorize the spirituality of feminists on paths other than one's own. For Christ the question was fundamentally that of divine transcendence, which she had come to reject, in part because it reduces nature deities to idols or demons. Stripped of transcendence, the biblical God became to her nothing more than his symbols. No conceptual operation could detach the liberating aspects of that symbol from the misogyny, aggression, and intolerance that compose God's other face.

Evil as a Theo(a)logical Problem:
Immanence or Transcendence

The rejection of divine transcendence also affected Christ's construction of the Goddess. When she looked to ancient Goddesses for a religious legacy, she had in mind not the cult of the Goddess and King but the pre-patriarchal Goddesses reconstructed by Marija Gimbutas and others. This Goddess was not the "nature" in a Romantic nature-culture dualism, nor was she to be equated with the Romantic or Jungian "feminine."[11] But the Goddess did represent for Christ the duality between *patriarchal* culture and a more holistic culture, reconciled to mortality and change. Neither this Goddess nor her female devotees were "feminine" in the Romantic or Jungian senses. Their separatist strategies did not necessarily entrain either separatism "as a total worldview" or the religious exclusion or subordination of men. However, Christ observed, the Goddess does afford women an unambiguous spiritual affirmation. She could not understand why Ruether would not be supportive of that. For Ruether, however, the lack of moral nuance in Goddess feminism's affimation of women was exactly what was most worrisome.

While Ruether was defending nature from its patriarchal detractors and the transcendent God from feminist detractors, Christ was identifying the notion of transcendence as itself a *symbol* for the divine, and a questionable symbol at that. In a 1983 typology of feminist symbols for the divine, she suggested that "God," both in his maleness and his purported transcendence, "may have outlived its usefulness as an exclusive mediator between humans and the ultimate reality that grounds and sustains our lives."[12] She did not notice, however, that she and Ruether meant different things by divine transcendence. Ruether wanted God as the ground of moral transcendence, which she believed could be extricated from metaphysical dualism,[13] while Christ rejected both moral and metaphysical dualism. Still employing Ruether's critique of metaphysical dualism as theoretical backdrop for her own rejection of God, Christ could not account for why Ruether had shown "less interest in female symbolism for God than [have] many other feminist theologians."[14] In actuality, the tone of Ruether's writings on contemporary Goddess worship had ranged from skepticism to suspicion.[15] That was due not to any vestigial antinaturalism but to Ruether's abiding moral and rational interests.

Christ, for her part, denied God's traditional perfections in order to reject the absolute transcendence of disembodied spirit, not to wallow in banal immanence. In treating Goddesses and Gods as *symbols*, she did not mean that they were purely artifacts of the conscious mind, to be manipulated at will, but rather that they operated in the medial region between articulate consciousness and the "deep mind" that intuits the "nature of being." In Goddess spirituality, as she understood it, feminist consciousness shapes and is shaped by women's deepest intuitions of being. While it "would be foolish" to suggest that Goddess imagery alone empowers women, she argued, it could assist women to "no longer feel that the feminist political struggle is against the tide of history or the course of nature." Nor was Christ suggesting that the transition from Goddess to God "was a simple transition from matriarchy to patriarchy"; she found "no convincing evidence" of this. But it was clear to her that the superiority so often assigned to the biblical God on the basis of his presumed transcendence over nature was "tainted with apologetic pleading."[16]

Ruether did not see herself as condemning Goddess spirituality but as proposing dialogue and synthesis. In 1985 she wrote of the need for a "consciously pluralistic" feminist theology and asserted that "the legitimacy of encountering the divine as goddess" was the one *uncontroversial* issue among religious feminists.[17] But again she conceived the central constructive challenge of feminist theology in ethical and rationalistic terms that did not adequately address the mystical and aesthetic aims so central to the Goddess movement. Beyond condemning the misogynist myth of Eve and evil, Ruether argued, feminists must "explain *our* understanding of good and evil." She described this task in terms that encoded her theology of fallenness: feminist theology must "rightly name our authentic potential and that which corrupts it," so as to lead women "to a more mature and responsible humanity, and not simply to a reversal of patriarchal distortions."

Again, Ruether's equation of evil and inauthenticity was predicated on a rationalistic view of being as good. Feminism's basic religious intuition, she contended, is "the belief in a divine foundation of reality which is ultimately good, which does not wish evil or create evil, but affirms our autonomous personhood as women." To illustrate a religious intuition that many women find revelatory, Ruether told the story of a woman who, in the moments after being raped, envisioned God as a crucified woman. Ruether herself expressed some uneasiness with this image, recalling that the cross has long disserved women as an image of passive victimization. Her mention of the Christa on this and other occasions as an instance of primary religious experience, notwithstanding these reservations, seems to be a combined effect of her notion of divine transcendence and her theological focus on injustice. If the divine transcends female power and every other immanent good, it most often will appear obliquely as that which stands against injustice, and directly only as momentary "proleptic" glimpses of an eschatological good.[18]

Christ was among those invited to reply to Ruether's essay, most of which she found "so thoroughly sound and utterly uncontroversial" as to wonder why it would warrant responses.[19] On the other hand, she contended that Ruether's proposals "must sound heretical to most Christians," especially her statement that feminist theology is a new beginning rather than a restatement of previous revelation or a return "to some original good moment in the past." For Christ this new beginning meant not only allowing the legitimacy of Goddess spirituality, but naming Christianity's "fundamental antagonism" to paganism, "idolatry," and Judaism. These antagonisms, she recalled, were political as well as intellectual, and that applied also to the contemporary situation. Ruether was sensitive to the power dynamics with which feminist theology in Christian institutions becomes entangled, but Christ felt she had ignored the distinct needs of religious feminists in secular universities and other non-Christian settings. While Ruether was right to protest the destruction of women's writings, Christ argued, women's bodies and lives have also been injured and destroyed "for the crime of being true to their own spiritual visions and experiences."

In remembrance of this history, Christ seemed to think, the line between patriarchal and feminist religion should be drawn more rather than less sharply. She could not fathom how feminist theology as Ruether outlined it could expect to appear historically as part of the Christian tradition, or why exactly it would want to. From Ruether's viewpoint, for feminists to call themselves "heretics" was to concede to patriarchal Christianity an authority it ought not to have. But for Christ the theological meaning of the Christian tradition was a more empirical than speculative question. The preponderance of historical data indicated to her that spiritually gifted women do function as "heretics" and "witches" in relation to patriarchal religion, tearing the veil of transcendence behind which its God is revealed to be only man. While Ruether wanted Christ and others to defend these judgments in terms still drawn from monotheistic rationalism, Christ was interested in discovering what new religious insights might emerge were women to stop forcing elemental experience into this old conceptual grid.

But Ruether remained more interested in historical and ethical questions, and in a 1987 article she directed a number of these specifically at Christ.[20] Though Ruether emphasized that her disagreements with the Goddess movement were over "important but secondary matters," she also offered a detailed critique of Christ's version of Western religious history. In Christ's work, Ruether espied what amounted to periodizations and typologies based on simplistic divisions of good and evil. It was wrong, she contended, to make a one-to-one equation of monotheism with a male God, class hierarchy, and female subordination, or to equate Goddess worship with female social power. Early Byzantine Christianity, for example, far from "killing the Goddess" as Christ had suggested, had seen an increase in female sacred symbols. That gain was ambiguous, reflecting the importance of imperial women in the East rather than a general empowerment of women. Ambiguous too, she noted, is the relation between gender and class liberation, which not only have distinct dynamics but may even assume an inverse relation. That is why the biblical God could lift up the poor while exacerbating male dominance. Moreover, it is why ancient polytheism could affirm the sacrality of femaleness while blessing slavery and class hierarchy.

But if the moral equivocity of history made history a poor source of theological norms, that was because Ruether continued to conceive those norms in terms of a transcendence that rendered immanent deities definitionally inferior. Symbols, she proposed, should be assessed in terms of their historical functions. On those grounds, she suggested that Goddesses had little inherent connection with specifically female liberation and none at all with the liberation of poor women and men. At the same time, however, she defined the biblical God as essentially beyond his historical vices. The shift from polytheism to biblical monotheism, she contended, was not the triumph of a single male deity over a single female deity but "the supercession of a *pluralistic* concept of deity with many distinct male and female personifications by a *unitary* concept of deity, one beyond literal personification but imaginable in either male or female terms."[21] The male and female *images* of this God have often reflected and supported patriarchy, but the God itself, being "beyond literal personification," was not indicted for the behavior of its symbols in quite the way as were immanent deities.

Ruether's deity, as I will show, represents a transcendent reconciliation of moral goodness and ontic power. That eschatological reconciliation, however, cannot be predicated on the broken world. Here and now, therefore, she conceives of God goodness-first, as a principle of justice applied ever anew to the repair of the world. To her it seems as morally perilous to define the sacred power-first as to relinquish the notion of divine transcendence. In this vein, she asked Christ and others to reflect on the ugly resemblance between certain forms of post-Christian paganism and the nationalism, fascism, racism, and militarism of the twentieth century. Paganism, she asserted, has been used to "revitalize those power drives" which were embedded in "the repressed aspects of post-European culture."[22] Though she noted that fascist power was "not what egalitarian, antimilitarist feminists seek," these 1987 warnings about pagan fascism certainly echoed her previous comments about Goddess feminism and the "repressed animus" of patriarchy.

A brief rejoinder afforded Christ only the opportunity to respond in a general way to Ruether's historical questions. Contrary to Ruether's assertion, Christ wrote, she had not blamed Christianity for "killing the Goddess." In fact, Christ's view of pre-patriarchal Goddesses and their suppression was considerably more complex than Ruether had reported. These Goddesses, she believed, had been suppressed as "patriarchal, slave-based state societies emerged from more egalitarian and peaceful clan-based neolithic agricultural societies in the fourth millennium B.C.E." In Christ's view, Ruether's refusal to consider studies based on archaeological data had generated a consistent oversimplification of the theories put forth by Christ and others about the relationship between social structures and Goddess symbolism. Christ thought there was room in her own theory for the complexities of history, had not Ruether overlooked that complexity in order to create a less-than-credible Goddess. Ruether answered that she was well aware of Christ's theories of neolithic Goddesses; she had referred to them in her previous article as theories of "a matriarchal, Goddess-centered religion believed to have existed in an ancient, pre-patriarchal stage of human culture." But Ruether still rejected these theories on methodological grounds. "It is impossible to prove from only archaeological artifacts without written record what ancient people's social structure was."[23]

Clearly the written dialogue between these scholars, which ended for Christ with this last exchange, has not been fruitful. One reason, as I have already observed, is that embedded in their respective definitions of the divine were certain prejudgments about the inferiority or oppressiveness of contrary spiritualities. Another reason was that Ruether's characterizations of "matriarchal feminism" and theories of "primitive matriarchy" were determined more by her individual reading of nineteenth-century Romanticism than by constructive dialogue with feminist contemporaries who are not unaware of these and other historical questions.[24] In the process, many strong criticisms were laid at the doorstep of the Goddess movement that seemed to discredit all its proponents without sufficient attention to individual positions. Christ's work, for example, did not precisely involve the notion of what Ruether called "primitive matriarchy"; nor did Christ belong to Ruether's typology of "matriarchal feminists."[25] In adverting to "more egalitarian" societies prior to the fourth millennium B.C.E., Christ was simply working on the premise that patriarchy had historical beginnings, and that it is meaningful to imagine what may have existed before.

There were many missed opportunities for dialogue in all this, which might still be taken up among Christian, Jewish, and postbiblical feminists. Christian and Jewish feminists, for instance, ought to be challenged by Christ's comments on how the prevailing notion of the divine within religious studies continues to skew the study of ancient Goddesses. Pre-patriarchal Goddesses, she has pointed out, cannot be conceived as divine when the divine is predefined as "rationality, order and transcendence, as opposed to the alleged irrationality and chaos of the finite world, the world we call nature."[26] Methodologically, she argued, this mistrust for "the nonrational, the physical side of religion" resulted in religious studies' monogamous devotion to texts and its relative disinterest in oral traditions and ritual as evidential bases.[27] That, in turn, makes it academically unrespectable to theorize about pre-patriarchal times for which written records are not available.

Ruether, for her part, raises important questions to feminist neopaganism about how, absent the premises of ethical monotheism, it intends to found a social ethic or even maintain a modicum of self-critique. Her observations about the historical disjunctions among oppressions based on sex, race, and class remain extremely relevant to all theorizing about the historical development of social ills, and relevant as well to all serious efforts to forge political bonds among women in the present. Those observations should not be dismissed even though they are often confusingly phrased in theological paradigms that Goddess feminists reject, such as that of original sin and fall.

Ruether: Making Sense of Patriarchy

That confusion about whose paradigms are whose also marks *Gaia and God*, which includes Ruether's most recent criticisms of Goddess feminism. In this text, she focuses on Daly and Christ, placing them under the rubric of "ecofeminism" and describing the latter as a "new fall story" in which an original paradise of benignity is said to have been lost to the external force of malevolent patriarchy. Yet she also observes that Christ has consciously jettisoned the myths of redemption and fall.[28]

Perhaps this oddity is explained by Ruether's own ambivalence about the myth of the fall, an ambivalence centered on the dangers she perceives in the belief that there ever was or could be a time without sin. Construing feminist theories of pre-patriarchal history as a search for this type of "dreaming innocence," she concludes that Goddess feminism remains unreflectively under the spell of the myth of the fall. Yet it could as well be said that it is Ruether who retains a loyalty to this myth, albeit in carefully demythologized form. Theologically, the myth rests not upon historical literalism but on the characterization of human existence, insofar as it is touched by evil, as estranged being. Demythologization only strengthens this paradigm by clarifying that the problem it addresses is perennial rather than circumstantial. In this sense, Ruether might more appropriately complain of Goddess feminists that they do *not* think of the world as fallen, that they underestimate the realm of sin as limited by time, geography, or sex, failing to grasp that sin is a species condition of humanity, covering the whole of our history.

Gaia and God adds some new wrinkles to Ruether's thinking about a pre-patriarchal era. She cites James Mellaart at length, contending that his studies have been misused by Marija Gimbutas, Riane Eisler, and Christ. Still, Ruether's own theory has more in common with those of Goddess feminists than ever before. She speculates about the beginnings of patriarchy and about what came before. No longer counting on written sources to establish the bearing of physical evidence on social structure, she considers paleoanthropological theories based on fossil and archaeological evidence. From this evidence she hypothesizes that early homonids were matricentric, and that women developed tools, fire, and agriculture. In Neolithic farming villages women enjoyed great prestige, female fecundity was the "primal expression of the life force," and male virility was "celebrated" but felt to be dependent on the female. Moreover, she observes, these agricultural, women-honoring societies became the "main line of human development."[29]

Why then place this new theory in *opposition* to Christ and other ecofeminists? Again, Ruether's crucial concerns, though cast in historical terms, are theological. Though she now allows that Old European cultures may well have been more egalitarian and female-identified than what followed, she argues that feminists should not weave this into "a comprehensive story of an Eden-like world." Christ in her view has done exactly that, extending a "paradise-fall story" about Old Europe to the whole of the ancient world.[30] For Christ and others, theories about the rise of patriarchy have taken on a "mythical" role, providing a "warrant for the faith" that a feminist social vision might one day be realized. Ruether's theological point was that "faith claims need to be sorted out from what we can prove or not prove about prehistory."[31]

Christ, it should be noted, had already reflected in depth on the existential importance of pre-patriarchal history and Goddesses for contemporary women's spirituality.[32] The issue, then, is not that Goddess feminists remain unreflective about the link between faith and history.[33] Rather, the issue is the methodological relationship between historical and theological claims—a relationship that looks different depending on how one defines the divine. On the assumption of a transcendent God, faith claims may appear categorically different from historical claims. On immanentist or polytheistic assumptions, though, theological and historical claims must be drawn together more closely, since theological meaning cannot be referred to a higher order of being.

Ruether now accounts for the origins of patriarchy in terms of the "internal psychosocial weakness" of matricentrism. Though matricentrism is the permanent core of human society, it thwarts the appropriate need of males for social prestige and power. The "insecure, resentful male," alienated from the basic processes of life, then tries to assuage his wounded ego through hierarchical relations and fitful approximations of absolute power. This chronic problem, Ruether suggests, is best resolved by the careful construction of male social powers and honors that parallel those that matricentrism affords females.

Ruether's account, it seems to me, is akin to the critique of the patriarchal ego by a number of Goddess feminists.[34] The physiological bond between mother and fetus or child is as "natural" as anything gets for human beings, and to say that men resent these bonds is very like saying that they resent the basic natural processes with which women are associated. Yet even this new theory became a critique of Goddess feminists, who in Ruether's view have failed to learn the historical lesson of matricentrism and its patriarchal backlash. By reducing the male to the "son of the Great Mother," they do nothing to enhance male maturity and so help perpetuate the patriarchal ego.[35] Again, Ruether's position is predetermined by a theological principle that has as its assumptive backdrop a Christian worldview. Evil must be understood not as external or circumstantial in origins but as resulting from a universal proclivity for sin, while sin must be understood as a derailment of the very same forces that would otherwise lead to the good. If, as Gimbutas argues, patriarchy came to Old Europe through the invasion of Kurgan "bad guys," then, Ruether still wants to know, "how did the bad guys get bad?"[36]

*   *   *

What, then, might feminist religious reflection be for? In Carol Christ one sees a feminist thealogy that exists mainly for the purpose of cultivating and reflecting on women's religious experience. Rosemary Radford Ruether's feminist theology, on the other hand, aims to make justice credible as the ground and potential of life and to actualize moral faith through a realistic politic. It will be the purpose of the next chapters to highlight Ruether's distinct contributions to the moral consciousness of feminist theology, and Christ's distinct mystical and aesthetic voice. In the process, we will see how each system is troubled by the ancient surd of women's suffering and the ancient knot of suffering and fault.

Suppose, for example, we take seriously the pointed critique of male character advanced by Goddess feminists, while considering with Ruether the possibility that these characterological scars have roots in the sheer physical exigencies of life. Suppose, beyond Ruether's work to date, we reflect on how these scars harden into social roles without ever passing a clear boundary between necessity and freedom. Then we are confronted with the tragic, not confined to the borders of our lives but pervading the world in which meaning must be made. Or suppose we contemplate with Carol Christ the fact that patriarchy, like other structures of privilege, develops a complex inner causality far beyond any psychosocial needs human beings may share. Then we are face to face with conflicts of truly elemental depth between the privileges of manhood and the well-being of women—conflicts that, while not eternal, still cannot be resolved without destruction and loss. And if, beyond Christ's thealogy to date, we note that "women" and "nature" themselves comprise a cacophony of interests and powers, then feminist ethics cannot be cast as simple acceptance of life over against patriarchal necrophilia. If evil is not the Other, neither is good the One, and there is nowhere to retreat from the defiling aspects of moral responsibility.

To suggest that patriarchy involves tragedy is not at all to say that patriarchy is a "no-fault" situation. Quite the contrary: tragedy in the strong sense is a state not only of suffering but of fault, a state in which life places people in the wrong. Moreover, this moral defilement does not affect people evenly but, for example, selectively fosters male cruelty toward women and female victimization by men. The world of patriarchy, whatever its origins and whenever it may end, is such an absurd state, plainly negating any absolute right or reason, and the need to stanch this chaos has provided enough "mythic" motive to send blame volleying blame back and forth between the sexes for millennia.

In its efforts to make "sense" of patriarchy and make "right" its wrongs, feminist religious scholarship has a new opportunity to turn the rich compost of the tragic and name the insights that grow there. As a theological heuristic, the tragic highlights elemental conflict as *question-worthy*, holding open the telling wounds of absurdity and fault rather than closing them with preemptive appeals to faith. A tragic sensibility may also assist in the differentiation of the many *kinds* of questions proper to religious studies. There are questions to oneself or one's community, questions to others, questions to life as a whole. What counts for "answers" may then appropriately range from awe and lament to ritual or strategies for social change. To make such questions worthy of sustained scholarly attention is perhaps to commit the final infidelity against the God of the Fathers—to relinquish the Ideal for the creative expression of the real. Then women might speak more truly and shape more imaginatively the elements in which their lives are lived.

CHAPTER FIVE

RENATURING A FALLEN WORLD
THE THEOLOGY OF
ROSEMARY RADFORD RUETHER

> *When we model our God after emperors and despots
> who reduce others to dependency, then we have a
> problem of theodicy. But the cross of Jesus reveals a
> deeper mystery. The God revealed in Jesus has
> identified with the victims of history and has
> abandoned the thrones of the mighty. In Jesus' cross
> God abandons God's power into the human condition
> utterly and completely so that we might not abandon
> each other. This is perhaps why those who struggle for
> justice do not ask the question of theodicy. They know
> that the true God does not support the thrones of the
> mighty, but is one with those who struggle.*
>
> —*Rosemary Radford Ruether*[1]

> *[The raped woman's] vision of God as a crucified
> woman . . . filled her with a sense of relief since she
> knew that she would not have to tell a male God that
> she had been raped. God was a woman who knew what
> it was like to be raped. Such a story astonished and
> compelled us. . . . The divine is present here, not as
> representative of the male who is the victimizer, but on
> the side of the female victim, one with the female
> victim, one who knows this anguish, who is a part of
> it, and who also heals and empowers women to rise
> from the dead, to be re-created beyond and outside the
> grasp of this negative power.*
>
> —*Rosemary Radford Ruether*[2]

THERE IS a clarity about profound suffering, especially the kind of
suffering that results from human brutality and callousness. On the thresh-

old of this awful sanctuary, as Gustavo Gutiérrez observed, the hand should cover the mouth. Here one cannot speculate about whether God is just, as if "no" could be afforded, or as if "yes" would give relief. At this extremity, we can only choose to help or not to help. Familiar theological questions may begin to seem useless or even cruel. For the questions that remain, only change counts as an answer.

This clarity is the wellspring of Rosemary Radford Ruether's theology. The most ubiquitous injustices of our time, she believes, can be primal religious experiences, points of revelation. Who are we? Who is God? What in the world is "natural"? In Ruether's work these questions are locked together in the hard embrace of suffering, and it is only by unlocking what is unnecessary in suffering that the answers may be dimly discerned. Rather than defending God as just, she enlists theology in the service of making justice true. Rather than elucidating the goodness of power, she pours out the power and authority of Christianity for the sake of victims, especially Christianity's own victims.

If patriarchal theology is Ruether's Scylla, Goddess feminism is her Charybdis. Her purpose is not to discredit the latter as a religious choice but to mark a path for a distinctively Christian feminism. In doing so, she has to make meaning of the long-standing evil of patriarchy, while bearing in mind that our very patterns for interpreting evil often serve to shore up injustice. For that reason, no matter how real and pervasive evil seems to be, she will not posit a permament, ontological principle of evil—for example, matter in Gnostic ideology, or maleness in some feminist ideology. Nor will she revert to the Romantic holism that refuses to speak of evil at all.

As we have already seen, Ruether's solution to this perennial dilemma is a carefully revised and demythologized version of the Christian notion of a fallen world, with its distinctive combination of rationalism and dualism. By means of this paradigm, she can affirm the world as essentially good, yet observe that that goodness is everywhere distorted. She can recognize that evil has the solidity and force of social structures, yet still assert that evil has no ultimate reality. She can posit that justice and compassion are worth trusting and believing in, yet understand that this is a matter of faith rather than a judgment about history.

Her theological method is founded on this faith that there is "an original base of meaning and truth before corruption," that "truth is more basic than falsehood and hence able, ultimately, to root out falsehood," that even our most radical criticisms of the world are grounded upon "a deeper bedrock of authentic Being."[3] This faith is a theistic one, since it posits an ultimate unity of goodness and power, the ideal and the real.

That unity is broken in the fallen world, in which, as Ruether frequently notes, "is" and "ought" are not the same. Here, where innocence is so often victimized and power so often becomes domination, God/ess as Ruether defines it stands with the victims. To stand with victims, imitating the divine, becomes for her the primary expression of faith.

Ruether's theological interest in women, then, is as "the oppressed of the oppressed,"[4] not as bearers of any distinct ethics, cultures, or religious experiences. And while her theological response to women's suffering issues in feminist political action and advocacy, that is not where she begins or ends. For her, to stand with victims is to believe that no suffering is ultimately unredeemed, even that which remains beyond the reach of our best efforts. Against Mary Daly, for whom "tortured women remain only victims," Ruether senses a "depth of divine presence in female suffering itself."[5] Given the schism of goodness and power in the fallen world, the divine is revealed within suffering that indicts oppressive power—suffering like that of the crucified woman. Ruether's feminist critique of patriarchy and its idols is therefore not a tragic accusation of God. For her, God *is* the protest against evil, and so cannot itself be protested against.

Dualism is perhaps the last word Ruether herself would use to describe her position, since for her that term names the broken symbolic world she wants to mend. If, however, dualism is understood fundamentally as a way of thinking about good and evil and only secondarily as a way of thinking about spirit and matter, then Ruether's theology, like androcentric theology, does have a dualistic shadow. Since Ruether is committed to the position that good is more true, authentic, and ultimate than is evil, she too must conceive the realm in which evil exerts power as a lesser or counterreality, a fallen world. Her chief revision of the tradition is her attempt to authorize this *moral dualism* without reference to an essentialist distinction between spirit and matter. In effect, she has tried to disengage moral dualism from its roots in metaphysical dualism, hoping in that way to convert alienated Christian consciousness to the service of justice.

The difficulty with Ruether's diagnosis of patriarchal theology is that metaphysical dualism, whatever its influence on Christian symbology, has never been strictly consistent with Christian doctrine. Monotheism, as interpreted by Christianity's intellectual elites, cannot admit the existence of a metaphysical principle essentially independent of and opposed to God. Ruether is, of course, right to try to disengage from metaphysical dualism, but it is important to notice that this is not a feminist innovation in theology. From Augustine on, the best efforts of those elites have been marshalled to exorcise the cosmological backdrop of spirit/matter dualism. However, those efforts never succeeded and they are not succeeding for feminists, either. The reason for that failure, I believe, is the ongoing theological suppression of tragic multiplicity, which cannot but divide reality into the ideal and the nonideal. Even when Christian theology has been willing to give up the fantasy of pure spirit, it has not been able to give up its faith in a pure, inclusive, and invulnerable good. Even though it has recognized that the world is a place of innocent fault, guilty power, and conflicting goods, it has insisted that precisely as such, the fallen world *is not to be believed in* as the original or ultimate truth.

Ruether is acutely aware that the fall, like other theological traditions, has been etched in deeply misogynist tones. But reversal and distortion of truths are just what she expects of a fallen world. Characteristically, she looks for revelation at the very spot where the truth has been entombed, so that the symbols of patriarchy admit what they have crushed and hidden. Hierarchical domination, justified in patriarchal theology as divine creation or punishment, becomes for her a sign that the world is not what it can and should be. Nature, which has been demonized and inferiorized, is vindicated as the site of human life as divinely intended. Transcendence, envisioned by patriarchal asceticism as an escape from women and the body, becomes a conversion of persons and societies back to the mortal body, the finite earth, and egalitarian human relations. Following these closely related themes, the basic outlines of Ruether's system emerge and, more faintly but still unmistakable, the shadow of the metaphysical dualism that she has tried so hard to exorcise.

Sin as Injustice

> *Social sin seems to me to be a different kind of negativity from experiences of tragedy or finitude, which belong to the nature of mortal existence. Social sin, on the other hand, is fundamentally culpable. However, our moral traditions of individual sins do not give us a good handle for analyzing the nature of culpability for social sin. Social sin continues across generations. It is historically inherited. Individuals are socialized into roles of domination and oppression and taught that these roles are normal and right. Discovery that the social system of which you are a part is engaged in chronic duplicity and contradiction, then, comes as a shock and an awakening.*
> —Rosemary Radford Ruether[6]

For Ruether what makes something worthy of theological questioning is that it needs to be changed and can be changed. More than individual sin, social sin urgently needs changing and, unlike mortality or finitude, it *can* be changed. Social sin or injustice therefore draws the circumference of her theology, and within that circumference she has found no shortage of subject matter.

In focusing on injustice as her main theological problem, Ruether has an eye on her foundational differences with Goddess feminism. Within the women's movement, she observes, there are "women who take the need for a new culture or spirituality as primary, and therefore start with the need for a new women's religion." On the other side, there are women "who are mainly concerned with a new social order and who assess the negative or positive role of religion in relation to this social agenda." Her own position, she states, belongs more in the latter camp.[7] In contrast to Goddess feminists, Ruether approaches religion with primarily moral concerns, and these concerns establish the criteria by which she assesses the mystical and aesthetic dimensions of feminist spirituality.

Like every circumference and every theology, Ruether's also has an outside; certain possible questions are excluded from the range of theological inquiry. "The reconstruction of the ethical tradition," she argues, "must begin by a clear separation of the questions of finitude from those of sin." Finitude, mortality, and the quotidian sufferings attending them belong, in her view, to the tragic dimension of life. She connects tragedy with finitude, necessity, and mortality; injustice, in contrast, belongs to the realm of freedom, sociality, and culpable fault. In practice this line may be hard to draw, since the "boundaries between fate and freedom are fluid, and humans have greatly extended their power over things once thought unchangeable."[8] She means to take advantage of this fluidity, finding the room for change and renewal within the finite world and enlarging the realm of freedom and compassion.

The principle behind this practice is that evil must be construed not as a feature of finite being but as a rejection of finite being. In fact, Ruether seems to construe the relation between these two ways of framing the question of evil as virtually inverse. To raise moral questions about finitude itself, as patriarchal theology has done, is, in her view, to conflate suffering that cannot be changed with suffering that can and should be changed. Injustice can then be legitimated as a feature of earthly life as divinely created or ordained. To question injustice, on the other hand, is to accept the limitations of finitude and to search for ways of living equitably within them.

Like liberation theologians and political theologians, Ruether deepens theology's disbelief in the tragic. Not just "in the end," she believes, but here and now, what has been called tragic must be subjected to the severest ideological suspicion. Here and now, evil is not to be accepted, and what must be accepted is not to be thought of as evil. In Ruether's view, the notion of innocent fault may resonate with aspects of experience, but it also serves to foster passivity and blame victims.[9] Similarly, she interrogates apparently disparate truths to detect whether they might be refractions of ideologically distorted consciousness. And when vital goods are said to be incommensurable, she asks who makes that claim and whether they possess such goods in disproportionate measure.

For Ruether this ideological suspicion appears to be not only a moral strategy but also an expression of anti-tragic faith. Her theological warrant for justice always involves the tacit or explicit claim that justice is ultimately more true than injustice. Most often, this warrant operates obliquely, through the characterization of injustice as a species of *falsehood*—for example, as "duplicity," "contradiction," "deceit," "inauthenticity," "alienation," "estrangement."[10] Injustice, as she understands it, inverts the true patterns of biotic and social interdependence. It acts as if finite resources were infinite, as if "matter" depended on consciousness, as if slaves needed their masters. Injustice for Ruether is in no way a necessary consequence of life's physical exigencies. On the contrary, it is an aberrant fruit of human consciousness, which possesses a peculiar capacity to become alienated from the conditions on which consciousness itself depends.[11]

Consciousness takes an enigmatic place within Ruether's analysis of social sin. She has argued that consciousness reflects but does not create social structures.[12] In this sense, consciousness is *ideological*—an epiphenomenon of social, political, and economic structures, subject to their laws and mirroring their injustices. Ideological consciousness, Ruether notes, can pervert moral ideals into social legitimation, poisoning the very well from which social reform would otherwise be drawn. On the other hand, one also finds throughout Ruether's work another proclivity of consciousness, which is *moral* or *transcendent*. In this respect, consciousness creates the crucial distinction between "is" and "ought," which for Ruether is the source of all meaningful theological questions.[13] Moreover, genuine moral and theological consciousness rests, in her view, on a "bedrock of authentic Being." On the strength of that deeper intuition of "what is," moral consciousness can correct ideological consciousness in its shallow obedience to what-is-but-ought-not-to-be.

From the viewpoint of Ruether's effort to get rid of metaphysical dualism, there is a difficulty here: in pointing to a perfect good, moral consciousness also seems to point beyond the world in which finitude and injustice are so intertwined. As Ruether herself has observed, this is why moral consciousness is so susceptible to ideological distortion. In its search for a world order transcending "present ontological as well as moral limitations," moral consciousness "concludes by having to destroy the world."[14] Her corrective has been to distinguish ontological limitations, which must be accepted, from moral limitations, which must be overcome. This anchors her moral ideals to certain empirical standards—for example, they must be possible and sustainable within the parameters of finite and relational life.[15]

Possibility and sustainability, though, do not in themselves distinguish justice from evils such as patriarchy, which has proven to be both. What seems more decisive is her own moral dualism, her a priori equation of Being and Goodness, which persists even when stripped of the cosmology of spirit and matter. For if injustice is assessed as ultimately false, this is only on the presupposition that somewhere, in some sense, there is a perfect justice. A line between freedom and fate, even if fluid, can be imagined only on the assumption that somewhere, in some sense, there is an absolute and unconstrained freedom; otherwise, one would contemplate the degrees and types of limited freedom in all forms of life. Ruether does not make humanity responsible for what is beyond our power, but she does believe that no injustice actually is beyond the range of culpability or, in principle, beyond the range of freedom. No matter how "natural" or "fated" injustice may appear, no matter how intractable in practice, those appearances do not, for Ruether, reflect an ultimate truth. Indeed, even sufferings that might seem entirely unredeemed or forgotten cannot be without divine compassion and solidarity.

Absolute freedom, inclusive goodness, and transcendent truth are, in fine, attributes of God, and they cannot be conceived without imagining a reality not bound by the conditions of existence in time and space. Such a reality can only be apprehended through faith, and indeed Ruether early on identified the doctrine of justification by faith as the hub of her theology.[16] More recently she has likened it to Matthew Fox's idea of "original blessing," in which encounter with "our true selves" leads to "a new state of being" and "breaks the hold of false power" on us. Shorn of the "dualistic anthropology," which blames alienation on embodiment, original blessing "is the truth to the Protestant and Augustinian teaching about salvation by grace alone, without the works of the law."[17] In other words, Ruether assumes that it was only the denial of *embodiment* that made those theological traditions go awry. She does not notice that they— and she—also want to find a way out of the guilt and conflict that attend even our best moral efforts. Her dual description of consciousness, as torn between ideology and moral faith, thus continues to imply two kinds of reality—one ultimate, true, and authentic, and one less than ultimate precisely insofar as it is distorted by injustice.

The enigma of consciousness is also the enigma of religion in Ruether's theology. In her view, as we have seen, the ideologies of oppression display a "single root pattern" which she calls "sacralism," "established religion," or the "religion of the sacred canopy." All these terms indicate for her forms of ideological legitimation in which dominative power relations are ascribed to divine creation or command.[18] Metaphysical dualism justifies domination with reference to the relation of spirit to matter, but that is not the only form sacralism can take. More than once she has suggested that religious traditions in which the divine is purely immanent may be less able to distinguish "is" and "ought" and hence less able to correct for sacralism.[19] Sacralism has been "the dominant religious practice of humanity,"[20] both before biblical times and since. Indeed, the link between religion and that ancient form of domination, patriarchy, is so thick that "one is tempted to suggest that religion itself is essentially a male creation" and to wonder "whether religion or spirituality is what [feminists] should be about at all."[21]

This nearly materialist assessment of religion, however, is mitigated by Ruether's claim that all religions bear within them some inner corrective to sacralism.[22] It is the prophetic traditions of the Bible to which she constantly returns to describe this transcendent dimension of religion. Prophetic faith bore a "revolution of consciousness," introducing to religion "a new concept of divine-human relations."[23] In the prophets there is a "social shift of religion." No longer solely a "panegyric of the powerful, in the name of the gods," religion could now criticize itself and society in the name of a God who takes the side of the poor and marginalized.[24] Prophetic God-talk is "destabilizing toward the existing social order and its hierarchies of power."[25] Even the secular revolutions of the modern era, she argued in an early work, take their *élan* from this biblical tradition, which could only be activated as a political force after Christianity had been disestablished.[26]

At its best, religion as Ruether envisions it supports a dialectic between a community's self-affirmation and its self-critique. Sin is denounced, but in the name of the community's own authentic identity and promise.[27] Yet she expects this dialectic to break down as a matter of course. In the language of the early Ruether, religion reflects a human tendency to "fall from spirit to flesh, from the Rule of God to the Kingdom of the Prince of the World." In the language of the more recent Ruether, the corruption of religion is symptomatic of "the relationship between

God/ess (or ultimate truthful and good reality) and human sin (failure to live in harmony with the ultimate truthful and good reality)."[28] In both cases, the divine object of religion is defined in such a way that actual social life is bound to betray it. The betrayal is due to something more than injustice, since injustice remains correctible in all its concrete forms. It is due, more profoundly, to the categorical difference that must stand between ultimate truth or goodness and relative truths or goods.

Ruether's theological interpretation of patriarchy has also employed the paradigm of original sin and fall, which she turned on its head to indict the paradigm's own traditional misogyny. What fallenness says about sin is just what Ruether wants to say about patriarchy. Feminism "claims that a most basic expression of human community . . . has been distorted throughout all known history." That primary alienation "is reflected in all dimensions of alienation"—from the body, from other races and cultures, from the divine. In this sense, feminism "continues in a new form, the basic Christian perception that sin, as perversion of good potential into evil, is not simply individual, but refers to a fallen state of humanity, historically."[29]

More than any other single feature of her theology, Ruether's innovations on this paradigm have allowed her to cut a path different from both Goddess feminism and patriarchal theology. It is perhaps significant that she first essayed this theory in 1973, the same year Mary Daly published *Beyond God the Father*.[30] But if the fall has solved certain theological problems for her, it has also made her heir to others, especially that of evil's origins. For a long time, she embedded this question within the quite different question of the origins of patriarchy. When, in *Gaia and God*, she contemplates the beginnings of patriarchy while still rejecting the notion of a paradisiacal era, it becomes clearer than ever that the most significant issue for Ruether is not the historical origins of evil but its ontological status. That status, for her, is definitely not one of necessity. That is the point of associating evil with sin rather than tragedy, with sociality rather than physicality, with sexism rather than sex. But she does see sin as a permanent human proclivity, and that confers on evil a certain inevitability. That, it seems, is the theological point of her insistence in *Gaia and God* that sexism is not the only or the earliest form of evil.[31]

But if sin is more a rejection of reality than a reality unto itself, why is this rejection more or less inevitable? If there is something about life that we always reject, is there something about life that *warrants* rejection? Ruether has traced social sin to the rejection of the body and, less consistently, to the rejection of guilt.[32] In the first case, for example, men may project sexuality and death onto women; an example of the second case is when the affluent blame the poor for their own poverty. To date, Ruether has not spelled out the relationship between these etiologies of injustice, but each has its own puzzle. To say that the rejection of the body is a root cause of sin is to imply that this rejection is in some sense inevitable, that the body is in some sense alien to human identity—precisely the position Ruether wants to refute. On the other hand, if the rejection of guilt is the basic problem, then there must be some sense in which we really *are* guilty, originally and always. In any case, there cannot be a perfect symmetry between the rejection of the body and the rejection of guilt, since even if the acceptance of the body can be unequivocal, the acceptance of guilt cannot be.

What might it mean to "accept" guilt as the frame of human existence? In a worldview that admits the tragic, such acceptance would mean that this *unacceptable* situation really is true, that it cannot be answered by speculation or faith but only by protest and struggle. In the kind of Christian worldview that denies the tragic, "accepting" guilt means founding ourselves on faith in a God beyond fault, before whom we are both guilty and forgiven. But if God is beyond fault, does this not imply that the ultimate source of guilt is simply the fact that creation is not God? Here, in the relation between nature and God, we encounter a second major theme of Ruether's theology.

Nature and Fallenness

> *The basic meaning of this messianic hope lies in the continued human experience of a tension and contradiction between the is and the ought of life. This being so, it is not enough to examine this reality and the way it contradicts the visions of ideal beatitude. We must also examine the ideals themselves and the appropriateness of their tension with present existence. That is to say, we must not merely ask how the situation is judged in relation to the ideal, but also whether the ideal is an authentic expression of the proper "nature" of creation. We must assume not merely a future or eschatological pole in relation to present existence but also a primordial pole that stands for the appropriateness of the ideal in view of God's "original intent" for His creation.*
> —Rosemary Radford Ruether[33]

For Rosemary Radford Ruether, as we have seen, justice is the art of living well within the limits of nature as divinely intended. Even her most radical calls for moral reform are intended as mandates to become what, in the deepest sense, we already are. But the human relationship to nature is peculiar, because for us, unlike other creatures, it is possible *not* to be who we are. This estrangement runs much deeper than the familiar hypocrisy in which we know the good but fail to do it. Beyond that, Ruether observes, our very ideals of the good and the natural are deformed in the image of domination and deceit. In her estimation, metaphysical dualism has been an encompassing feature of these distorted ideologies in the Christian West. In naming this dualism as the original sin of Christian theology, she hopes, by a kind of homeopathic cure, to renature her tradition, restoring something of its distinctive truth and promise.

Ruether's theology of nature employs, at different moments, the dualistic view of evil as a counterreality and the rationalistic view of evil as ontic privation. In its earliest phase, dualistic tones prevailed. Nature as divinely intended functioned as both the necessary and sufficient condition of the human good. Theologically, true nature was equivalent to grace, and the alternative to grace was not nature but *sin* masquerading as natural. A second phase began in the 1980s and culminates in *Gaia and God*. Here, nature remains the necessary condition for the human good but is no longer sufficient. From a Protestant schema of sin and grace, Ruether returns to the three-tiered world of classical Catholicism, in which nature is better and more real than sin but worse and less real than grace.

In Ruether's earliest writings on nature, she often signaled the dualism of sin and grace by pinching the term *nature* in quotation marks. This little syn-tactic, it seems, was intended to raise the red flag of ideological suspicion over all *ideas* of the natural, which may be distorted by injustice.[34] Only patterns of living that are just and equitable, Ruether thought, deserve to be considered authentically natural. That kind of natural existence, she wrote in 1971, is an entirely "possible possibility." But our "unbalanced world transcendence" has "made the most possible things impossible."[35] Living between "nature" and nature, the human task is to "cultivate the garden," blending the "transcendent consciousness" that distinguishes humanity with the finite parameters of earthly reality.

Yet transcendent (or moral) consciousness, as we have seen, is part of the problem: on one side, it is tempted to collapse into immanentism; on the other, to flee the world altogether.[36] Once transcendent consciousness puts quotation marks around "nature," questioning what is in view of what ought to be, there is for Ruether no going home again. Or rather, home is forward; the goodness of creation is refreshed only on a moral journey toward an ideal that remains transcendent and yet is nothing more than authentic nature. Between "nature" and nature, one could say, there appeared in Ruether's writings a breach reminiscent of the old joke with the punchline "you can't get there from here."

The refractions of nature have also been of vital importance to Ruether's theological anthropology. Her aim has been to debunk ideological notions of human nature, especially those surrounding sex difference. She insists that human nature in itself must be thought of as good, emphatically refusing not only the inferiorization of the oppressed but also the demonization of oppressors. For example, feminists must "not confuse nature with the Fall; we do not confuse . . . males with the system of male domination; and we do not confuse the demons we seek to exorcise with the human beings we seek to liberate from demonic possession."[37] For both sexes, our claim to natural goodness must involve repentant acknowledgment of sin. Between creation and final redemption, human "nature" remains unknown even to humans.[38]

In addition to the idea of fallenness, Ruether's theology of nature beginning in the 1970s has drawn upon the covenantal tradition of the Hebrew Bible. By developing this tradition in a contemporary context, she hoped to abet the uneasy alliance between Third World movements for economic liberation and environmentalism as framed by the industrialized nations. In the covenantal vision, she wrote, "nature no longer exists 'naturally' "; it becomes an "ethical sign" of the moral quality of human life. Injustice breaks the covenant of nature, and from that brokenness come "poverty, social oppression, war and violence . . . and the polluted, barren, hostile face of nature." The restoration of justice could be envisioned as the "peaceable kingdom," harmonious and beautiful, "where nature experiences the loss of hostility between animal and animal, and between human and animal."[39] In the early 1980s she also associated Hebrew covenantal theology with the Christian notion of fallenness. In "Hebrew thought," she wrote, the "struggle to restore justice in society and harmony with nature becomes a historical project that defines the fallenness and hope of humanity."[40]

Nature, in these writings, is fundamentally a category of ideality, echoing Immanuel Kant and Karl Barth. Like Kant, Ruether seemed to posit a *categorical* difference between "nature" as we know it and nature as Ideal—a difference predicated not on any notion of "matter" as ontologically inferior but on the inability of consciousness to grasp nature-itself in a direct and immediate fashion. With Barth, she understood creation, redemption, and eschaton as existing in dynamic unity. Like him, too, she rejected the idea of a supernature, and like him presupposed the priority of faith and grace. However, for Ruether faith had to be at every moment a mandate for moral action, and for this reason she objected to Barth's treatment of the "shadow side of creation" (what Ruether would later call the "tragic") as a "frontier" between the goodness of creation and the radical evil of chaos. Ruether wanted no overgrown frontier but the clearest possible boundary between the two, so that injustice could not be hidden by the ground cover of natural suffering.[41]

That boundary has not been easy for her to uphold either, because a morally perfected nature is more an object of faith than a program for social action. Lions, after all, do not lie down with lambs, and in a world where this could happen lions no longer would be lions, and lambs no longer lambs. Nor, perhaps, would people be people if our "natural" sufferings and our "social" wrongs could be cleanly divided. As Ruether crafted a more detailed and realizable vision of eco-justice in the 1980s, nature had to become more than a cipher for whatever would be left if we got rid of injustice. Nature, as Ruether now described it, includes human and nonhuman life; it changes, exercises freedom, and transcends itself by creating forms of life, including human intelligence. Within these changes, she identified certain constants of eco-justice, including "a human scale of habitats and communities, an ability of people to participate in the decisions that govern their lives, work in which everyone is able to integrate intelligence and creativity with physical participation, a just sharing of the profits and benefits of production, an interpenetration of work and celebration, a balance of rural and urban environments."[42]

In this fuller vision of nature, conversion became Ruether's model for optimal change. Conversion implies that there is no going back to a pristine state, nor evolving forward as if there were no end to our resources or powers. Conversion is a matter of bringing life back to center by creating new patterns of justice within the exigencies of a finite and interdependent world. It can never be achieved once and for all, because nature itself changes and because chaos and sin are among its permanent proclivities. Linking the idea of conversion to the sabbatical and jubilee traditions of the Hebrew Bible, Ruether proposed, we must imagine forms of periodic renewal that not only correct human imbalances of wealth and power but also bring humanity back into right relation with animals and the land.[43]

Alongside these traditions of periodic renewal, however, Ruether continued to invoke the tradition of the fall, which places the whole of history between a perfect "beginning" and a perfect "end." For example, she could still characterize the whole of patriarchal history as "a big lie," beneath which the "harmony is still there, persisting, supporting, forgiving, preserving us in spite of ourselves."[44] Moreover, she continued to present its eschatology as the feature that distinguishes Christian spirituality from the natural cycles of paganism and the historical renewal traditions of Judaism.[45] But how could this perfect future be understood, if not as a future point of historical progress, a heaven beyond mortality, or a cosmic beyond? Ruether wanted to remove the idea of a good creation from these mythic encasements and replant it in the earthly garden. But she also wanted to buttress the moral authority of that ideal creation with the ontological primacy of its Creator—a procedure which, I would argue, draws whatever credibility it has from the tenacious dualism of spirit and matter.

In *Gaia and God*, partly as a point of disagreement with Goddess feminism, Ruether once and for all removes the halo of grace from nature. The book is meant to convert Christian transcendence to the care of the earth, but it is as much meant to say that Gaia is *not* God. The finite world, she now implies, is a necessary but not sufficient condition for human moral fulfillment. This insufficiency is now due to more than false consciousness; it pertains to the earth system itself. Because evil is not "some 'thing' out there," she argues, "it cannot be escaped" and is only worsened by attempts to do so. Evil is a matter of "wrong relationship" between good beings. Yet wrong relationship is a permanent tendency within each species, which wants "to maximize its own existence and hence to proliferate in a cancerous way that destroys its own biotic support." The implication for her theology of nature is clear: "Nature, in the sense of the sum of cosmic life, was not originally paradisiacal (benign for us) and is not capable of completely fulfilling human hopes for the good, in the sense of benign regard for individual and communal life, which is the human ideal."[46] Nature, it seems, is no longer equivalent to grace; it remains the arena of works but cannot be the object of faith.

Ruether's etiology of sin in *Gaia* centers squarely on the rejection of the body and on dualism, its philosophical corollary, which she now defines as "the rejection of mortality."[47] But what does it mean simultaneously to identify sin with the rejection of physicality and yet to suggest that the earth system is in fact *not* good enough for us? It means, I suggest, a return to that ancient pattern of thought in which the world bound by finitude is a *lesser* good than the absolutely transcendent good, which is God. In Ruether's case, as in the tradition preceding her, the unity of that hierarchical universe is always compromised by the irresolvable categorical difference between the swarm of immanent goods that comprise the earth system and the inclusive, invulnerable good that is God. Ruether senses this problem when she links metaphysical dualism to a notion of God who is "unrelated to earth, body or mortality," and who "is absolute good against absolute evil in a way that is unrelational."[48] Yet her God still remains absolute good, with the proviso that this good is to be imagined in relation to life—that is, not as disembodied "spirit."

But this is precisely the problem: Can any good be conceived as both absolute and relational, as embodied but not subject to the moral in-adequacies of embodied life? The root problem is the nature and destiny of moral consciousness, strung as it is between Gaia and God. It is true, Ruether notes, that the limits of the world affect our moral freedom, that the notion of unavoidable fault does resonate with experience, and that the "life force itself is not unequivocally good." All this entails a stronger sense of the tragic than had appeared in her previous work. But the tragic limitations of Gaia now establish, more firmly than ever before, the difference between Gaia and God. Against Goddess feminism, Ruether argues that "merely replacing a male transcendent deity with an immanent female one is an insufficient answer to the 'god-problem.'" Humanity needs "a vision of a source of life" that can account for and foster "consciousness and altruistic care." "To believe in the divine," she con-tends, "is to believe that those qualities of ourselves are rooted in and respond to the life power from which the universe itself arises." Precisely in grasping that the body and the earth system do not fully answer the question of moral consciousness, we are driven to ask: Is it "a universe in which it makes sense to speak of values, of life and death, good and evil, as meaningful distinctions within which we can hope for a 'better world'? Is it a universe with which we can communicate heart to heart, thought to thought, as I and Thou?"[49] Her own answer, unmistakably, is that of Christian faith.

Transcendence and Theological Truth

Christianity is a historical community, not by having a fixed and closed past (which would make it a dead and fossilized entity) but by having a redemptive future. . . . However much it must look back in memory at these past experiences as its foundations, these experiences them-selves point Christianity to the future, the yet uncom-pleted future. This future is one in which every tear will be wiped away, every form of injustice and enmity over-

*come. It is this redemptive future, not past events, which
is ultimately normative.*

—Rosemary Radford Ruether[50]

Ruether's feet are planted in the world that is, but her eyes have always been fixed on a vision of what ought to be, a vision in which our moral destiny is also our ontological ground. That vision is the linchpin of her entire theological methodology, which she has described as dialectical and historical. Its guiding principle is that societies and religious traditions are to be criticized in terms of their own inner norms. In this way, criticism becomes an affirmation of essential goodness, but essential goodness is never affirmed uncritically.[51]

Herein lies the method's own inner problematic: goodness is our origin and destiny, but that destiny is no more a *literal* future than ideal nature is a literal past. Ruether's theological norm, in other words, comes from something beyond history and nature, something bearing the traditional attributes of God. Can this eschatological future grow out of the rocky past? Can this essential goodness be preserved outside the cool sanctuary of metaphysical spirit? This is the question of transcendence that riddles Ruether's stated method and that operates as well in her biblical theology and Christology.

One finds in Ruether's work a tension between theological and historical truth. In her regard for historical truth, she has refused either to cover up wrongs or to minimize complexity. In fact, her accounts of the Bible, Christian history, and theology owe their sophistication partly to the fact that her theological norms are drawn from elsewhere. Her feminist critical principle, for instance, is that "whatever diminishes or denies the full humanity of women must be presumed not to reflect the divine or an authentic relation to the divine, or to reflect the authentic nature of things, or to be the message or work of an authentic redeemer or community of redemption." This claim, however, does not pertain to history, in which it has been "fundamentally distorted." Indeed, to affirm this principle "is itself an act of faith in the true ground of our being over against all that has distorted and alienated us from our authentic humanity."[52] The same can be said of her claim that patriarchy is "a strong social additive, but not the *norm* or essential nature of the Judaeo-Christian tradition." That norm is "the prophetic-iconoclastic-messianic tradition" and "without the recognition/conviction that this, and not patriarchy, is the normative biblical faith, none of my writing makes any sense."[53] Again, the norm is *manifest* in history, but it has never been Ruether's claim that the prophetic tradition has been historically *predominant*. Nor does its theological validity hinge on its future success.

Ruether thinks of revelation as a dialectic of judgment and promise, and that shapes her method as well as her Christology and biblical theology.[54] In ideologies of injustice, she believes, this dialectic is broken; judgment is aimed at "them," while promise is saved for "us." The conditions of ideological distortion appear to be dangerously entangled with the conditions of revelation; in both cases, the promise points to the truth of our being, while the judgment condemns what is not truly us. Everything, therefore, depends on a precise understanding of the sense in which it can be said that good is more true than evil.

Considering the Bible, the question has two sides. How should the obviously oppressive texts within the Bible be interpreted as to their meaning and authority? What is revelatory and liberative in the Bible, and in what sense can those elements be claimed as truer and/or more authoritative than the opposite trends? The oppressive elements in the Bible, Ruether has consistently argued, should not be explained away; these include misogynism and patriarchalism as well as anti-Semitism, slavery, and ethnocentrism.[55] Frankly denying the theological authority of these biblical themes, she has rejected all theories of the "uniform 'inspiration' of Scripture" together with the notion of revelation as "a finality *in the past*."[56] Revelation, for her, is not a fixed content, but a process in which the meaning of liberation is discerned in new contexts.

For Ruether the Bible is revelatory insofar as it inscribes a transcendent God and an authentic moral consciousness. As we have seen, she finds in the Bible something that departs from most of what has been called religion: a prophetic God who *destabilizes* existing hierarchies of power and promises a messianic life of justice on earth.[57] These critical and visionary themes, central to the mission of Jesus and the prophets, constitute in Ruether's view "a tradition that can be fairly claimed, on the basis of generally accepted Biblical scholarship, to be the central tradition, the tradition by which Biblical faith constantly criticizes and renews its own vision."[58] The ideological deformations of this tradition, she argues, are criticized within the Bible itself; in this way, the Bible gives us a prototype for the ongoing critique of injustices that are not recognized as such in the Bible.[59]

Still, it has been tricky to show how the prophetic-messianic tradition is the truest or most authentic dimension of the Bible, other than on the a priori assumption of its moral superiority. This normative tradition, she has insisted, is not a textual "canon within the canon."[60] And although it has historical bases in the practice of Jesus and early Christian communities, "the application of ancient language to modern issues is not historical exegesis but analogical *midrash*."[61] In analogical interpretation, old meanings can be radically recontextualized, and meanings unforeseen in the original context can emerge. She disputes the hegemony of the historical-critical method among scholars, which in her view functions as a way of convincing ordinary people that the Bible is beyond their comprehension. Since "the prophetic texts themselves are written from the standpoint of the oppressed," oppressed people know how to "connect up the Bible with their social experience."[62] The "biblical liberation tradition," she argues, "is precious to all concerned with social liberation because it is the cultural prototype of all such movements in Western society." That vision of liberation "cannot be discarded simply because it has been formulated in an androcentric and ethnocentric optic."[63]

Ruether's judgment in favor of the Bible, notwithstanding the Bible's oppressive features, is clearly more theological than historical or exegetical. That is why it has been able to survive her increasingly severe feminist critique. Initially, her feminist hermeneutic was a method of correlation in which feminism stands to women's experience as the prophetic tradition stands to the Bible, each functioning in its own realm as a principle of authenticity and critique.[64] This meant that feminism did not have to look to the Bible for authority, but also that the Bible had an authority of its own. "One can stand within this tradition and claim to be renewing it only if this principle is, at the deepest level, the true principle of the Scriptures and tradition as well, in spite of all distortion by the sin of sexism." And this, in fact, was exactly Ruether's conviction: that "the biblical tradition, despite all distortion, does indeed intend the full humanity of women as created and redeemed."[65]

To whom, however, did this intention belong? Not to those who wrote the texts or shaped them into the biblical collection, she concluded within the same year. "The Old and New Testaments have been shaped in their formation, their transmission, and, finally, their canonization to sacralize patriarchy." Though "between the lines" they may contain shards of women's memories, "in their present form and intention they are designed to erase women's experience and to mention women only as objects of male definition." Their norm for women is not liberation but "absence and silence."[66] On this basis, she concluded, the Bible should not be allowed to circumscribe the canon of sacred writings for women. Neither, however, was it to be excluded from the emerging feminist canon. In part, her rationale for this was that openly misogynist and patriarchal texts continue to exert oppressive power, which should be defused through ritual exorcism rather than abandoned like nuclear waste. In part, too, her rationale continued to be that texts with some liberative meaning can be "radically recontextualized" for feminist use.[67] However, the latter rationale has grown less pervasive as Ruether has variously presented feminist hermeneutics as extending or as flatly contradicting the Bible.

Apparently, then, Ruether's ongoing attribution of theological truth to feminist hermeneutics relies on a habit of thought so familiar in Christian theology as to have become unnoticeable: the ethically good is equivalent *ipso facto* to ultimate truth, while evil—though true enough in its own sphere—is a distortion of what is ultimately true. Whatever is unjust in the Bible thus becomes, *definitionally*, a distortion of its theological truth, mirroring the distortions of a fallen world. The "language of ethical struggle and judgment" that the Bible gave to the West, she argues, "presupposes an alienated world in conflict between a distorted and evil present reality and a lost option pointing to an imagined future." In repudiating that biblical language, she believes, Goddess feminists retreat to "the dreaming innocence of an unfallen world."[68] In other words, behind Ruether's biblical hermeneutic one again sees a worldview that belongs very much to the theological tradition, but not to the Bible itself.

Ruether's Christ, too, is the liberating Word of God, whose true meaning can only be discerned in the ongoing struggle against oppression. No symbol has been more influenced by patriarchy, she observes, but she sees these influences as ideological distortions of Christ's real meaning.[69] Dualism, in various forms, is the structure of ideologically distorted Christology: the dualism of creation and redemption, the spiritual and the political, the ruling male Logos and the obedient female nature.[70] In contrast, Ruether's Christ is a critical, dynamic, and innerworldly principle, which destabilizes injustice without abrogating life's built-in limits. He is historically manifest in the Jesus of the synoptics, but, like revelation, his theological meaning "goes ahead of us" and may now be sought "in the form of our sister."[71]

Like her biblical hermeneutic, Ruether's Christology presupposes a theological dimension of meaning that transcends the vicissitudes of history. Adapting traditional terms, she thinks of Christ both as Redeemer, which for her means liberator from injustice, and as Logos, which for her encompasses the inner Wisdom of created being.[72] To say that both are Christ is to say that liberation is nothing more than the restoration of creation. But this unity of moral good and ontic truth is transcendent for Ruether; between the two, here and now, the fallen world intervenes. The Logos must not be identified as "the foundation of the powers of the world"; otherwise Christology deteriorates into sacralism. Instead, "*both* the original and true being of things [must be] set over against the oppressive powers of the world," so that "Christ continues to be a symbol of our authentic selves over against systems of injustice."[73]

This eschatological, proleptic dimension is the distinctive feature of Ruether's Christ, though he shares much with the ethos of the Hebrew Bible. Among the commonalities are his prophetic critique of religion and society on behalf of the oppressed, his references to the jubilee renewal tradition, and his vision of a messianic age on earth. But Jesus, in Ruether's telling, expands these traditions by renouncing hierarchy as such, repudiating "the nationalist revenge-mythology of much of the messianic tradition," and attacking the love of wealth, status, and prestige which are the roots of oppression.[74] He functions as a principle of perfect justice, standing not only beyond this or that specific wrong but against all wrong. To affirm that "Jesus-is-the-Christ," she has argued, is to recognize that the "powers and principalities of systemic evil continue to exist," but "their legitimacy has been unmasked." One "no longer believes in them" and can now resist them "with the fearlessness of one who has *already seen* their point of termination."[75]

As such, Ruether's Christ is more of a formal idea than a concrete historical reality. That may explain, for example, why the maleness of Jesus is of no ultimate theological significance for her, despite its enormous impact on the christological tradition.[76] Her feminist Christology does have evidential bases in history—for example, the roles of women within the Jesus movement as implied by the synoptics, or the more egalitarian christologies that inhabit the edges of the theological tradition.[77] But "the element in Jesus' teaching that seems most important for feminism," she contends, "is its pervasive and radical iconoclasm and anti-hierarchicalism."[78] Christ, in other words, goes out ahead of all symbols and social forms, and to reduce him to patriarchal Christology is to miss his theological meaning altogether. She has even likened the denunciation of Christ among post-Christian feminists to Christian anti-Semitism. Jesus criticized "bad scribes and Pharisees," but Christians were wrong to read that "as a denunciation of the Law itself as *essentially* hypocritical." The contemporary analogue "would be the difference between a person who denounces a patriarchal reading of Christology and a person who denounces Christology as essentially patriarchal."[79]

Of necessity, the eschatological good of this Christ represents a certain challenge to the gritty goods and strategies of political life. The issue looms large in Ruether's treatment of kenosis as the relational power modeled by Jesus. Kenosis is power expressed as service, outpoured to empower the oppressed. In Jesus, she suggests, we see the kenosis of patriarchy itself.[80] Kenosis is typically misunderstood, she recognizes, either to sacralize elitist power or to enforce servitude. This does not mitigate its theological truth, for "neither existing lords nor existing servants can serve as a model for this servanthood, but only the Christ, the messianic person, who represents a new kind of humanity."[81] To share power and autonomy, one must already possess them, and for oppressed people, Ruether emphasizes, that calls for an end to servitude. Kenosis, then, prescribes the limits and uses of power once gained, but it does not seem to govern the struggle for power on the part of the oppressed.[82] Yet it also implies the free relinquishment of privilege—something the privileged rarely do—and so, as Ruether suggests, may be best grasped by the oppressed. Ruether expresses this mythically when she presents Mary Magdalene as interpreting the salvific meaning of Jesus' death in kenotic terms, in contrast to the triumphalism of the male disciples. "So this is why [Jesus] had to die," Ruether's Magdalene concludes, "to teach us to give up our fantasies of power and revenge."[83]

Behind Ruether's thinking on kenosis, it seems, lie the premises of her Christian theism. In kenosis are joined power and goodness, and that joining, though small as a mustard seed, discloses the ground and destiny of life. But amid the hierarchical and often demonic powers of the world, an absolutely good kind of power will look more like powerlessness, just as divine goodness, in the face of human self-righteousness, may appear as the blamed victim who "becomes the sin" of the oppressor. This, I would suggest, is a serious danger in the Christa image, which remains symbolically welded to the cross of Jesus and the soteriology of kenosis. That soteriology, more than serving as a practical model for social behavior, appeals to a faith that what seems like powerless love may "in the end" be powerful, and what seems like sheer victimization may "ultimately" be redemptive. Ruether in no sense holds the Christa up as a model for emulation, but she does want to link women's suffering to those christological claims and so inherits their political liabilities.

In Ruether's Christology as in her biblical theology, then, we see the implications of a method in which the liberative dimensions of a tradition, however suppressed, are imputed to the tradition as its true meaning. Though these liberative dimensions are proleptically manifest in history, the claim for their truth and normativity is theological, where "theological" pertains to an absolutely transcendent good. Those presuppositions have enabled her to render exceptionally critical and nuanced accounts of the Bible, Christian history, and Christian theology. At the same time, they have dislodged the normative center of her theology from the moral ambiguities of a fallen world, to float free in the airy regions once inhabited by the metaphysical God.

Assessment:
The God/ess and the Dance

Feminist theology involves, not simply an exegesis of past texts, but a retelling of the story of redemption from women's experience. It entails a feminist spirituality that must precede a feminist theology or exegesis. Women need to be able to experience the divine in their own image and create the dance, the poetry, the music and the story that express this experience. They need to be able to gather in communities of feminist consciousness-raising and creation of primary religious images. It is out of this generation of a new feminist religious culture that the development of feminist theology will flow.
—*Rosemary Radford Ruether*[84]

First the god, then the dance, then the story.
—*Robert Palmer*[85]

In 1954 Rosemary Ruether entered Scripps College, intending to become a painter. But when she left Claremont some years later, she held a Ph.D. in classics and patristics, and her intellectual journey pointed toward historical theology. The turn from art to theology was effected partly under the influence of Robert Palmer, whose fingers remained steadfastly on the pulse of the religious experience of ancient Greece and Rome. Despite himself, Palmer represented to Ruether the possibility of a revitalized religious scholarship, a scholarship that would be unafraid to question doctrinal verities and that would draw its insight from the dance of lived experience.

In Ruether's readiness to begin again from the primary data of religious experience, there is the promise of a new answer to the question, "What is theology for?" Traditionally, much Christian theology has existed to authorize the ethos of Christian elites as a reflection of God's nature or will. Whether that elitism took the form of imperial Christendom or secular patriarchy, the basic intellectual operation remained the same: what is true is also right, on earth as in heaven.

In contrast, as we have seen, the initiating move of Ruether's theology is her categorical distinction between "is" and "ought," which, more often than not, she has embedded in an ingeniously revised theology of the fall. Ruether's feminist sin against patriarchal Christianity has indeed been an original one, and the fruit she has stolen has made her wise. Intellectually she has achieved a richer and less contentious picture of Christian history than have many of Christianity's patriarchal apologists and a number of its feminist detractors. Morally the advantages of her theology come not only from her passionate sense of what ought to be, but from her earthy realism. She has renounced the luxurious illusion of academic neutrality in favor of clear political positions and practical social visions. In order to craft a theology that can make a real difference in the world, she has become what she once called a "generalist *par excellence*,"[86] absorbing encyclopedic quantities of data from relevant nontheological disciplines. And while she has stood with historical victims, she has not succumbed to valorizing "the oppressed."[87]

But alongside the distinction between "is" and "ought" that divides the fallen world, Ruether also presupposes an ultimate unity of the real and the ideal. Like the tradition preceding her, she pictures history against a transcendent backdrop, and against that backdrop the tangled world must be adjudged less than finally real. We have seen this pattern of thought in her analyses of injustice, nature, and transcendence. In each case, the analysis hinges on the supposition of an inclusive and transcendent Good that, although the ground of created being, can never be fully actualized and/or known. In this vital respect, Ruether retains a basic, but now highly questionable, premise of Christian theology: that particular ethical positions can be authorized against their opposition by invoking "God" as the highest court of ontological appeal.

Ontological language as such is not in question here. Ethical proposals should be defended as to their practical possibility and foreseeable consequences, as Ruether often does. On such earthly grounds as ecological sustainability and political equity, her work compels the most serious attention. Beyond this, however, a surplus of ontological authority is invoked for her theological-ethical norms, a surplus that in fact purports to be infinite. Ruether has complained that Niebuhrian-style moral realism, in its emphasis on the absolute distinction between grace and works, flattens the moral differences among human works—differences that, if relative, are nonetheless vital.[88] But although she has made a life's work out of elucidating these relative differences, she does not want to say that relative differences make all the difference, that they are in this sense absolute. Instead, in the face of profound conflict, she appeals to a divine transcendence that purports to reconcile all genuine truths and goods, without having to demonstrate this reconciliation concretely. In this way, the fading *imprimatur* of religious authority is stamped on positions better defended on more intrinsic grounds.

The cul-de-sac in Ruether's method is the same as that of theology as a whole, insofar as the discipline has relied on a metaphysical authority. In liberation-oriented theologies like Ruether's, this authority is poured out in the service of innerworldly goods, which are articulated with the help of disciplines such as economics, the ecological sciences, political theory, and psychology. The appeal to a higher order of Being, which clinches the arguments called from other disciplines, may then become the only distinctively *theological* move within the entire method. It is also a self-contradictory move, since it undermines the ultimacy of the innerworldly goods that liberation-oriented theologies take as their expressed ultimate concerns.

As the metaphysical God becomes unbelievable and theology casts about for a new self-definition, we will have to rethink fundamental terms such as the divine, the moral, nature, and sociality. If divinity and morality have no otherworldly referents, then they too partake of plurality and change and so cannot be appealed to as a means of adjudicating among profoundly conflicting claims. If consciousness and sociality are part of nature, then injustice too is "natural," as are compassion, beauty, and freedom. Cosmic eggs have only the fragile nests of social and biotic community in which to hatch. Whatever persuasiveness our moral dreams and mystical visions have comes from the power of a living community to "make good" on its truth claims and "make true" its moral claims. And when the dreams become repugnant or the visions incredible, that is due to the shifts and fissures of community. To think critically about religion, as theologians should do, is more a matter of attending to these shifts and fissures than of holding religion up to the blinding light of absolute transcendence.

Ruether is certainly cognizant of the social limitations of religion, but for her this has the negative connotations of "sacralism." Sacralism, moreover, in her usage implies a falsification of the proper and transcendent object of religion. Such a transcendent object, however universal in appearance, remains, like all universals, a masked particularity. Since particularity is all we can have, that does not count against Ruether's program or any other. But it does expose the shakiness of moral terms such as "inclusivity," "diversity," or "sustainability," which, when stripped away from the backdrop of an absolute Good, show themselves to rely on an a priori consensus about what is worth including and sustaining, which differences are desirable and which are not.

It could be argued that the appeal to God functions as a way to shape and express such a consensus. But again, the existential force of that appeal comes from actively struggling for the agenda that God is said to endorse. That is why, as Ruether has observed, those who struggle for justice do not ask the question of theodicy. But it is also why those who fight back to keep their status of privilege so often feel that God is on their side. To their proponents, the "ideologies" of oppression feel rather like genuine ideas, heartfelt faith, righteous wrath, and moral commitment. Ruether's analysis of this, as we have seen, is a version of the doctrine of justification by faith. It is the need for self-justification, she believes, that makes us blame our victims; the corrective is to work continually for social reform, while understanding that we are saved, not by our always imperfect works but by a gracious God. That God, I have argued, has always been intellectually problematic because of the impossibility of conceiving an absolute goodness outside the framework of metaphysical spirit. Of late it has grown even more politically problematic, because it plays the wild card of infinity into the calculation of limited and conflicting goods, obscuring the costs of what we choose to create and destroy in the world.

Faith in a goodness beyond tragedy also upholds Ruether's theology of the fall, a tradition of which she shares both the genius and the problematic. She has not perceived the extent of her own continuity with this tradition, focusing instead on dismantling its metaphysical dualism. This focus, I have suggested, misses half the mark. The oversight is a signficant one, for her diagnosis of patriarchal theology as "dualistic" has been perhaps Ruether's most influential contribution to theology. Conflating dualism with hierarchicalism, she hopes to cure both by replacing spirit with authentic Being and the idea of a natural hierarchy with a presumed natural equality and harmony. However, neither strategy resolves the moral dualism with which metaphysical dualism is so closely quartered. Ruether, with her insistence that evil is nothing more than alienation from authentic being, shares in the privation theory and its rational values. But she does not notice that the privation theory presumes greater and lesser degrees of being, so that even if one repudiates the notion of a hierarchy of created beings, one is still left with the ontic inadequacy of relative goods in contrast with the Absolute. The notion of a fallen world, in sum, presupposes that we are estranged from God on two counts, not just one—both by sin and by our very creaturehood. Even when employed as a critique of injustice, therefore, that worldview can never be fully converted to earthly life as its ultimate concern.

Ruether's notion of transcendent goodness has served her moral and political interests well. But it has done little for the aesthetic and mystical sensibilities of her work, which remain rather understated. Transcendent ideas are thin spiritual fare, with little of the sustenance that sticks to complex particularity. Ruether's call for a new feminist religious culture is a welcome step in this direction, as is her vision of the feminist theologian as an "organic intellectual" within a community of faith.[89] But as long as women are interpreted only as "the oppressed of the oppressed" and the cultures of women only as critical correctives to patriarchy, can anything really new be expected? For Ruether, the primary religious experience of feminism is that women are in the image of a God who intends justice and liberation for all.[90] But the idea of God as a cipher for the Good is far from new. Might there be a difference between assimilating feminism to this old image of God and reimagining the divine through the experience of women? The same questions can be raised about the rituals in Ruether's *Women-Church*, which almost without exception provide religious blessing for predefined political goals. The goals are worthy ones, and they need the energy of ritual. But when the divine becomes more authoritative Idea than elemental energy, ritual loses much of its ecstasy and creativity; its power to open up new moral and political insight is then diminished.

It may be that between Ruether's theology and my own there is a difference of religious experience—a difference that calls for acceptance rather than judgment. Despite the analytical tone of her work, Ruether's theology, at least in its feminist dimension, does center on a kind of religious experience: an experience of the most profound victimization, in which women are scarred by internalized shame and self-blame. She is very sensitive to this spiritual suffering within the physical and social damage inflicted by patriarchy, and she believes that it *must* in some way be a wellspring of transformation. With the force of religious experience, she feels that this inner defilement cannot be true for us, that women can become aware of this injury only because there is a depth of our being that it does not touch. Her God/ess is this depth of being, distorted and suppressed but never corrupted.

My different intuition is that even the capacity to feel ourselves unworthy of brutality, even the power of resistance, is nurtured or crushed in the web of relational life. That is how fragile we are; that is what it means to live without metaphysical guarantees.[91] What comes first, it seems to me, is not any incorruptible goodness but the dance of life, where the goddesses and gods appear and dissolve again. To abandon faith in a God who protects us from tragedy does involve, as Ruether senses, a real risk of passivity and despair. For me, though, the risk of drowning in the tragic is not as great as that of clinging to a boat that no longer floats. But these are great risks and fundamental religious choices, and it would be wrong to absolutize any single way of risking and choosing.

Within the framework of Ruether's own choices and heritage, there are several ways in which her system might be developed to reflect more deeply on the tragic. The prophetic and covenant traditions of the Hebrew Scriptures, which she has adapted to good effect, can be placed in dialogue with Jewish traditions of religious questioning and lament.[92] The fall tradition can also be read as an account of the tragic dimension of life, if separated from the idea of a perfect beginning and end and relieved of the exaggerated negativity often laid onto the world as a foil for faith. Then too theologians might see the beauty and power that have always sustained ordinary folk in the midst of suffering and fault. Finally, Ruether might look to women's religious cultures not just for new forms of spirituality but for patterns of theological insight more organically related to women's creative and spiritual practices.

As Reuther knows, this search must go on beyond the walls of patriarchal paradise. To date, her own escape from this paradise has been an exodus journey toward an ever receding horizon of unambiguous good. Now it is time to make the world home for women and other aliens, and for that we may need to invoke other, less pristine powers.

CHAPTER SIX

A DESIRING NATURE
THE THEALOGICAL QUEST OF
CAROL P. CHRIST

Imagine a life-and-death struggle between two angels,
the angel of love and the angel of wrath, the angel of
promise and the angel of evil. Imagine that they both
attain their ends, each one victorious. Imagine the
laugh that would rise above their corpses as if to say,
your death has given me birth; I am the soul of your
conflict, its fulfillment as well.

—*Elie Wiesel*[1]

The day I read The Gates of the Forest, *the laughter of*
Gavriel entered my bones. I found myself laughing out
loud and put the book down. I laughed for hours and
hours. All my private, personal suffering during my
first two years in graduate school flashed before my
eyes and was dissolved in laughter. . . . Though I have
never forgotten that day and have always viewed what
happened as a kind of spiritual experience, I have not
written about it before, because it seemed so personal,
because people do not usually think of laughter as a
spiritual experience. Recently, after writing about the
laughter of Aphrodite, which I experienced in Lesbos, I
began to think about the laughter of Gavriel again. I
now understand that laughter can be the mediator of
transformation. Gavriel's laughter, like Aphrodite's,
enabled me to distance myself from pain, opening a
new perspective on my life.

—*Carol Christ*[2]

A funny thing, laughter, what's it for?

—*Doris Lessing*[3]

WHEN WOMEN gather around what is sacred and powerful for us, laughter may resound as much as lament. Carol Christ has allowed that laughter to resound in her heart and to stir her mind. Before it God himself has shrunk and retreated. Even without God, she has found plenty to laugh about—mysteries, joys, beauties, and enigmas that are part of life and not just symptoms of injustice. Her emerging thealogy is centered more on what she is for than on what she is against. And what she is for is no abstract ideal; it is immediately, richly present in the deepest desires and pleasures of women. Religious feminists before her had begun to restore the moral perspectives of women to theology, but Christ, in a unique way, has made women's mystical experience and aesthetic sensibilities the stuff of religious reflection.

Driving out God the Father, though, may not be the same as leaving paradise. In patterns characteristic of Goddess feminism, Christ reconfigures the rationalism and dualism with which Christian theology has walled off the tragic. This is despite the fact that in Christ's own view she has thoroughly repudiated the Christian interpretation of good and evil. Everywhere in her work one sees a sharp critique of what she takes to be the most deleterious features of patriarchal rationalism—the God above change and finitude, the morality aimed at a disembodied Good, the scholarly myths of objectivity and neutrality. Everywhere, too, Christ jettisons both metaphysical dualism and the moral dualism of sin and grace. But her thealogy still dreams of the oneness that has entranced Western rationalism. Though not "higher" than the world of injustice, her Goddess is certainly more basic and, though not above change, can endure without fracture life's hardest tensions. Christ's ethic is based on desire and pleasure rather than on sacrifice, but desire is still presumed to be fundamentally good. And again, the One creates the Other. Christ's thealogy too is haunted by what it excludes—natural wholeness by the broken world of sociality, eros by violence, the true Goddess by the false but powerful God.

Christ's primal wholeness, then, is bedeviled by the same multiplicity that undermined God's purchase on universal right or reason. The paradox is one she shares with other forms of Romantic holism: on one hand, the primal whole is said to heal and reconcile binary oppositions; on the other hand, that whole is itself established only by excluding the world of division and domination. In correcting these lacunae, however, we ought to be accountable to a precious truth that Christ articulates perhaps more strikingly than any other feminist scholar of religion: however severe may be our moral critique of the world, that critique ought not to be symmetrical with our sheer love and enjoyment of life. For Christ the world is sacred, so there is no unholy place where moral refuse can be discarded. If feminists want an earth-centered spirituality, they must be able to integrate and in this sense "accept" even the most profound negativity, without adverting to a supernatural resolution.

Christ's thealogy aims to effect such an integration by drawing on the integrative powers of life itself. Exploring her theory of women's spiritual quest, her construction of the Goddess, her ethic and method of eros, we hear a thealogical voice that echoes elemental truths, but from a particular social location. Goddesses, like Gods, are local after all, and intuitions of the primal whole, like visions of absolute transcendence, illuminate and bound particular worlds. Thinking on those boundaries, we may share Christ's bemused laughter while also questioning her Goddess.

Is the Rainbow Enough?
Christ's Theory of Women's Spiritual Quest

It is on his deathbed that Martha Quest's father wonders out loud what laughter is for. The "creatures fussing around his bed" appear to him like "animals with clothes on who made strange noises with their mouths and noses to communicate and to express feelings." In that moment, what makes them unintelligible is not their animality but their clothes, not their grunting participation in life but their flight from its naked contradictions. Martha, too, loses patience with the facile equilibria of convention. Laughter, to her, is "a kind of balancing mechanism, a shock absorber," and giggling is "a retreat away from facts which needed to be faced." Crying, even over human corruption, seems trivial and unrevealing. Managing reality with moral distinctions also appears shallow, even in regard to the misogynist sadism of her lover Jack. "Shorthand words like evil" might seem to fit the case, but in fact they only cause one "to be done thinking about it."[4]

Still, Doris Lessing construed this thinking as a "quest" for something that is already there—a hidden wholeness, in which contradictions inscrutably coexist. Already there, too, was what Martha called "the watcher," a "dark receptive intelligence," the "only part of me that is real—that's permanent anyway."[5] Christ calls it "the core" of a woman's self, a felt inner connection with nonpersonal, elemental power. It was exposed to her first in *The Four-Gated City*, in response to which she began to formulate her theory of women's spiritual quest.[6] Here Christ saw a female character truly "experiencing her own experience," rather than reenacting the stories of men; in this and similar stories, women could find "the power to create new being."[7]

This new being, however, grew out of an organic, preexisting wholeness. That is evident in Christ's expectation that women's literature be imaginative and realistic. Realism, as she understands it, encompasses an understanding of the alienation, violence, and misogynism of patriarchal culture, while imagination encodes a feminist vision of social transformation.[8] In principle, those criteria seemed perfectly congruent with the standards of feminists who looked to women's literature only for stories of social quests. But Christ's realism is itself mystical and imaginative, a kind of depth description of the great natural powers manifest in and pushing through the surface of convention. In literature she sees women connecting with those deep forces, integrating negativity in a realistic fashion, and in the process developing extraordinary capacities for insight, healing, and creativity. What makes the literature spiritual for her, in other words, is a certain alchemy of the mystical and the moral, acceptance and transformation, and this was what she wanted to articulate and preserve with her theory of women's spiritual quests.

To Christ, the grounding of feminist social ethics in women's spirituality looks quite different than the authorization of Christian patriarchy via God. God, she came to believe, had functioned as a pure, infinite, changeless Good; modeling itself on this Good, Western patriarchy tried to explode natural limitations and make itself impervious to organic change.[9] Women's literature, in contrast, suggested a different model of the sacred, a different view of authority, and a different stance toward change. Since nature is both within and beyond humanity, it empowers women while reminding us that human powers are only a small part of the whole and must be exercised in harmony with it. Since nature itself changes, nature can teach means of change that are more organic and less violent than those of patriarchy. And since nature is finite and relational, to confront it is to accept human limitation and interdependence. For those reasons, Christ refuses to assimilate women's literature to androcentric theories of religion and literature, instead hypothesizing that men and women may be disposed, by inculturation and/or biology, to distinct forms of religious experience.[10]

Still, her procedure remains congruent with that of the theological tradition in one very important way: she wants to ground ethical proposals about social life in a unity of the real and the ideal, a unity more basic, more enduring, more fundamentally *true* than its contradictions. That elemental unity, in other words, enjoyed the same immunity to moral critique as did the Christian God and, like God, was distanced from the world by its very perfection. Her religious idealism, like that of her theological predecessors, was anti-worldly in this respect, but she saw hers as different because it opposed a particular, alienated world, and did not imagine a spiritual plane beyond finitude and change. But the crucial issue, as we saw in Ruether's case, is whether the ideal is granted an ontological status that the nonideal lacks, not whether that status is based on an essentialist distinction between spirit and matter. When "nature" gains this status, it may travel conceptually as far from sociality as "heaven" is from earth, even without leaving the ground. Given this congruence, it is not surprising that the distinction between Christ's theory and androcentric views of spirituality remained more slippery than she had anticipated.

Christ discerns four stages in women's spiritual quests—nothingness, awakening, mystical insight, and new naming. In the original edition of *Diving Deep and Surfacing*, she describes nothingness as analogous to the "dark night" of classical mysticism, especially as interpreted by Michael Novak. But for women, she observes with Mary Daly, nothingness is also a sex-specific condition in which one's own story is silenced. In continuity with the tradition, though, she finds something positive in women's experience of nothingness: the absence of *social* power becomes the point of breakthrough for deeper "powers of being," and for that reason women may be better positioned to receive mystical experience than are men.[11] Women's awakening is akin to what has been called conversion, except that conversion implies surrendering the self to a higher power, while women's awakening strengthens rather than submerges the self. But the epistemic shift Christ attributes to awakening is just as disjunctive. "To one who has 'awakened,' conventional notions of reality seem as unreal and illusory as the world of dreams does to a person abruptly aroused from sleep."[12] She characterizes mystical insight in terms borrowed from William James as ineffable, transient, noetic, and unitive or integrative, and in Evelyn Underhill's terms as embracing and changing the whole self. But against their penchant for metaphysical transcendence, she gladly gives nature pride of place in women's mystical experiences. She also discerns mysticism in the social and sexual experiences within women's literature, but these, too, as we will see, rest on the transpersonal or impersonal forces of nature.[13]

The "new naming" of great powers is a different matter; from the start, Christ has defined that in opposition to patriarchal religion, especially to the Christian perspectives that dominated the field of religion and literature. Women's stories disclose "a basic defect in the perception of ultimate power and reality" in patriarchal culture. Through new naming, the mystical experiences of individual women could be solidified and validated by others, realizing what Adrienne Rich called the "dream of common language" that might overcome the dualistic thinking of Western culture.[14] By the second edition of *Diving Deep*, the chasm between patriarchal religion and feminist "new naming" had widened. There, Christ allows that it was only through the "deformation of language" that she had been able to apply androcentric terms to women's spirituality. For example, it was not just that women's nature mysticism was *as good as* the so-called "higher" mysticisms, but that the "higher" amounts to a "flight from the real conditions of our lives." The nothingness suffered by women is not a matter of universal "finitude and limitation" but of social arrangements in which males strive for infinity at the expense of women and the planet.[15]

While in the first edition Christ treated patriarchal religions as partial truths, by the second edition she seems to regard the patriarchal cosmos as a false and evil whole. The difference, I would suggest, is not great, since partial truths, insofar as they claim universal jurisdiction, generate totalized counterrealities. Nor is the difference great for the ontic status of the ideal whole imagined by feminist spirituality. Whether it stands to patriarchal religion as whole to part or as truth to falsehood, in either case it possesses a kind of being that the God of patriarchy lacks. Interpreted this way, feminist spirituality did not address the possibility of clashing "worlds," conflicting truths, fundamentally different ways of configuring the parameters and possibilities of life. Differences of that kind cannot be reconciled by a shared intuition of wholeness, since visions of wholeness may themselves conflict.

The difficulty of separating women's spirituality from patriarchal religion is matched by that of collecting women's stories under a single theory, for women, too, inhabit and imagine different worlds along lines of race, class, culture, and sexuality. The theory Christ had drawn from works of Doris Lessing and Margaret Atwood represents only one such world. The nothingness experienced by Martha Quest and by Atwood's unnamed protagonist is primarily intrapsychic—passivity, emotional numbness, an anemic sense of self. As Christ shows, this nothingness is how the characters experience conventional femininity, and they overcome it only by facing their own involvement in the destructive side of life. For Atwood's protagonist that entails coming to know death in two forms—the drowned body of her missing father and the suppressed memory of a traumatic abortion. For Martha Quest it means accepting her own involvement in the violence of the twentieth century, on which she had been "conceived, bred, fed and reared."[16]

Traditional theological language could not do justice to these stories. For example, Christ notes, destructive forces such as what Martha calls the "self-hater" are recognized, but there is no attempt to conquer them in the way Christian spirituality tries to conquer "sin" or "the devil." Rather, they are cautiously accepted as part of life and that, paradoxically, quiets their ferocity.[17] Moreover, the "great powers" disclosed in these stories are impersonal. The protagonist of *Surfacing* must learn, in Christ's words, that in the state of mystical union, "individual human identity has no meaning." Life feeds on life; indeed, Christ reflects, "the original guilt may be that we must kill to live." In *The Four-Gated City*, too, psychic and interpersonal forces are interpreted as natural and as impersonal. As Lessing writes and Christ quotes, sex between Martha and Thomas is a force "as impersonal as thunder or lightning or sunlight or the movement of the oceans"; so is the madness that envelopes Lynda and Martha. When Atwood's protagonist conceives, in harmony with the moon but eschewing personal relation with her lover Joe, Christ envisions the virgin Goddess, "complete in herself, the male being incidental." Though the harsh impersonality of nature strips these characters of what Christ terms a "typical female delusion of innocence," it also empowers them to refuse victimhood and to take responsibility for their lives.[18]

Neither novel, however, is in Christ's view easily connected with women's social quests. Her early work on *The Four-Gated City* had found Martha socially relevant as the "medial woman" or "wise woman," whose politics stand on mysticism.[19] By *Diving Deep*, however, Christ had grown discouraged with Lessing's social pessimism and her reliance on conventional forms of messianism.[20] *Surfacing* was troubling for its ambiguous conclusion, as well as the apparently apolitical character of its mystical intensity. Christ ferrets out of *Surfacing* a rudimentary ethic of killing and sacrifice, and she argues that its ancient wisdom about death and life marks a direction for social transformation "that would be beneficial for women and all life."[21] Still, she allows, "if feminism is defined primarily in social terms," *Surfacing* and *The Four-Gated City* could only be considered "protofeminist" or "transitionally feminist."[22]

In an initial study of Lessing, Christ had used the words of Euripides to express her hope that women's stories might "let the world's great order be reversed."[23] Now, with additional hindsight, we can observe that *Surfacing* and *The Four-Gated City* were by and about women of relative privilege, women who, like Medea, nonetheless find themselves denizens in the lands of men. That double situation helps account for the painful isolation of these characters, but it also affords them and women of similar means the solitude so vital to spiritual quest as Christ defines it. It may also explain their sense of the connection between power and guilt. Finding themselves to have been complicit in injustice without malice or deliberation, it becomes vital to grasp that only the completely powerless are completely innocent, and that they are neither. What feels revelatory is therefore the amorality of power, the insignificance of the individual self, the fluidity of the boundary between the wrongs women do and the wrongs we suffer. Still, the detached equanimity that is the great achievement of these spiritual heroines may not be the goal of women whose daily survival is more closely bound with the success of their social quest, such as Ntozake Shange and Adrienne Rich, who were also among Christ's subjects in *Diving Deep*.

In Shange's *for colored girls who have considered suicide when the rainbow is enuf*, Christ reads the "double burden" and the "double strength" of being black and female in a society defined by white men. But she argues that "the heart of the experience of nothingness" in the choreopoem "is a woman's loss and debasement of self for love of a man." Strength is found through black sisterhood; in Christ's terminology, an instance of "communal mysticism" expressed in the imagery of nature. The "colored girls" become a rainbow with, in Shange's words, "as much right and as much purpose for being here as the air and the mountains." That, writes Christ, is a "mystical insight—being does not require justi-fication, it just is." The openness and vulnerability of Shange's ladies, she notes, do not guarantee love; but may even make them more threatening to the men they desire. The black woman "may not be able to find a man to love her," but she can at least "refuse to be a victim." Finding God in herself and "loving Her fiercely," she grounds herself in larger powers, and no longer needs "to imitate whiteness or depend on men for her power of being."[24]

Of all the writers discussed in *Diving Deep*, Christ discovers in Ad-rienne Rich's poetry "the clearest vision of the path toward the integration of spiritual vision with social reality." In *Diving into the Wreck*, Rich faced the nothingness of patriarchal marriage and politics, and was led "to an ontological insight, a *new seeing* or revelation of 'what is,' which then requires a *new naming* of self and world." On one side, the revelation concerned the violence and emotional deadness of men; on the other, the life-sustaining powers of women manifest in motherhood, sisterhood, and lesbian love. Like Rich's "rose-wet cave," those powers echoed an-cient Goddesses. In Rich's *The Dream of a Common Language*, Christ hears an emerging language common to women, a language naming those sacred powers and concretizing new modes of being and of loving. She is particularly touched by Rich's acceptance of solitude and her willingness to share responsibility for a failed relationship rather than feeling "tragically doomed." Surveying "the forces they had ranged against us" as well as "the forces we had ranged within us," Rich accepts: "this we were, this is how we tried to love." Even in the ruins of relationship, Rich discovers in Christ's words, "what remains is essential." The "great light" filling that primal circle is for Christ "a place in the mind where all is understood as part of patterns larger than the self and accepted without sorrow, regret, or desire."[25] But unlike Rich, for whom "two people together" is "a miracle," "a work heroic in its ordinariness," Christ finds "heroine-ism more in the years I and my women friends have lived alone than in relationships with women or men." She is also uneasy with Rich's utopic view of women's community and her almost unrelievedly negative view of men.[26] Even here, where Christ finds the strongest connection between spiritual and social quest, the passage between the two seems somewhat arduous.

In retrospect, it could be added, marrying the works of Lessing and Atwood with those of Shange and Rich was more arduous still. *Surfacing* and *The Four-Gated City*, for all their challenge to traditional Christian spirituality, are still primarily absorbed with intrapsychic matters; the major change undergone by the characters is an enlightenment felt to be of intrinsic worth regardless of its immediate relevance to social change. But this is less the case for the works by Shange and Rich, where psychic revolution occurs in concert with other women and is complicated by the vectors of racism, poverty, and compulsory heterosexuality. There are important intrapsychic changes in these works, especially the gains noted by Christ in personal autonomy and responsibility. But these are not freighted with the claim, which Christ draws from Atwood and Lessing, that the core of the self is separable from the particularities of her relations. A different sense of the sacred, too, arises from these social locations. Nature is central in each, as Christ rightly points out, but in Shange and Rich the connection between humanity and nature humanizes nature rather than depersonalizing humanity. Shange's sacred rainbow is made of "colored girls," and Rich's Goddess is a Mother, disclosed in the most passionate, pleasurable, and particular of relationships. That contrasts sharply with the Goddess imaged in the dispassionate conception of *Surfacing*. It also contrasts with Martha Quest, who, as Christ mentions, could find motherhood spiritually meaningful only in relation to people who were *not* her biological children.[27]

Most significantly, we can observe in these texts differences in the treatment of power and victimization. "To refuse victimhood" has become a feminist maxim, but its meaning is not univocal. For Atwood's and Lessing's protagonists it means recognizing that power is not only external but internal, and that with power goes the potential for destruction and guilt. But for "colored girls" to refuse victimhood is to also externalize the blame they have ingested. Rich knows that her love affair was undermined by "the forces ranged within us," but she also names the enemy without. And even in the world of lesbian separatism, Rich does not seem to feel utterly separable from her relations, not even from her bad relations. There may be more poignancy than equanimity, too, in Shange's claim that "the rainbow is enuf." It *has* to be enough, but for women who remain black in a white-supremacist context, or heterosexual in a misogynist context, or lesbian in a heterosexist context, personal power is that much less detachable from the success or the failure of concrete relations. If spirituality is conceived in primarily intrapsychic terms, women like these may appear more interested in social than in spiritual matters. Or their spirituality may seem to be a retreat, what Martha Quest would call a "shock absorber" for social defeat. In short, to define women's spirituality in a way that privileges the natural over the social can recapitulate the lines of social privilege that divide women.[28] What appears to be an intrinsic tension between the spiritual and the social may actually be a tension between different social worlds.

Kate Chopin's late-nineteenth-century novel *The Awakening* is an interesting case study in these tensions. Christ's essay on the novel is subtitled "spiritual liberation, social defeat." Edna Pontellier, Chopin's protagonist, rejects the sensual and emotional deadness of bourgeois marriage and motherhood, searching for what Christ terms "wholeness— for a total sexual and creative life as a woman." Edna reaches for that wholeness through sexual freedom and artistic creativity. But, like a snail without a shell, she cannot find social housing for her new energies. Finally she commits suicide, drowning herself in the sea, image of "the limitless potential of her soul." Christ perceives this shattering of self as "a common feature of mystic experience," complicated in Edna's case by the lack of viable alternatives to patriarchal life. But she also blames Edna for "insufficient self-consciousness and dedication in both her art and her life." In her finest moment, Edna appears to Christ as the sensual woman-unto-herself, "imperious and triumphant, like a queen or Goddess." But Edna has not "learned to stand alone"; she clings to the fantasy that her happiness depends on her lover, Robert. Though Edna's demise is imaged ambivalently, as rebirth as well as death and bondage, still Christ is disappointed with Chopin's inability to envision a better ending.[29] The disjunction of spiritual and social quests is, as the essay's title suggests, "tragic." But tragedy, though perhaps socially realistic, seems to remain in Christ's view thealogically misguided: eros was supposed to connect a woman to life, not to drown her. Still, if the core of the self is transpersonal, then, as Atwood writes and Christ quotes in her essay on *Surfacing*, "nothing has died, everything is alive, everything is waiting to become alive."[30]

Edna's awakening, and those of other women, might be read differently if eros and other elemental powers were transferred from the realm of ideality to that of social reality.[31] In the latter realm, eros appears as a malleable energy, mirroring the limits and the possibilities of social imagination. When eros challenges *dominant* conventions, that is not by dint of a sacred transcendence but by virtue of the "faults" in the social order itself. In those cracks and discontents, new forms of life may grow, which are nonetheless shaped and misshaped by the prevailing order. The crack in Edna's virtue occasions such a growth. In Edna's own view, what breaks through is "nature," whose ways sometimes seem to her brutal and monstrous in their anonymity.[32] Yet these pains are as socially constructed as is Edna's acute pleasure in transpersonal sensuality; indeed, throughout the novel, the two are tied together in tones of romantic masochism. Perhaps, then, this bourgeois lady's erotic satisfaction presupposes the social freedom to "drown," to surrender, to be freed from the burdens of love in the concrete. In any case, to imagine oneself devoid of social bonds is itself a privilege many cannot afford, and the visions of wholeness conjured in such isolation may rest on the brokenness of other women and men.

Since the beginning of her work with women's literature, Christ has been conscious of differences of privilege among women, acknowledging that "women's experience" is not one but many things.[33] The shortcomings of her theory in addressing these differences are by no means unique. They reflect a long moment, through which we have yet to finish passing, when Euro-American religious feminism has not fathomed the depth of the difference that race, class, culture, and sexuality make to women. On the other hand, Christ's work on women's literature has contributed insights that remain unique. She has highlighted the need to root moral vision in the mortal earth, to temper and ground political idealism in a world far older and greater than humanity. Far from commending the romantic escapism of which Goddess feminism is sometimes accused, the impulse behind Christ's work on spiritual quest is to encounter the real even in its harshness and mystery,[34] and that represents a real gain in the *religious* depth of religious studies. Moreover, by refusing to assimilate women's stories to the doctrines of men, she has established women's literature as a thealogical source that, while still largely ignored by androcentric religious studies, has become vital to most religious feminists.[35]

To speak more deeply to differences among women, Christ's theory would need to relinquish the notion of a single or ideal whole beneath women's diverse experiences. In the absence of that ideal, both literature and life warrant the mixture of acceptance and questioning that I have characterized as a tragic sensibility. Among the most pressing questions are whether and how women's social quests are supported by our spiritual quests. In places, as in her work on *Surfacing*, Christ seems to suggest that nature is amoral,[36] from which it would follow that social ethics must be found elsewhere. Yet nature mysticism is at the heart of her theory of women's spiritual quest, and the *feminist* relevance of that theory has always hinged upon its relation to the social quest. From the viewpoint of feminist postmodernism, this difficulty is related to the problem of difference: since ideas of nature are themselves social products, they do not point to a whole traversing social difference. But they can illuminate the heterogeneity of sociality itself, in which change may grow. The feminist critic, then, needs to be cognizant of her own social location in relation to the text. Finally, the creativity of women, so much a part of Christ's style in *Diving Deep*, must also enter thealogical inquiry as part of its substance. For the real, whether at a given moment we are apprehending it mystically or transforming it morally, is itself a *creation* of persons-in-relation. And if creativity is not the imitation of a perfect God but a movement of powers diverse and dangerous, then creativity is itself never innocent, nor are the sacred powers in which it participates.

Journey to the Goddess:
Eros as Knowledge and Ethic

For Elie Wiesel the entangled laughter of God and humanity became a form of continued relationship, a way of holding open the questions that each presents to the other about power and goodness. For Christ, who wrote her dissertation on Wiesel, the questions Wiesel had raised to the God who permitted the Holocaust grew into questions about the God who presides over patriarchy. For her, too, raising those questions was initially a continuation of relationship. Drawing upon the story theologies of Stephen Crites and Michael Novak, she raised women's voices as midrashim on the biblical story. But when she repeated Wiesel's spiritual exercise of imaginatively changing places with God, the change held for Christ in an unexpected way. The "still, small voice" that told her "in God is a woman like yourself," though first imagined in biblical metaphors, would become a voice from off the biblical stage, the voice of the Goddess. And the laughter of Aphrodite, that divine woman-unto-herself, would signal the end of relationship with the biblical God. Accepting tension and contradiction as part of life, Christ would laugh away the God who renders the world fundamentally questionable.[37]

Christ's rejection of God was based partly on historical judgments. The biblical God, she concluded, was a male war God, mirroring the historical association between patriarchy and large-scale warfare. Relying on Morton Smith and Raphael Patai, she hypothesized that Yahweh's claim to exclusivity was a historical fiction created by the "Yahweh alone party" to legitimate its eventual victory over the long-standing polytheism and Goddess-worship of ancient Israel and Judah. The threat of violence, then, was always the Other side of chosenness, mandating the historical persecution of pagans, witches, and heretics, both inside and beyond the Hebrew and then the Christian people. She realized that her own biblical history was to be found with those outsiders, not lying dormant within prophetic visions of social justice. The prophetic discourse, at least in its written form, was the product of "a relatively comfortable, urban (and, it should be added, misogynist) priestly class," and for every denunciation of the rich, it included a threat against the worshipers of other deities. That threat, Christ believed, would have been felt not just by foreign Jezebels but by the rural poor. It would have especially targeted women, who retained important religious powers within Goddess worship.[38]

Still, Christ's primary concerns were "with the function of symbolism," not with "the historical truth of the Exodus stories, with questions of how many slaves may or may not have been freed, nor by what means, nor with questions of the different traditions that may have been woven together to shape the biblical stories." Like liberation theology, she was concerned with the present-day function of symbols. Whatever the class context of biblical warfare, she argued, a warlike God cannot be morally acceptable in a world of nuclear arms. And whatever the appeal of Yahweh or Jesus to poor women, still in both testaments women could be saved only at the sufferance of a male God.[39]

The peculiar perniciousness of this symbol, as I have noted before, lay for Christ in its claim to transcend all symbols. On the wings of that transcendence, God could evade responsibility for his historical crimes, claiming to include as his "real meaning" only what is good. For Christ, however, God's inclusivity was like the cat who swallowed the mouse, achieved only through violent suppression. As an attribute of the one and only God, maleness had become generic humanity, and chosenness an inferiorization of the unchosen. The hybrid "God-She" and other symbolic revisions were not sufficient to redeem God, she argued; one must also question the ideas of transcendence, monotheism, and perfection that serve to hypostatize God's symbolic contents.[40]

The Idea behind this symbol, Christ came to believe, was Plato's changeless and disembodied Good.[41] Like Ruether and influenced by her, Christ attacked that Idea as dualistic. But for Christ to deflate spirit was also to dismantle the moral dualism of sin and grace. Since there is no grace "higher" than the natural processes of change, decay, and death, there is nothing of sin in life's destructive side. The problem beneath "the problem of evil," as it struck Christ, has been the effort to divide the painful side of life from its joys and creativity. God represented that eviscerated Good, and she wanted no more part of Him. So, returning from her peregrinations in patriarchal history, she began to seek a Goddess within nature, who she hoped would be truer to experience and better for the planet and its creatures.

Though Christ's personal spirituality was captivated by the classical Greek Goddess Aphrodite, she interpreted Aphrodite and other patriarchal Goddesses as fractured vestiges of pre-patriarchal Goddesses. In patriarchy, as Pomeroy had commented, insecure males divide positive female characteristics among a variety of Goddesses; adding those traits together, one might come up with "a female equivalent of Zeus or Apollo."[42] Christ came up with more: "the prehistorical Goddesses of life, death and renewal," of which sexuality, represented by Aphrodite, is one powerful manifestation.[43] Aphrodite and other virgin Goddesses represented the separation of the Maiden and Mother aspects of the more ancient Goddess. Even so, they were never fully subordinated to male interests, recalling the degree of autonomy that women under patriarchy may still find outside marriage.[44]

Studying the works of feminist scholars such as Merlin Stone, Anne Barstow, G. Rachel Levy, Ruby Rohrlich, Jane Ellen Harrison, and Marija Gimbutas, Christ concluded that Paleolithic and Neolithic cultures had been relatively stable, irenic, and without profound class conflict. Archaeological evidence suggests that women in these cultures were not subordinate to men and enjoyed a power and prestige that were further enhanced in the Neolithic era by women's invention of agriculture. The images Christ terms the "Lady of the Animals" come from the Neolithic era and later, including, for example, the sculpture of Catal Hüyük (6500–5650 B.C.E.), the Sumerian Lilith (ca. 2000 B.C.E.), and the Minoan Snake Goddess (ca. 1700–1450 B.C.E.), and from cultures as varied as Egypt, Japan, and the Americas. She saw a link between these images and the Upper Paleothic "Venuses." Moreover, she wrote, these images "must be interpreted in relation to the cave art of the Paleolithic era." The caves, in which rituals of burial and hunting were performed, may have functioned as aniconic images of the Lady of the Animals.[45]

But Christ came to believe that to appreciate the sacrality of these images as well as their social significance, religious studies would have to undergo a thorough shift of paradigms. She argued that by defining history as conterminous with written texts, androcentric religious studies had placed pre-patriarchal times outside the pale of knowledge; in marking time by Jesus and the Hebrew patriarchs, it had exiled pre-patriarchal religion from the center of academic significance. Most importantly, Christ linked the "myth of objectivity" to Western, androcentric notions of divinity and truth with roots in the Platonic Idea and branches in Enlightenment reason and scientific method. That myth, she argued, derives its subjective credibility from the idiosyncrasies of male psychology, and cannot accommodate the experience of Paleolithic and Neolithic peoples, for whom "magic and science were not yet separate, and . . . divinity, humanity and nature were not understood as inhabiting separate spheres."[46]

Christ has defined the Goddess as woman and as nature,[47] and her view of the divine, too, implies a view of knowledge. That connection is clearest in Susan Griffin's allegory of the cave, to which Christ often refers in describing the implications of the Goddess for religious studies.[48] Griffin's cave, literally the inside of the earth and metaphorically the vagina, reverses Plato in treating earth and body as the site of revelation rather than illusion. In the sentient, intelligent earth-body, there is a communion of knower and known, and, as in lesbian lovemaking, knowledge of the self and of the beloved are mutually arousing. Women participate in the sacred and reveal it, but Christ's intent is less to deify women than to sacralize life. Women's wills, for example, manifest the Goddess, but only when exercised in harmony with other beings. Women's eros, which reveals the Goddess, is not simply any desire but the deepest desires disclosed in mystical experience, confirmed by other women and expanded by contact with new points of view.[49]

At the center of things, for Christ as for Griffin, is the moving reality of connection, the creative activity of desire. And if that is what is most sacred and most real, then knowledge in general and religious knowledge in particular are an expression and a development of one's connection to life. That, too, was the moral power of thealogy for Christ. The commitment to the correction of historical injustices, which is one of her criteria of thealogical adequacy, is a matter of restoring and deepening connection. Thealogy ought to "strike a deep chord in our experience" and "help us better to understand, love and enjoy the life that has been given us."[50] Methodologically, this relational ontology called for greater attention to ritual and symbol as well as to physical evidence. Ritual "opens channels of understanding that could not be reached through study alone."[51] In the Goddess movement, Christ has found, women gather around common symbols but allow different interpretations to coexist fruitfully in the living soil of experience. She noted, "My theological training tells me I must know whether Goddess is one or many, personal or impersonal, whether she is in nature or more than nature," but "I am not certain that these questions can be answered. The answers do not seem to be required for participation in ritual."[52]

Christ's search for the pre-patriarchal Goddess, then, has been deeply bound to her participation in the contemporary Goddess movement. She likes to repeat Elie Wiesel's story about a series of Hassidic *rebbe* who over the generations forgot the sacred place, the prayers, and the ritual, but who remembered and retold the story of their people's longing for God. For God, Wiesel wrote, the story was sufficient. For Christ the "heartfelt desire" of the *rebbe* to communicate with their God "sheds light on the desires of many women and men today to enter into relation with ancient Goddesses."[53] Like the *rebbe*, she chooses to believe her desire and to search for its history. Her own "deep experience of the power of Goddess symbolism and ritual," she relates, makes her skeptical about "the oft-repeated scholarly cliché that Goddesses always and everywhere support male power, functioning merely as the lap of the king."[54] It also makes her disbelieve the androcentric paradigm of religious history exemplified by Mircea Eliade, which assumed, for example, that hierarchical sex arrangements are endemic to human nature, and that religious consciousness aims to transcend, often by violent means, the "profane" world.[55]

For Christ, as for Elisabeth Schüssler Fiorenza, whose method she adapts, the feminist critique of religious studies is a matter of veracity.[56] But it is also a question of values, which interact with facts, methods, and hypotheses to create the scholarly paradigms that may erupt into intellectual revolutions.[57] That was why Eliade's religious history, notwithstanding its points of overlap with feminist scholarship, remains, in Christ's opinion, fundamentally wrongheaded. In Eliade's case, as in the case of androcentric scholarship generally, she notices that the *mythos* of objectivity is also an *ethos*,[58] replete with value judgments in the questions that are asked and those that are ignored, the rhetorical applause for patriarchy and the lack of moral approbation against the crimes of men and their Gods.

Christ names her alternative paradigm a method of eros and empathy, where eros means "a passion to connect, the desire to understand the

experience of another, the desire to deepen our understanding of ourselves and our world, the passion to transform or preserve the world as
we understand it more deeply." Rather than pretending to speak universally, the feminist scholar should articulate the eros driving her work,
which for Christ is the desire to find and reinvent what Anne Barstow
called "a religion created, at least in part, by women." [59] The normative
center of this method cannot be objectified; for Christ it is "my own
experience, as shaped, named and confirmed by the voices of my sisters."
While ancient Goddesses are an important source, "they are not normative
for me in the way that scripture and tradition have been normative for
Christian theology, halachah and scripture for Jewish thought."[60] Beginning with desire does not encase one in solipsism, she holds, because
eros itself flows toward empathy, the desire to understand others on
their own terms. In its empathic moment, feminist scholarship does not
differ very much from the ethos of objectivity. But its beginning remains
distinct, as does its endpoint. New insights are woven into an expanded
viewpoint, but remain grounded "in an ever-expanding community of
knowledge and scholarship, which in turn expands [the scholar's] standpoint."[61]

The notion of eros clearly plays a central role in Christ's thealogy,
combining an ontology, an epistemology, and, perhaps most significantly,
an incipient ethic. Against Gordon Kaufman she contends that the poign-
ant pleasure we take in this mortal life provides a stronger basis for
ethics than does agapic sacrifice, which signals an inability to love "this
life which ends in death."[62] In relation to received norms of order and
morality, eros is disruptive and sometimes painful. Christ has felt those
effects powerfully in her personal life, but along with them the power
of eros to open new avenues of creativity.[63] Her praise of eros parallels
her view of the pre-patriarchal Goddesses, who appear chaotic "when
viewed from the standpoint of rational control," but who "have their own
inner logic," following "rhythmical patterns which are regular, though
not entirely predictable or controllable."[64] Drawing on Lorde's "Uses of
the Erotic," she suggests that by feeling deeply into their eros, women
can find the vision and energy to build an integrally satisfying world.[65]
In contrast, the patriarchal eros of war numbs the soldier's sense of
connection with those he kills, rapes, and enslaves.[66]

By positing Goddess-nature as an immanent unity of the real and the
good, Christ has been able to renounce "objectivity" without ceding her
claims for truth. Against Sheila Davaney's postmodern nihilism, she contends that "truth may be relative, but we are relational beings, and in
our lives, there are relative truths." In her own life, "commitment to

feminism does not have the same ontological status as commitment to patriarchalism." Feminism is experientially "more true," and none of the facts of patriarchal history shake Christ's belief that "women are fully human," nor her judgment that patriarchy "has inhibited the possibilities of life on this earth."[67] God might evaporate in the postmodern critique of transcendent truth, but the Goddess will not.

But if the Goddess can outlive transcendent truth, can she survive the death of essential goodness? That remains a problem for Christ's thealogy, which, for all its repudiation of Platonic rationalism, inherits the assumption that true eros is good. The Platonic soul might hope to ascend from lower loves to higher; Christ descends from rarefied agape to chthonic eros, to which all true desire flows.[68] Christ, I believe, is right that much unnecessary negativity comes from the rejection of unavoidable limitations, and that some dimensions of injustice can be healed by feeling more deeply. The question is whether this strategy can be absolutized on the thealogical assumption that "real" eros is inherently creative. Can this idealized eros speak to the obvious plasticity of sexuality, which can mold and harden around war, violence, and domination quite as well as around mutuality? Can women of relative privilege hope to persuade our less privileged sisters when we argue that injustices, even those from which we benefit, are but obstructions of our *true* desires, that social oppression is only the hardened shell of psychic repression?

There is a theoretical sleight of hand here, which has a long history in Western rationalistic responses to evil. If some negativity is acceptable and some is not, then everything depends on telling which is which. But to define the unacceptable kind of negativity simply as the nonacceptance of acceptable negativity, or to reduce destructive sexuality to the repression of "true" desire, is to retreat from ethical discernment into formal circularity. The goodness of eros, like the goodness of God, is marshalled to authorize whatever ethical positions one already holds, but we are none the wiser as to how those positions might be explicated on more intrinsic grounds. For Christ the problem is more severe, since she has explicitly repudiated the Idea of a Good that transcends all negativity. If moral discernment has no other referent than the conflicted world, then it cannot be achieved by appeal to formal principles but by the political work of constructing and deconstructing shared values—a work that has to include saying "no" as well as saying "yes."

Christ's formal equation of truth and goodness is a methodological problem as well, for it alone provides the thread linking everything that she has called Goddess. In what sense, for example, could images from widely varied cultures and periods be gathered under the name of "Lady of the Animals"? In what sense could it be claimed that for Paleolithic people, "both the cave and the female body were understood to be images of the creative power of the Goddess"[69]—as if the Goddess were the "original" and the cave or body mere "representations"? And in what sense could the Goddess symbol as experienced by contemporary women refer to that same reality? For Jungians these data may be welded together under the concept of the "feminine." But for Christ, who has long been skeptical of the Jungian feminine,[70] the Goddess stands for organic processes of integration in which women participate. However, those organic processes do not of themselves provide historical connections among the data that Christ calls Goddess. This is not to gainsay the historical connections that may in fact exist, but only to observe the logical problem in positing an essence, however organic, as the referent of historical meaning.

In the years since the Goddess movement began, the meanings of sameness, difference, nature, desire, and representation have been greatly problematized by postmodern discourse, which aims to "denature" or "de-doxify" all objective givens. Christ, I think, is right in sensing a link between the old objectivism and the new nihilism, asking why, if reality is relational, relative claims do not count as truth or as value. But there remains a difference between *relative* truths, each partially disclosing a greater whole, and *conflicting* truths of the kind that encode clashing interests and generate disparate paradigms. Others, like Christ, conceive desire as playing a role in constructing reality, but desire no longer appears one and the same, not even within the contested boundaries of the "self."[71] To the degree that wishing does make it so, reality is then immersed in the (not always creative) chaos of desire. That, I have suggested, stirs up the most elemental questions about truths, goods, and their multiple relations, questions that the Christian theological tradition has for the most part evaded.

Yet they are properly thealogical and theological questions, insofar as theo(a)logy aims to connect history, culture, and ethics. That will to connect is probably also the major source of academic skepticism about religious studies, which is perceived as intellectually tainted by its lingering attachment to religious values and communities. No doubt it also accounts for why mainstream religious studies, trying to secure its shaky academic status, is embarrassed by feminist scholars whose work challenges canonical facts and values. The doubts and the embarrassment, however, are not entirely reducible to moral bad will. There *is* a difference as well as a connection between truth claims and evaluative claims, and if feminists expose the connection we must also reconceive the difference.

Evil, I have suggested, is that difference, where "evil" refers not to an essence but to the negative moral judgments that infect morality with fault and reason with absurdity. For example, when Christ writes that *for her* patriarchy lacks the ontological status of feminism, the validity of that claim is admittedly provisional; it obtains for "finite and limited individuals and within finite and limited communities" where feminists' desires may be actualized.[72] However, she does not contemplate those trackless regions where judgments of truth and of value diverge, where patriarchy, though bad "for us," is unfortunately still true "for us" and is evidently good "for them." To think about evil is to think about the boundaries of intelligibility and value, and if on those boundaries there is an infinity of loss, there also is the promise of finite gain. Precisely because scholars can sometimes agree on matters of truth even when we disagree on values, it is possible to expand our regional intelligibilities and soften the borders between them. Precisely because moral agreements are not upheld by an inclusive truth, it is possible to create forms of social life that are more hospitable to benign diversity. At the places where agreement cannot be achieved and paradigms clash, what we are witnessing is not the reemergence of the Goddess or any other essential truth, but the costs of community, which it should be the special job of the thealogian to count.

The suggestions I have made in relation to Christ's work on literature, about rethinking nature, social location, and the relation of thealogical and ethical claims, apply as well to her work on Goddesses. In addition, her thealogy would benefit from reflection on polytheism, which to date she has consigned to the netherworld of unimportant doctrinal questions. A polytheistic thealogy might better address the multiplicity of worlds and their guiding spirits while dissolving the aura of essentialism that surrounds Christ's references to "the Goddess." Moreover, as I have suggested before, in a more polytheistic world nature is less a foil for society than an encompassing life-world.[73] By combining her intuitions about the creativity of desire with a sharper sense of life's tensions, Christ's thealogy could avoid objectivist approaches to nature without abandoning physicality for the solipsistic sociality of nihilistic post-modernism.

Methodologically, thealogy might heed Christ's own call for greater scholarly attention to the religious experience of nonliterate people,[74] which so far she has applied more to Goddess religions than to the biblical traditions. Like most theologians, she reads the latter through the viewpoints of literate elites, overlooking the ordinary people who, aside from the coercive imposition of orthodoxy, have always incorporated what elites regard as heterodox but without thinking of themselves as pagans, heretics, or even syncretists. From the viewpoint of feminist thealogy, this admission need not be a loss. On the contrary, it might contribute to the sophistication of Christ's religious historiography, even while deepening her thealogical judgment about the meanings of Goddess and God. What is true for people must also be true for our deities: only the powerless are innocent. To know them in their historical complexity is to weigh sacred levity with moral judgment. Whatever can fly then, human or divine, will have earned its wings.

Thealogy as Wonder: An Assessment

Only a few contemporary theologians have invited us to understand their work in the context of their lives, and Carol Christ is one of them. In ancient times Augustine did the same, though his *Confessions*, unlike those of feminists, never counted much against his credibility. What came to be Christ's thealogy began with the startling realization that there was no place within religious studies where what she found sacred could be named as such, or where her questions could serve as research hypotheses. Discovering in Doris Lessing's novels a disturbing but illuminating resonance with her own experiences of sacred power, Christ had to question the established canon of sacred texts and the well-worn paths of religious interpretation. Learning from her own experience "why women need the Goddess"[75] and from others how varied the meanings of Goddess are, she could not but reject the presumption that religious symbols point to a single transcendent referent. This was less a matter of positing a single female essence than of suspending androcentric assumptions about generic humanity and inclusive truth in order to clear a space in which women's questions could be asked.[76]

If women's quests count as religious questions, what will count as answers? Where traditional theology has been persuaded by order, Christ's work stands out for its attraction to beauty and power, by its intellectual fascination with what is *not* understood, its ability to recognize sacrality in what is *not* pure. As she once said of Aphrodite, "I am her priestess not because I understand, but because I do not."[77] Her work, I have said, is moved by acceptance, but that acceptance has never been facile, nor is the wholeness she seeks homogeneous. Her thealogical inquiry expresses the profound and permanent *wonder* that is religious experience. Entering that mixture with her, one finds not only power and beauty but real intellectual gain; it becomes possible to wonder about history, about the sacred, about power and pleasure in ways that were not possible before.

I have found in Christ's work two areas of difficulty. One concerns women's differences and is most evident in her literary work; the other concerns the truth and goodness of eros and is most evident in her thealogy. These difficulties, I propose, come not from her departures from theology-as-usual but from her unacknowledged continuity with it: the belief that ethics can and must be authorized with claims about the essential nature of things. There is, however, some ambiguity in her work on this point and, in that ambiguity, room for movement. For in Christ one finds both an immanent Ideal called nature or Goddess and an unusual sense of the unsettling, disturbing character of sacred power. In that immanent Ideal, Christ has tried to join desire and knowledge, spiritual and social quest, ancient Goddesses and contemporary ones. But in the disturbance of that Ideal, arising from her own experience and from many other quarters, comes a new opportunity to thealogize about how truths and goods might join and disjoin in a radically plural world.

In pointing to differences between women's desires and men's, Christ is implicated, for better and for worse, not only in the death of andro-centrism but in the death of humanism, in the end of an era when beneath the changing surface of sociality there were unquestionable referents of meaning. Now that "essences" are no longer persuasive as causes and "origins" are suspect as explanations, every construction of meaning is stripped and scrutinized for its political aims. Stripped that way, Christ's work shows that the intellectual challenges of postmodernism, however abstruse, are indeed tied to the political problems facing feminism as it struggles to regroup beyond identity politics. As Judith Butler has argued, feminism is now troubled by the radical multiplicity of gender.[78] That is also trouble for the ideas of patriarchy upon which Christ, Ruether, and other Euro-American feminists have depended and against which they have conferred upon women a strained theoretical unity. Now the effort to "include" all oppressions in a single systematic analysis has become as unsteady as the chaotic company of "the oppressed."

Christ has not engaged fully with these intellectual and political crises, because she remains docked on an essence, not of spirit, not even of rational intelligibility, but of a goodness that she hopes to find at the heart of nature. For Christ that goodness is immanent, changing, complex, and, to date, otherwise undefined. But it remains an essence—an object of faith-*stopping*-understanding—as long as Christ, having repudiated the Christian language of sin and guilt, has no alternative name for moral wrong.

Here, however, is exactly the point at which feminist thealogy might not simply adapt to the postmodern situation but shape it, because "evil" is still the intellectual hot potato that benights scholarly work precisely because it cannot be thought about. Feminist scholars of religion, overturning ancient Gods and pursuing forbidden desires, show that what has been called evil can indeed think. Now, perhaps, it is time to think about the fact that what *we* adjudge evil, too, has voices, desires, and intelligibilities of its own, and if those desires cannot be included in a benign whole, neither can they be excluded without cost and damage. To paraphrase Adrienne Rich, "wholeness," in such partial ways as we can create it, is a matter of "pulling the tenets of a life together / with no mere will to mastery, / only care for the many-lived, unending / forms in which [we] find [ourselves]."[79] That may not yield a common language, but it promises a gentler touching of worlds.

CHAPTER SEVEN

A WORLD OF COLOR
THE PROMISE OF A
TRAGIC HEURISTIC

*I'm here. I lasted. And my girl come home. Now I can
look at things again because she's here to see them too.
After the shed, I stopped. Now, in the morning, when I
light the fire I mean to look out the window to see what
the sun is doing to the day. Does it hit the pump
handle first or the spigot? See if the grass is gray-green
or brown or what. Now I know why Baby Suggs
pondered color her last years. She never had time to
see, let alone enjoy it before. Took her a long time to
finish with blue, then yellow, then green. She was well
into pink when she died. I don't believe she wanted to
get to red and I understand why because me and
Beloved outdid ourselves with it.*

—Toni Morrison[1]

SETHE, WHO welcomes color on this new morning, was recovering
from a kind of color blindness. Theology has suffered a similar ailment,
whether damning its Others as demons or whitewashing them with neutrality. I have suggested that a tragic heuristic takes much away from
theology—familiar warrants of certitude, paths on which to move with
confidence from what is to what ought to be. But in the wilder world
beyond the walls of paradise, something is also restored. This place has
paths of its own, though traditional theology has not been trained to
discern them and it is too soon to make a map. For now, it is enough to
wonder at the colors.

The return of color, I have suggested, is an event at once political,
intellectual, and moral. On that tide, with the multiple tones of humanity,
comes a riddling plurality of truths and goods. So color is the most mixed

137

of blessings and Sethe, who heralds it, is a haunted woman. She can celebrate green and blue and yellow and brown, but she can hardly bear red, that most colored of colors.[2] It is red that has covered her hands and broken open her heart, red that carries the shock of elemental mixture, of passion with guilt, love with rage and loss. But the flower of moral consciousness is born with this shock of contradiction in its heart, and each new blossom opens around the knowledge that its contradictions will outlive it.

Literature is not the only theological source to which a tragic heuristic might be applied. Tragedy, as I define it, is not just a set of stories; it is a way of telling stories so as to wonder about elemental conflicts. Any meaning-making activity of a historical community can be wondered about that way. The questions belonging to a tragic heuristic can also be raised around stories belonging to androcentrically defined canons. But in relation to those stories, the critical distance needed to reflect on *women's* lives is very great—so great, in fact, that once women have attained it, they often find that they have backed themselves into other, more female-centered stories. Though religious feminists have a variety of opinions about the redeemability of androcentric stories, there is a consensus that their own emerging or reconfigured canons need at least some women-created stories. In that spirit I turn to literature by women, though without presupposing that other women's stories are *ipso facto* my stories. My model, rather, is one of dialogue with these novels, putting my story down next to theirs, as did Sethe's lover with hers.[3] For in fact the stories of women have been woven next to each other, and it is a task of religious feminists to inquire about what that has meant and might be made to mean.

In commending attention to aesthetic, mystical, and moral functions and to their communal context, I do not have in mind a return to "raw" experience. Art, as a theological source, is especially good at dispelling the illusion of simple facticity. But no matter what sources we use to explore the religious functions of a community, those sources ought not to be construed as conduits to the really real but as information about where and upon whom our religious reflection stands. Those grounds are not "natural," but cultured, peopled with histories and full of meaning well before a theological word is spoken. Moreover, they are bounded by neighboring grounds, and to know where we are we must also inquire about them. I approach literature by women, then, not as an Archimedean point from which a moral critique of "patriarchy" can be launched, but as a cultural site where meaning is negotiated and invented. I find theological hope not in turning from theory to experience or from the social or cultural to the natural, but in exploring the creative, abrasive non-homogeneity of culture and society themselves.

I have chosen these stories, all of them by contemporary women writers from the United States, partly for their variety, which is an end in itself and does not claim an ark-like inclusivity. Louise Erdrich's story is of the Chippewa people, Dorothy Allison's is of the white Southern working poor, Marilyn Robinson's novel concerns white Anglo-Saxon Protestants, and Toni Morrison's *Beloved* is about African Americans. Each of these stories exemplifies mystical, aesthetic, and moral functions and dysfunctions within a given community. In each, elemental powers are encountered in their plurality and ambivalence, beauty and pleasure are wrenched from conflict, creativity emerges in the midst of constraint, and moral transformation grows from the compost of guilt and loss. The tone and styles of the stories differ, from Morrison's solemn monument to slavery to the gentle levity of Robinson's ruminations on death. Allison's and Morrison's novels are more exclusively tragic in tone, Erdrich's and Robinson's more tragicomic. But each leaves the reader richly unfinished and full of elemental wonder, longing to lay one's story next to these and to make them, together, go on.

Beloved

But none of that had worn out his marrow. None of that. It was the ribbon. Tying his flatbed up on the bank of the Licking River . . . Stamp caught sight of something red on its bottom. . . . He tugged and what came loose in his hand was a red ribbon knotted around a curl of wet woolly hair, clinging still to its bit of scalp. He untied the ribbon and put it in his pocket, dropped the curl in the weeds. On the way home, he stopped, short of breath and dizzy. . . . Rested, he got to his feet, but before he took a step he turned to look back down the road he was traveling and said, to its frozen mud and the river beyond, "What are these people? You tell me, Jesus. What are they?"
                                        —*Toni Morrison*[4]

The people whose humanity Stamp questions, upon finding this evidence of a drowned black girl, are white people. His friend Baby Suggs agrees. "There is no bad luck in the world but white folks," she pronounces, as she quits the world and retires to bed to think of "something harmless."[5]

Color, she hopes, will be that harmless thing, and she demands of Sethe one hue after another, anything but white. But red is not harmless at all; together with white, it wears her out.

Beloved, set in Cincinnati in 1873, is a story of color within a frame of white. Its focus is within the frame, but it also protests the frame itself, which has squeezed so much unnecessary suffering and intractable conflict onto African American life.[6] Whiteness, here, takes its meaning from U.S. history. In that context it is both a racial and a moral quality, joining delusions of innocence with pretensions to omnipotence. "Good," explains Baby Suggs, "is knowing when to stop," and from sixty years of slavery and ten of freedom, her conclusion is that white people "don't know when to stop."[7] Refusing limitation and repelling mixture, whiteness presents itself as an elemental power, malevolent and practically immovable, setting the bounds within which other conflicts must be negotiated. The novel is in this sense the accusation of an elemental power, the historical power of whiteness.

Reading this story as a white woman, I am struck by its contrast with mainline Euro-American culture, in which African Americans spring everywhere as messianic figures for whites. For example, there is the Whoopi Goldberg of *Ghost*, or the Morgan Freeman of *Driving Miss Daisy*. The black messiahs are always isolated from their own communities, so that they can enter the white world as solitary, unthreatening figures. They are uncannily patient with the foibles of whites and even with what Delores Williams calls "white racial narcissism."[8] They become veritable channels of grace, valorized out of complex humanity to provide whites with healing and forgiveness. Thus the souls of black folk are used to jump-start those of whites, when whites have been benumbed by privilege or lost touch with their own spiritual traditions.[9]

There is profound moral wisdom in the literature of African American women, and a number of religious feminists are turning to that literature as a theological source.[10] When Euro-American feminists listen to these sources, it is important to hear them from where *we* are, marking and learning from the distance. *Beloved* helps us do that, because it makes us witness something that is, in one sense, no business of whitefolks to know. The story pushes me back, but it also compels my attention. Even as it tells me that I am not to seek salvation here, it shares with me the great, mixed blessing of an African American community's struggle to heal and forgive itself.

The accusation of whiteness in *Beloved* spills over into the accusation of God for the evident failure of providence. When Baby Suggs retreats from whiteness, she also resigns from preaching, because "God puzzled her and she was too ashamed of Him to say so."[11] The accusation of God is implicit, too, in Morrison's presentation of "Sweet Home," the place of enslavement for Sethe, Baby's daughter-in-law, and Paul D., who later becomes Sethe's lover. Sweet Home is a bitter parody of Genesis 2 and 3, a place of enforced childhood where whiteness approximates omnipotence in its control over black life. The evil of such an imitation of God becomes evident when Mr. Garner, the first and more humane master, dies and is replaced with the sadistic "schoolteacher." But what became evident then was true all along, muses Paul D., realizing that slavery is exactly the state in which one's worth is conferred or revoked at the will of another.[12] In a world where goodness is clearly not all-powerful, could an omnipotent power, whether human or divine, ever be good?[13]

Like Eve, Sethe will taste her freedom whether or not her husband can follow suit, but her exit from paradise is an escape rather than an exile. She does not lapse from moral freedom to sinful compulsion, but refuses unjust compulsion in favor of a freedom tempered by tragedy. After schoolteacher's boys steal her mother's milk, Sethe protests to Mrs. Garner. But her protest earns her a brutal whipping that leaves her back looking like a chokecherry tree in bitter red bloom.[14] This imposed and brutal scarification is a forced initiation into moral adulthood. With a baby in her belly and a tree on her back, Sethe knows in her flesh the weight and the cost of moral freedom in a cramped and conflicted world.

Sethe gets herself and her three children across the Ohio River, birthing her fourth along the way. After twenty-eight days of freedom, the central tragedy of the novel occurs, an event so horrible that the rest of the story pushes away from it as if by centrifugal force. Entitled by the Fugitive Slave Act, Sethe's former owner comes with the sheriff to return Sethe and her children to slavery.

> And if she thought anything, it was No. No Nono. Nononono. Simple. She just flew. Collected every bit of life she had made, all the parts of her that were precious and fine and beautiful, and carried, pushed, dragged them, out, away over there where no one could hurt them.[15]

Reaching the woodshed with all four, Sethe grabs the second youngest, "already crawling" but not yet even named, slashes her throat with a saw, and is stopped from killing the others only by Stamp's intervention. Eighteen years later, this baby returns as the demonic, love-hungry ghost who calls herself "Beloved," an uneasy resurrection that, far from promising that "every tear shall be dried," only shows that "them that die bad don't stay in the ground."[16]

After the sacrifice of Beloved, Sethe goes off to jail with her head held high, denying the white law and her black neighbors the right to judge her and, most poignantly, the power to forgive her. Though made within terrible constraints, her action was a decision, a response of her integral being, and she will not renounce it.[17] Sethe knows in her flesh that power and goodness are not the same, that there is no benign force guiding history toward a just end. Knowing that, she understands that it is not possible not to choose; she cannot mistake passivity for innocence. The mother who gave life must therefore choose how it will end, and Sethe does choose, mingling her mother's milk with the blood of her sacrificed baby and soaking her remaining days in red. The circumstances of her choice are extreme, but also common—common in this fictional world, where they resonate with those of Ella and of Sethe's own mother, common in the historical world where they echo the acts of Margaret Garner and other slave women.[18] In extreme but common circumstances, Sethe shows us, moral creativity is also a power of destruction, a defiled and defiling thing.

Morrison could have made this story one of madness or sheer compulsion, or told it simply as a story about the sins of whites. Those also could have been "true," illuminating stories. But instead she makes this a story about a *necessary sin*, conveying that elemental shock as moral information, something we need to know in order to make our national story go on less tragically. Thus she claims for slaves the aristocratic conventions of tragedy, and expels the masters from center stage. In the process, the genre itself is transformed, the audience judged and dumbstruck by the tragic sin it witnesses.

The moral grief that permeates this story could easily rend its fabric, were the story not threaded through with goodness, humor, and beauty. White folks *are* bad luck, but the Garners and Amy Denver are, at moments, genuinely kind. The agonized gait of a Georgia chain gang becomes, in Morrison's glance, a silly two-step dance across the fields. The presence of beauty in contradiction is evident especially in the living world around humankind, rendered by Morrison with a cruel beauty that at once heightens moral horror and bestows the promise of renewal. Trees are often the bearers of this shameless beauty. It is a tree he calls "Brother" that witnesses Paul D.'s degradation and shelters him from insanity, and a trail of blossoming trees that leads him North to freedom.[19] We may wish that trees were not indifferent to the children who hang in them, but they are, and that, the story suggests, is educational. For to recognize that terrible beauty is also to know the fierce tenacity of creativity, in which we humans have a share.

Certainly, the strongest example of joy in the elemental mixture of things is the sermon in the Clearing, delivered by Baby Suggs to her black neighbors. First she orders the men to dance, the women to cry, and the children to laugh.

> It started that way: laughing children, dancing men, crying women and then it got mixed up. Women stopped crying and danced; men sat down and cried; children danced, women laughed, children cried until, exhausted and riven, all and each lay about the Clearing damp and gasping for breath.[20]

Then Baby Suggs, "Holy," preaches to the people, not that they are spirit but that they are flesh, not to love their enemies but to defy their enemies by loving themselves. The message is more than words; it moves, and she dances it with her twisted hip.

But this ability to hold mixture together remains fragile, dependent on the community's power to protect black personhood from slavery and its inner reverberations. The breakdown of community is partly responsible for the death of Beloved, since the neighbors could have warned Sethe of the sheriff's approach but did not. That betrayal, we are told, was their response to the extravagantly generous feast that Baby Suggs had thrown the evening before. Gratitude gives way to resentment as the neighbors wonder how this crippled ex-slave could give as if without measure. The next day, they have the same reaction, multiplied exponentially, to Sethe, who takes life as if unbounded by morality or law. These women, like whitefolks, seem not to know when to stop. For this *hubris* they are effectively excommunicated and handed over to the angry past, which haunts Sethe almost to death. Even her lover Paul D., who was a slave with Sethe, leaves her when he learns of the killing. "Your love is too thick," he tells her. "Thin love ain't love at all," she replies.[21]

The judgment against Baby and Sethe redounds upon those who make it and who cannot bear to remember their own defilement by slavery. That defilement, they know, was never a matter of abrogating limits; it was a matter of getting hit with what life throws back when you push hard against them. In that sense, what is shocking about Sethe and Baby Suggs is not that they reject limits, but that in the presence of limits—that is, in the *absence* of a limitless and transcendent good—they take responsibility for sin and grace into their own hands. Nobody wants to know, after all, that sin can be necessary, or that grace walks on a crippled hip.

In the end, community is restored when all begin to own their complicity in sin and in grace. Stamp Paid persuades Paul D. to return to Sethe by relating how Stamp himself had wanted to kill his wife after she was forced to have sex with her owner. In blaming his wife for her own victimization, Stamp comes to see, he has abandoned her to her shame, and that was his sin. The community of women, contacted by Sethe's daughter Denver, reclaims the starving Sethe from the insatiable ghost by giving gifts of food out of their own poverty, repeating the defiant generosity of Baby Suggs. And, too, they remember their own tragic choices; Ella, one of the women who comes in a group of thirty to exorcise the ghost, remembers how "she had delivered but would not nurse, a hairy white thing." It is that memory which sets her and the others to shouting, taking "a step back to the beginning,"[22] when there were no words, only sound. From that female roar and lament, there arises once again the power "to beat back the past," at least enough to wrest from it a present.

I hear this black, female sound from just beyond the Clearing's "ringing trees," near enough to hear the promise, but distant enough to accept the judgment. White culture in the United States continues to rest substantially on racism, sometimes a racism that is actively defended, but, just as often or more often, a racism that is cloaked with unquestioned privilege. In that dim light, racism is thought to be only a psychological problem, a set of feelings and attitudes that have now been dispelled. That liberal delusion of innocence, however, has to be paid for by less affluent whites, who cannot help noticing that their tenuous racial privileges directly abut against the nonwhite poor.

My upbringing spared me the most virulent and defensive forms of racism, but not the subtle presumptions of race privilege. For example, I remember an afternoon years ago when I brought some small black children I was caring for to my home in a lower middle class neighborhood. It was summer, so when we went out on the deck of my second floor apartment the children could see the neighbors below, working in their yards and grilling on their barbecues. The oldest, who was seven, surveyed the scene for several minutes, then said with a heavy sigh, "there are sure a lot of white people here!" Already, he seemed to know that the absence of faces like his own was not coincidental but signaled danger for him. While the racial hostility and exclusivity of my neighborhood was something that I, till then, had overlooked, he could not afford to ignore it.

Recognizing racial privilege is a series of moral shocks, about inherited sins for which I nonetheless share responsibility, about the repercussions for others of my apparently innocent acts and attitudes. There is shame in the shocks, deepened by the derision that is directed at white social guilt from all quarters, even from our own quarter. In effect, the guilt is treated only as a psychological symptom that whites are ashamed to have and that we seek to cure, suppress, or wryly discredit. But there is important *moral information* in the racial remorse of white Americans, and until we absorb that information whites may turn from one another in shame or rage, generating self-justifying ideologies of both the racist and the righteously progressive sort. Turning to African-Americans to salve that racial remorse is clearly not the answer. For all of us, goodness is a fragile and costly thing, to be fostered in our own communities, not imported from abroad or imputed from beyond. That is the gift to whitefolks of Morrison's great monument to slavery; in the thickness of uneasy love, it returns us as well to our own communities, where the scars of racism must be faced.

Bastard Out of Carolina

Granny, my mama, uncles, aunts, cousins—all of us look dead on the black-and-white page.
—*Dorothy Allison*[23]

That is how Ruth Anne Boatwright, called Bone, sees her family as its disgraces and misadventures appear in newsprint. Like the red stamp of "ILLEGITIMATE" that defaces Bone's birth certificate, black and white establishes, with the certainty of an inherited sin, who Boatwrights of Greenville, South Carolina, are. "It takes a lot of money to make someone look alive on the printed page," explains her Aunt Alma, "to keep some piece of soul behind the eyes." Boatwrights do not have money, and that fixes their status as "trash," "liars," "thieves," and "drunks." But they do have soul, and that colorful matriline is also part of Bone's inheritance. Telling her family story, Bone makes illegitimacy the site of creativity and sings out her suffering as "purest gospel, a song of absolute hopeless grief."[24]

Bastard Out of Carolina is autobiographical fiction by a Southern lesbian writer. The ambiguity of that genre fits the Boatwrights, who love to tell stories. To outsiders, those stories are a mark of untrustworthiness, but for Boatwrights, they are a necessary fabrication from bare threads. Granny Boatwright acknowledges no distinction "between what she knew to be true and what she had only heard told," and in her stories, "everything seemed to come back to grief and blood, and everybody seemed legendary."[25] Autobiographical fiction mixes "fact" and "imagination" just as authoritatively, allowing Allison to read the bones of her childhood and prophesy survival.

To fabricate a story for herself, Bone must also give one to her mother, Anney. For Anney stories are shameful, and she neither wants to tell them nor to have them told about her. It is from others in the family that Bone learns of her father, a married man who left Anney pregnant at age fourteen, and of Anney's yearly, humiliating attempts to secure for Bone a birth certificate not stamped "illegitimate." Above all, Anney wants to be legitimate, to have a husband for herself and a father for her children. It is as if she has been voided by her illegitimate pregnancy. At Bone's birth she is "eight months gone" and "strictly speaking," says Bone, not present at all, but unconscious from a car accident.[26] Anney disappears again at the story's end, delivering Bone to the hospital as a raped and brutalized twelve-year-old and leaving her there without giving either of their names. It is Anney's husband Glen who has put Bone in this condition, and Anney is about to abandon Bone for him.

My Irish people are storytellers, too, and I have grown up on the stories of my immigrant grandparents, great-aunts, and great-uncles. Most of them emigrated between 1900 and 1913, except for my paternal grandfather, whose parents had come from Ireland the generation before. Often, they worked for the wealthy, cooking their meals or cleaning their homes. That, I imagine, had something to do with the diffident gentility I remember so well from childhood, lace curtains and demitasse cups in dirty tenements, crumpled dollars pressed into our hands from great-aunts and uncles who were visibly poor. After the Depression and World War II, in which my parents both served, the quiet legitimacy of a home in the suburbs became their goal. The house was what my father called a "handyman special," thrown on a cement slab and not built to last. It was a middle-class façade, but only as thick as the paycheck my father brought home from loading railroad cars at night.

My father tells these stories with relish and Irish sentimentality, and I listen the same way, for details and turns of phrase that might unearth some buried treasure. My mother is more reticent; for her the past seems finished. She was the same way with the company of women in our neighborhood, listening politely and cultivating a close friend or two, but mostly keeping her own counsel. The conversation of women seemed like gossip to her, and though she never said so, I surmised from her silence that she found it less than dignified. In that open silence, I have tried to imagine myself a female heritage and future. I long to know the minds of my maiden aunts, my great-grandmothers who died birthing their twelfth or sixteenth child, to conjure my grandmother at age seventeen in the hand-me-down clothes of her rich employer. Yet I am not someone those women would recognize as their own. "I think you'll never marry," my mother used to say to me, doubtfully at first but then with increasing certainty and with what I imagined to be an edge of pride. I would not follow her, it was true, and she would not guide me where I wanted to go.

Boatwright men and women, too, have sharply different roles in the family story. The men are boyish philanderers and alcoholics who land frequently in jail for "causing other men serious damage." Their vital energies seem to be drained directly from the Boatwright women, who seem "worn-down, and slow, born to mother, nurse and clean up after the men." Age comes early upon the Boatwright women, "the look" that sinks their eyes and sharpens their cheekbones. Despite themselves, the women forgive the meanness of the men and, within the family, even tame it. Boatwrights know that Boatwrights feel "bad," and while they wear that badness outside as a badge of defiant pride, inside they treat it gently, as a wound. "Ugly, ugly, ugly, ugly! You so ugly you almost pretty!" exclaims Granny to a grandson, and Bone she calls "pretty ugly" and therefore, "a Boatwright for sure."[27] A good kind of badness, a pretty kind of ugliness—that is the best a Boatwright can have.

"Trash" is not a word one hears much in the North, but it has its analogue. When I was a child, there was a house at the end of the street, owned by the Welfare Department, in which such families were placed. For a long time, those were white families. Nothing much was said about them, and I got the sense that that was a matter of politeness. When a black family moved in, though, there were meetings of some of the white neighbors to discuss "property values" and fight "blockbusting." Some months later, the house was found empty. The family had left some time before, with dinner still on the stove, obviously fled though no one would say so. Looking back, I can see how the tenuous class status of those who were white and held their own mortgages was etched on people like those in the welfare house, who could not hide their struggle or their color. In a way, it was like the female identity I gathered from my mother's circumspect intelligence, won by disowning those women with painted nails and teased hair whose femininity we did not wish to share.

Bone's stepfather "Daddy Glen" is a portrait of frustrated privilege, grown furious and destructive. "That boy's got something wrong with him," says Granny, an assessment eventually shared by all the Boatwrights. Classwise, Anney Boatwright is a step down for him, but as Bone tells it Glen was as much after the belligerent manhood of her brothers, aiming to "marry the whole Boatwright legend, shame his daddy and shock his brothers." Glen is like all men, says Aunt Ruth, "just little boys climbing onto titty whenever they can," but he is worse, at once an infant and a tyrant. People talk about his hands which are "big, impersonal and fast" and about his temper.[28] He inverts the relation of parent and child, demanding unconditional love from Bone and her sister, and blaming them for his failures. Bone becomes the special object of his malevolent desire, her illegitimacy highlighting his as her father or anyone else's, and her childhood threatening his utter dependence on Anney.

Glen will not countenance Boatwright stories and thus imposes on Bone a state of denial. It begins when he rapes her at age five, an event he never seems to think about, which becomes for her "a bad dream, hazy and shadowed" and resumes with a new cycle of abuse and beating when Bone is ten.[29] The combination of violence and desire bewilders Bone into the silence Glen tacitly demands:

> I could not tell Mama. I would not have known how to explain why I stood there and let him touch me. It wasn't sex, not like a man and a woman pushing their naked bodies into each other, but then, it was something like sex, something powerful and frightening that he wanted badly and I did not understand at all. Worst of all, when Daddy Glen held me that way, it was the only time his hands were gentle, and when he let me go, I would rock on uncertain feet.[30]

Anney knows about some of the beatings, but even her protective responses are laced with denial. "Why honey? Why do you have to act like that?" she asks Bone after Glen beats her bloody, while from the radio "came the low sound of Conway Twitty singing 'But it's on-ly make believe.' " Glen has his own stories to tell, and in the absence of Bone's story, his version of truth becomes the efficacious one. Anney's efforts to protect Bone without leaving Glen only serve to delay the inevitable, and they are as much a protection from Anney's own shame about the abuse. Bone learns to blame herself for Anney's unhappiness as much as for Glen's violence. "I'm sorry," she whispers to her mother, when a doctor treating Bone becomes enraged at Anney. But Anney's denial is also a societal one, expressed by the nurse who apologizes for the doctor: "He's young and he's not been here long."[31]

For Bone, Anney and Glen are two elemental powers, one wicked and one benign, each with the power to determine her fate. Till the story's very end, she believes that Anney could provide her healing and shelter, if only Anney would so choose. But these two powers are in fact allied with each other, and the results can only be catastrophic. The reasons for the alliance remain mysterious, given Glen's inadequacies as a husband and father. Anney says it is about love, but love, as Aunt Alma observes,

"has more to do with how pretty a body is than anyone would ever admit."
The spring of their wedding is full of bad omens, and when Bone is ten
years old the love knot made for them by Anney's clairvoyant aunts
unravels.[32] The love unravels, but the powers do not; try as she might to
extricate them, Bone must accept their entanglement, which will mark
her life forever.

Bone tries to untangle the good and the bad by being purely one or
the other. Gospel music is the good; it "made you hate and love yourself
at the same time," but it promises that the love will win out if only the
self will surrender. That was why Bone's best efforts could not save her
Uncle Earle's soul; he loved the battle but had no intention of losing it.
Gospel, her Granny says, is for women who will believe anything for love.
It soothes Bone's feelings of meanness and ugliness, but only by making
her repeat to Jesus the words she has said to her mother, "I'm sorry"—
for everything, "for being young and healthy and sitting there full of
music."[33] But Bone is too tough for self-surrender. What she really wants
is to sing gospel with her own voice and make the hard world surrender
to her. Unfortunately, however, her singing voice has at best an ugly
beauty.

Besides, as Bone learns through her friend Shannon Pearl, unmitigated
righteousness is the ugliest thing of all. Shannon is the albino child of
gospel promoters who deny her disability, pretending that she is an angel.
As a result, she becomes a monster with no shame to protect her, whose
ugliness repels sympathy, and who hates her tormentors as well as "nig-
gers" and "trash." If there is a God, if there is justice, Bone thinks,
Shannon's tormentors will burn. But it is Shannon who burns instead,
incinerating herself in a barbecue accident, her hair standing up "in a
crown of burning glory" and her features blackening.[34]

If being good is for women, being bad is for men, and Bone tries that
too. Anney said "don't ever let me catch you stealing," and Bone "took
Mama at her word, . . . planning not to get caught and not to tell Mama."[35]
When Anney does catch her in a petty theft, she tells Bone about a cousin
so bad he stole from his mother, as if Bone's crime too is an offense
against her mama's hard-earned respectability. In an act that humiliates
them both, she makes Bone apologize to the store manager, Tyler High-
garden, condescension incarnate, who bans Bone from the store for a
time. When she returns it is not by invitation but by break-in, and not to
taste the forbidden fruits but to wreck the place.

Good and bad, female and male, dark and light—Bone tries to sort
them out but in the end finds strength in the mixture. Feeling the resonance between the words "nigger" and "trash," she finds that black is

not pure Other, but is like her with her black hair, her dignity and anger. Black also carries a beauty that stands out against the ugliness of Shannon Pearl, or the pitted face of Bone's cousin Grey; Bone sees it in the face of a neighbor child, either "a very pretty boy or a very fierce girl." Bone's budding gender identity is the same kind of mixture. In her winsome but violent Uncle Earle and her Cherokee great-grandfather, she finds models for herself as rebel and warrior. She liked "being one of the women with my aunts, liked feeling a part of something nasty and strong and separate" but begins to worry when her body buds into that of a Boatwright woman, "born to be worked to death, used up and thrown away." She longs to be pretty, "more like the girls in storybooks, princesses with pale skin and tender hearts," but that is clearly not her destiny.[36]

In actuality, Bone's gender is neither male nor female as these are heterosexually constructed. She is something else—something that is given like a body but also made up like a story. From her Aunt Alma, Bone learns women can be dangerous and so, perhaps, can girls. From her lesbian Aunt Raylene, too, she learns what it means to create a self out of constraint. Just as Glen makes Anney choose between Bone and him, Raylene had forced her female lover to choose between the lover's child and their relationship. "I made my life," she tells Bone, "the same way it looks like you're going to make yours—out of pride, stubbornness and too much anger."[37] Desire, Raylene knows, is both creative and malleable, resistant and corruptible. So, she advises, "you better think hard" about the power of feeling and desire, so as to aim their effects.

Like her gender, Bone's sexuality is woven from what is available. In her fantasies, as in her life, force and violence become enwrapped with pleasure and safety. She masturbates to fantasies of struggling to escape a burning haystack or being beaten under the eyes of a sympathetic crowd. Release comes to mean vindication. "Fire, Burn it all," she thinks, when it is clear that her mother is withdrawing from her. Raylene finds Bone "seriously confused about love," and she is, but the tenacity of Bone's desires, for love and for sex, is also the stuff of her survival.[38] She does not choose or want the sexual experiences Glen forces upon her, but in and beyond those experiences her sexuality burns with its own energy and creativity, which she inherits by losing the myth of a sexuality innocent of power.

Bastard Out of Carolina ends with a rapid-fire series of rebellions and retributions that unfold with the force of fate, culminating in Glen's rape of Bone, and Anney's final decision to sacrifice child for husband. Before the rape and before returning to Glen, Anney had in effect asked Bone for advance absolution. But after the rape, Bone knows with clarity that it is her mother who has abandoned her, not the other way around. And while she fully and without remorse longs for Glen's death, her rage and hatred for Anney cannot but redound upon Bone herself. Looking in the mirror, she sees on her own face "the look" of a Boatwright woman, "eyes sunk in shadowy caves above sharp cheekbones and a mouth so tight the lips had disappeared." She appears to herself "older, meaner, rawboned, crazy and hateful. . . . I was who I was going to be, and she was a terrible person."[39] But when Anney returns for a moment, looking ravaged and aged, Bone again accepts love, in all its ambivalence.

> I pressed my face into her neck, and let it all go. The grief. The anger. The guilt and the shame. It would come back later. It would come back forever. We had all wanted the simplest thing, to love and be loved and be safe together, but we had lost it and I didn't know how to get it back.[40]

Bastard Out of Carolina is clear in its indictment of the destructive presumptions of sex, race, and class. But there are questions it does not raise, especially about the way women may betray their children for men. That those questions remain unasked is partly due to the child's perspective Allison wants to convey. And if she leaves her reader with work to do on the matter of child abuse, that is fitting too. But there is also a woman's wisdom in this book about how daughters need their mothers' stories, even if they have to make those stories up themselves. Anney cannot provide that for Bone; her farewell gift is only a birth certificate not stamped "illegitimate." It is nothing more and nothing less than a blank and aching space in which Bone can write her own story. Claimed and cut loose, Bone knows now who she is and wills to be—like Raylene, like her Mama, "a Boatwright woman."

> Who had Mama been, what had she wanted to be or do before I was born? Once I was born, her hopes had turned, and I had climbed up her life like a flower reaching for the sun. Fourteen and terrified, fifteen and a mother, just past twenty-one when she married Glen. Her life had been folded into mine. What would I be like when I was fifteen, twenty, thirty? Would I be as strong as she had been, as hungry for love, as desperate, determined and ashamed?[41]

My mother also did not give me the story I need for my life. Like Anney she has a look, but it is more on her hands than on her face. My mother's hands were never young; veins swelled and coursed like rivers on their backs. They embarrassed her but awed me, or perhaps it was my interest in them that embarrassed her. She did not mean to raise a lesbian, but she did. I look down at my keyboard now and I see those hands, my mother's hands, saying things that she would never say. It is evidence to me that creativity gets out of our hands, that desire, uncountenanced and unforeseen, may speak new stories.

Love Medicine

> *Our Gods aren't perfect, is what I'm saying, but at least they come around. They'll do you a favor if you ask them right. You don't have to yell. But you do have to know, like I said, how to ask in the right way. That makes problems, because to ask proper was an art that was lost to the Chippewa once the Catholics gained ground. Even now, I have to wonder if Higher Power turned its back, if we got to yell, or if we just don't speak its language.*
>
> *I missed Dot in the days that followed, days so alike they welded seamlessly to one another and took your mind away. I seemed to exist in a suspension and spent my time sitting at the window watching nothing until the sun went down, bruising the whole sky as it dropped, clotting my heart. I couldn't name anything I felt anymore, although I knew it was a kind of boredom. I had been living the same life too long.*
>
> *—Louise Erdrich*[42]

Lipsha Morrissey and Albertine Johnson, soulmates and second cousins, ruminate separately on their relations to elemental power. For Lipsha, the problem is that "Higher Power" has withdrawn and eclipsed in its shadow the imperfect but available deities of the Chippewa. For Albertine, the problem is one of weightless suspension amid the inertial forces of white culture. Neither of them is powerless; rather, like their people, they are *susceptible* to great powers, both historical and spiritual. By mediating power, they can survive, but survival is not equivalent to liberation. In white society, Indians sometimes survive but are possessed by destructive powers such as alcohol and poverty, sometimes survive but are alienated from powers that were once native. Even the past survives, like Lipsha's mother June, whose disappearance in 1981 and whose symbolic restoration in 1984 mark the circle within which the other stories are set. But the unresolved past, "them vast unreasonable waves,"[43] as Lipsha calls them, cannot solve the problems of Chippewa life in the present, when old "ways of asking" must be brought to bear on a new and hostile world.

Louise Erdrich, like her characters, belongs to a generation of Native American writers who live between worlds. Chippewa and German American, she was raised near the Turtle Mountain reservation in North Dakota, where *Love Medicine* is set. She tells the stories of her mixed people with a cycle novel, something between a novel and a series of short stories. *Love Medicine* is also between tragedy and comedy, neither pure levity nor pure gravity. The fourteen stories, rather than tunneling inexorably to a single end, illuminate a set of events and relations from different viewpoints and at different times. The effect is like a beadwork tapestry, composed of stunning and startling connections. The pattern, with its openings and inevitabilities, elicits flashes of tragic insight. But at other moments that same flash makes light and pleasure of contradiction. Like classical comedy, *Love Medicine* has stock characters and repetitious battles whose pointlessness is evident to everyone except those who enact them. But just as power is ambivalent here, so is humor. There is the hilarity of contradictions that can be accepted without regret, like the old-age lust that outlives a man's wits and a woman's beauty. But there is also the desperate round-and-round of abuse and addiction, which if they elicit laughter do so at the cost of hope, like the Norwegian joke told by Gordie while, within earshot, his drunken son abuses his Norwegian wife.[44]

Comedy and tragedy are the play of the elemental powers that toy with the Chippewa, and by returning the play, the characters can find relief and room for innovation within their tight-knit lives. To play artfully, however, people have to know what they are doing—specifically, who set them up to act in particular ways and who is affected by their actions. The answer, in *Love Medicine*, is as fixed as a punchline, but also as surprising: everyone. It is an inherited piece of Indian wisdom, which yet must be appropriated by each person and generation. To learn this truth is, on the one hand, to break through encrusted denial and, on the other hand, to be initiated into mystery. Denial gives way to mystery, because the relations of the Chippewa with each other and the white world are unfathomably complex. That is especially the case when this book is read alongside Erdrich's later works,[45] which further develop characters from *Love Medicine* and elaborate their relations. But even *Love Medicine*'s variegated patterns cannot all be viewed within this small a scope. I focus instead on a few central characters and connections: Marie and Lulu, who mother or grandmother nearly all the major characters and are therefore at the center of *Love Medicine*'s relational web, their mutual grandson Lipsha, and Nectar, Marie's husband and Lulu's lover, who connects the two women even as he divides them.

Nectar is reminiscent of the Greek hero Heracles, fodder for both comedy and tragedy. His demise closely parallels that of Heracles in the Sophoclean tragedy, yet his virility and passion can also deteriorate into the helpless, infantile gluttony depicted by Aristophanes.[46] Good things, Nectar says, "get handed to me on a plate"—good looks, intelligence, a modestly heroic status as a tribal leader. Like Heracles, he mediates between the worlds—in Nectar's case, between the white and Indian worlds. But the heroism is a thin one, due to the dramatic imbalance between Indian and white political power. The irony is immortalized in the painting "The Plunge of the Brave" for which Nectar poses as a young man, "stock still in a diaper,"[47] and which is later installed in the state capitol at Bismarck. Romanticized and infantilized, the Indian hero within white culture is consigned to the past, remembered as plunging gracefully to certain death.

For many non-Native Americans, no real Indian people have been available to us behind those caricatures. I grew up in a town called Massapequa, where all that was left of the Native people was their name and the solemn bronze-faced profile on the jackets of the high-schoolers. It was an almost palpable absence that I associated, as a child, with the rapidly disappearing woods where we used to play. Thinking back, I realize that we who settled on those lands in the post-war decades were ourselves mostly the children or grandchildren of immigrants, far from our own native lands and, by my generation, forgetful of our ancestors and their ways. How much, I wonder, has that alienation from our own old connections blinded Euro-Americans to the costs of our new connections to this continent—the cost for example, of the use of Native lands as dumping grounds for toxic wastes, or as their reduction to energy sources for consumer culture?

Nectar, for his part, never intended to die, even if he had to appear to die in order to survive. Plunged pictorially into the river, he planned to "hold my breath when I hit and let the current pull me, around jagged rocks." His sweet receptivity draws offers of jobs and of "candy between the bedcovers," but it is also his great fault, not as a noble *hubris*, but as a pathetic passivity before power. When he signs the paper permitting the tribe to reclaim Lulu's land, he feels "trapped behind the wheel" and "steering something out of control."[48] Later in life, his need for metaphorical sugar deteriorates into a more literal dependency, exacerbating the diabetes that erodes his memory and hence his sense of responsibility for the past.

Most of all, Nectar's passivity is evident in his relations with Marie and Lulu, the women who claim and divide him. Geese are the metaphor for that condition, and its binding magic. The love medicine that Marie and Lipsha concoct was to consist of goose hearts, on the theory that the lifetime mating patterns of geese might anchor Nectar's wandering passions to his wife alone. But from the moment in 1934 when he met Marie and she claimed him as her mate, Nectar was bound to both women, comically encumbered with a pair of wild geese on each wrist. Only once does he come close to making a decision, on the day in 1957 when he leaves a note of rejection for Marie and heads for Lulu's house with a love letter that reads like the title to his person. But finding Lulu not at home, and himself alone and unclaimed, he "accidentally" burns down her house, also nearly incinerating his own son, all the while telling himself, "I have done nothing."[49] Nectar gets his come-uppance when, in another dubious accident twenty-five years later, he chokes and dies on the love medicine administered by Marie. It is like a bad joke, suggesting that only death is the cure for love. But the joke is even worse, because even after death Nectar's ghost returns to each of his two women. The link between love and violence, it seems, is not purely gratuitous or remediable, so if love is strong as death, that is bad news as well as good news.

In his character, as in his caricature, Nectar is uncomfortably familiar to me. He is a disenfranchised person who nonetheless can pick some pockets of privilege, an affable beggar, better at winning favors than at building justice. That is a role I also know; it must be a temptation of many people in comparably mixed social situations. Nectar is not heroic, but he is more sympathetic for being less admirable. I understand his inability to take control of his life, which is rooted not only in selfishness but in a profound inhibition about making choices that injure others. Those of us who were not reared for power are unaccustomed to deliberating about whom to hurt and how much, and while that preserves us from callousness, it may feed the illusion that it is possible or even good "to do nothing" in this world. In this regard, Nectar teaches something that the character himself does not learn, about keeping your hands on the wheel though what you steer is only very partially in your control, about remembering whom you have hurt in order to learn to steer more skillfully.

Marie and Lulu, however, do eventually learn from the riddle of their embattled, intertwined lives. From the start, they are more alike than either wants to know, a matched pair, salt and sugar, as Nectar says. Each, at moments, shines like a golden Goddess, and both can run over men like trains.[50] Each in her own way abrogates the power of paternity—Marie by taking in so many children that Nectar can hardly remember which are his own, Lulu by choosing different fathers for her children and keeping their identities to herself.

But in matters of sex, race, and spirituality, the two women position themselves very differently. Marie, the salty one, is farther from her sexuality and her Chippewa heritage, closer to the white world and to Christianity. She absorbs self-hatred from her alcoholic parents the "dirty Lazarres" and from her teacher Sr. Leopolda (in *Tracks*, her real mother), for whom Indian men are devils and sex is the devil's seduction. For Marie and Leopolda, Catholicism represents what Doris Lessing called the "self-hater," yet both women attack this demon with Chippewa spiritual arts, to win his power for their own. Leopolda, like a hunter, spears her devil with a window pole, and when Marie attempts sainthood, it is to conquer Leopolda and the other nuns. Even when she leaves the convent, Marie transforms the fated roles of wife and mother into forms of personal power, claiming of Nectar that "he is what he is because I made him."[51]

Marie is a someone I partly recognize in myself, coming from a lineage of women whose moral rigor could calcify into the martyr's *rigor mortis* and who knew how to administer their families with the force of their suffering alone. Marie reminds her granddaughter of "rock cairns commemorating Indian defeats,"[52] but there is more than rock in her. At seismic moments she moves and is moved, she cracks and endures. At age fourteen, nearly paralyzed by her love-hate with Leopolda, Marie commands *herself* to "rise up and walk," a parody of its New Testament analogues.[53] In her greatest conquests and utter defeats, she breaks the force of gravity with sudden bursts of humor. When the nuns kneel to her, she imagines herself "Saint Marie of the Burnt Back and Scalded Butt"! Years later, Marie lands on her own knees, compulsively waxing the floor in her good purple dress, in order to be "the woman who kept her floor clean even when left by her husband." And again Marie, who "never went down on my knees to God or anyone,"[54] laughs at herself. When I think of the women who taught me moral strength, I think of Marie reaching across her just-waxed floor to rescue the husband she loves, who she now knows loves someone else. I have seen such acts in daunting, formidable women, women who do everything possible for love and then something impossible—they sustain connection by letting go.

Lulu Nanapush, like Marie, represents the forced choices of Chippewa women under the regimes of male and white power. But unlike Marie, who establishes her power in the social world, Lulu's energy comes from the beauty of the extra-human world, which she allows to fill her until "I wouldn't want anything more but what I had." She captures men sexually but leaves herself free. When her former brother-in-law comes to claim paternity for one of her sons, he himself is reduced within hours to one of "Lulu's boys." Sex for her is transpersonal—"angels in the body make us foreign to ourselves when touching,"[55] she believes—and, as such, is allied with death and decay. Her first sexual explorations, at the age of seven, are with the corpse of a male transient, and it was then, she remembers, that "Lulu Lamartine cried all the tears she would ever cry in her life."[56] Tears, to Lulu, represent shame and regret, and her resistance to them is her resistance to conventional femininity—because "as we all know, women are supposed to cry." She makes sex an apéritif before death, and death itself an aphrodisiac arousing the hunger for continuance. Feeling life in its full dimensions, Lulu disdains "numbers, time, inches, feet," as "ploys for cutting nature down to size" and as the means white culture uses to dispirit and despoil Native Americans. "If you're going to measure land," she argues, "let's measure right. Every foot and inch you're standing on . . . belongs to the Indians."[57]

In her love for Nectar, however, sex is personalized for Lulu, and she becomes supplicant as well as priestess. Through Nectar, too, she confronts the force that political power, despite its evident puniness in relation to the wide world, nonetheless retains. Being a Native American, she realizes, gives no immunity to that; the tribal council is nothing but a "red-apple court representing Uncle Sam" bribed by government money into setting Native Americans against each other. But if monetary greed can alienate Native Americans from their spiritual powers, so can the greed of passion. Lulu contemplates these truths in "the liquid golden last days of my oats," which she enters as a new and visionary phase of life. She and Nectar, she concludes, were "two of a kind," so immersed in their childish greed that "it took the court action of the tribe and a house on fire to pull us out." Recognizing the illusory, addictive side of their affair seasons and purifies her love, but does not purge it. Seeing Nectar in his old-age pathos, she thinks, "I wanted to stay and put my arms around him, simply, in the broad daylight of our old age."[58]

Marie and Lulu encounter each other after Nectar's death, when Marie volunteers to put drops in Lulu's eyes after surgery. Lulu will not pay for the connection with regret, but Marie has not come to exact a price, only to acknowledge in her own way the interdependence of wife and mistress. "There's a pattern of three lines in the wood," she observes, and, when Lulu does not get the message, "somebody had to put the tears into your eyes." Just as Lulu had forced Marie from self-seriousness to laughter, so Marie gives Lulu her first "good tears." Mourning Nectar with Marie, Lulu knows for the first time "exactly how another woman felt," and finds that it gives her "deep comfort, surprising." When Marie removes the bandages from Lulu's eyes, she appears to Lulu "like a dim mountain, huge and blurred, the way a mother must look to her just born child."[59]

The coming together of Marie and Lulu portends great possibilities for insight and reconciliation among the Chippewa. But they offer this possibility, paradoxically, by throwing light on structures of denial. Once the two women become "thick as thieves," Lipsha observes, they see "too clear for comfort," confronting people with "all the secrets they tried to hide from themselves."[60] Lipsha learns this personally when Lulu confronts him with his parentage, an open secret to everyone but himself. With that information he gains a father, Gerry Nanapush, whose murmuring heart gives Lipsha his freedom and an intelligence that does not reside primarily in the brain. Lipsha's other great gift, a "touch" for healing, also comes through Gerry, from Gerry's father Old Man Pillager, a Chippewa shaman. But in gaining the father he admires, Lipsha finds himself yoked with two women he has learned to despise as immoral—his mother June, and Lulu, who turns out to be his paternal grandmother. Gerry, however, is as distant from white law and convention as are June and Lulu. Believing in justice but not in law, he lives as an escape artist, almost as exiled from the world as is June, but more able to survive in a medial state. Moreover, Gerry's powers as a trickster[61] come from his mother Lulu and seem connected with the femininity that oddly underlines his hugely male physicality.

Congenital to these gifts and relations is the possibility of betraying them, and it is Marie, priestess of guilt, who initiates Lipsha into this part of his heritage. With Marie, Lipsha shares responsibility for Nectar's death, but for Lipsha there is an additional dimension: he cheated on the original recipe, substituting frozen store-bought turkey hearts and a stolen Catholic blessing. "I suppose you'll say, 'Slap a malpractice suit on Lipsha Morrissey,' " he theologizes, "but anybody ever go and slap an old malpractice suit on God?" Faith, he figures, was the heart of his mistake, counting on a Higher Power in view of which Chippewa healing traditions were just "strange superstitions." Faith of that kind is consent to unaccountable power, and it obviates the skill and acuity needed to exert the limited, ambivalent powers that actually are in our control. Watching his family kneel at Nectar's funeral like "rocks in a field," Lipsha notices "how strong and reliable grief was, and death."[62] Counting only on life's harsh continuance, beyond failure and loss, he decides to soften it where he can with healing and forgiveness.

But in the present social and political context, reconciliation among the Chippewa is not enough to guarantee a fully human life. In Lipsha's story, the marker of incompletion is his refusal to comment on his father's guilt or innocence in a murder. That information, which Lipsha holds like an initiation secret, also suggests that what constitutes moral adulthood for Indians is not something white culture is well equipped to assess. Albertine also indicts the "Scales" of white culture, telling the story of Gerry and his wife Dot, who are studies in solidity and girth, against the backdrop of a "weigh station" for trucks, where accuracy is never checked and imbalances never corrected. The Chippewa may be able to slip between worlds, but their right and need, like everyone else's, is to live in this one. In fact, there are several characters in *Love Medicine* who do not survive in a meaningful sense, but who are consumed by violence, from within or without.

In every case, these human disasters leave behind someone who might do more than endure and repeat. But to make that possibility into a likelihood for the Chippewa will take changes well beyond their control. So *Love Medicine*, for all the intoxication in its pages, is a sober book, offering nothing but enigma to those who want spirituality without justice or power without fault. Erdrich administers strong medicine, and if it chokes some of us going down, that may be more a matter of historical fate than of personal accident, a caution to remember what we have done and to whom we have done it, to learn "how to ask," not just how to take.

Housekeeping

To crave and to have are as alike as the thing and its shadow. For when does a berry break upon the tongue so sweetly as when one longs to taste it, and when is the taste refracted in so many hues and savors of ripeness and earth, and when do our senses know anything so utterly as when we lack it? And here again is a foreshadowing—the world will be made whole. For to wish for a hand upon one's head is all but to feel it. So whatever we may lose, very craving gives it back to us. Though we dream and hardly know it, longing, like an angel, fosters us, smooths our hair, and brings us wild strawberries. [63]
Marilynne Robinson

Housekeeping is a gentle, unreproachful lament for death and its intimations in love's every corner. It is a story that mourns with such depth and persistence that lament turns to poetry and loss materializes into creative desire. Its narrator is Ruthie, a midwestern girl of WASP heritage, whose heart has been broken open by a series of whimsical deaths, from accident, suicide, and age, but all viewed with a child's level bewilderment. Clinging to the particularities of face and family even as they come unmoored from the present, Ruthie is pulled into the evanescent world of dream and memory. There she discovers the past, living on in its own mode, seeing and desiring the present but not being seen, not being desired. For the present, at least as circumscribed by Ruthie's culture, shuts out the past the way a well-lit house shuts out the watchful, cradling darkness around it.[64] Longing for communion with the past and its forgotten inhabitants, Ruthie cannot but end up exiled from the land of the living.

"It's hard to describe someone you know so well,"[65] says Ruthie's Aunt Sylvie, trying to recall her sister Helen. It is equally hard to describe the elements in which our lives are suspended, but Robinson achieves that with a poetic prose that works the permeable membrane between contemplation and creation. *Housekeeping* does not construe its dilemma as moral, and for that reason it is not a tragic drama. When Robinson writes of the human tendency to death, she does not call us "mortal," which suggests a jealous comparison with immortals, but "perishable," like lettuce.[66] And, as if our perishability warranted a certain tact, she prefers delicate humor to bombastic protest. But Robinson's meditation on losses that, precisely in their intractability, are educational and somehow inspiring, suffuses *Housekeeping* with a tragic sensibility. She lets Ruthie wonder about the most elemental of questions, often in explicitly religious language, which Robinson uses deftly and for ends that are her own. In places the novel reads like a Buddhist meditation on impermanence, suffering, and desire, but the story works to purify desire, not to lose it. Its explicit religious language is Christian, but idiosyncratically so; the Creator, for example, is the biblical God, but imaged as an immature man who, at the start of creation, "had perhaps not Himself realized the ramifications of certain of His laws, for example, that shock will spend itself in waves. . . ."[67]

The color of this novel, then, is not red, not what stands out sharply and shockingly, but gray, the color of deep water. Fingerbone, Ruthie's town, is dwarfed by a massive lake, which is spanned by a railroad bridge. Below that is another lake, even deeper and older, and above it the misty air. Periodically the lake floods the town, reducing the artifacts of the present to relics of the past. Drowned in water and buried in earth, humanity interpenetrates its elements. When "Cain killed Abel and the blood cried out from the ground," Ruthie muses, the earth was given "a voice and a sorrow." Now, there is a human dread in the cries of birds, and the lake, full of people, groans with "giant miseries." Every living thing in Fingerbone suggests where human powers come from and where they end. On every puddle, "slight as the image in an eye," the past gazes up at the present, though the present sees only its own reflection.[68]

Ruthie's family has a particular association with water, since her grandfather Edmund Foster lodges in the deepest depths of the lake. Years before her birth, his passenger train left the bridge "like a weasel sliding off a rock"—an accident that, Ruthie tells us, would have been spectacular had anyone seen it. The change was not a dramatic one for Edmund's wife Sylvia, who had concluded early on in marriage that "love is half a longing of a kind that possession did nothing to mitigate." The pattern of love and loss repeats itself in her three daughters, who adore their mother but leave her without a backward glance, also drawn to water. Molly becomes a "fisher of souls," and Sylvie marries a man named Fisher. Helen, mother of Ruthie and Lucille, elopes with a Reginald Stone and, after he leaves or is left by her, sinks like a stone into water. In a suicide shocking for its nonchalance, she snacks on wild strawberries, then drives her borrowed car into the lake where her father reposes. Helen's children, Ruthie and Lucille, are left with their grandmother Sylvia, who receives them like the returned spirits of her disappeared daughters and tends them "like someone reliving a long day in a dream."[69]

But parenting, as Sylvia knew, is only fostering, because to give someone birth is to put them "out of house"[70] and send them on a journey to death. "Oh, it's your first time," my mother said to me, with a sympathy I found shocking, the day my brother died in a whimsically random car accident. I was twenty-one, so it was not really my first time, except in the way that a truth that has always been true can blast a fresh hole in your life. I felt Jim's presence quite sharply for a time, like an amputated limb, but I was afraid of it too, afraid of meeting him in the anguish of his death. So he began to meet me in the world of my dreams, where we are as close, still, as the present and the past are close, on the same spot yet unable to touch. In my dreams, I have learned how the present and the past long for each other, and that the longing is the bridge.

After Sylvia dies, her daughter Sylvie comes back across that bridge to foster Ruthie and Lucille. Sylvie is a transient and, we might say, a witch, a woman in tune with the elements but detached from the world of convention. She sleeps with her clothes on, waltzes in floodwaters, is unresistant to cold, and enjoys eating in the dark. She carries her head lowered and turned to one side "with an abstracted and considering expression, as if someone were speaking to her in a soft voice." Time, for her, is a "millennial present," and truth is an undifferentiated blend of fact and fiction. She is a woman unto herself, oblivious to her marriage and gazing upon Ruthie and Lucille "with the placid modesty of a virgin who has conceived." "Housekeeping," for her, is a matter of letting in the elements rather than keeping them out. When she takes up a broom, the corners of rooms begin to fill with leaves and bits of newspapers bearing such phrases as "Powers Meet" and "I think of you." Walking out on the railroad bridge, she flirts with death and, when the girls spot her, can only say, "I've always wondered what it would be like." Sylvie finds loss and sadness to be familiar and thus acceptable. When the neighbor ladies inquire about her social life, Sylvie said yes, she was lonely, "but she was used to being lonely and did not mind it," and, of Ruthie's sadness, "She should be sad . . . you know, who wouldn't be?"[71]

When I teach this book I ask students to remember Sylvies they have known, and it seems there was one in most neighborhoods. She was a woman considered frightening for being solitary and childless, and ugly for not having a man or not wanting one. We assimilated her to the Halloween caricature of the witch, so she was suspected of magical powers, mostly of the malevolent kind. She was eccentric, outside the circles of conventional society, and, within the circle of her own creativity, clearly growing something strange. It seemed that her yard was always overgrown, and if she had cats or dogs, they were too many or too attached to her. We dared each other to approach her, and some of us did, and some of us even befriended her. Some of us, since, have grown up to be her. As the years go by, I too am relieved by my eccentricities and breaches of femininity, and I grow less embarrassed to be seen with tilted head, listening for the whisper of perished things.

For Ruthie and Lucille, Sylvie's coming represents the return of their lost mother, the hope "that a substantial restitution was to be made." Prophecy, Ruthie figures, "is only brilliant memory" and memory can affect miracles, transfiguring the past. Soon the Sylvie who haunts their dreams becomes indistinguishable from Sylvie herself, and soon the girls feel themselves to be caught in Sylvie's dream with her. But while Ruthie is drawn to the convergence of dream and memory, Lucille is not. Her memory has fabricated a mother who could initiate her into conventional womanhood, but Sylvie sweeps in the opposite direction. Lucille tries to pull both herself and her sister into the world of the living, but to Ruthie it seems "that nothing I had lost, or might lose, could be found there," or "that something I had lost might be found in Sylvie's house." Finally,

Lucille escapes Sylvie's housekeeping for the more conventional domes-
ticity of her Home Economics teacher, and, as Ruthie tells it, "I had no
sister after that night."[72]

While Lucille develops into "a small woman," Ruthie becomes "a tow-
ering child," drawn to a different kind of ripeness. Since childhood she
has searched for sustenance in the darkness where her mother lives. But
growing up, she learns that the past needs her nurturance too, and her
compassion. One sees what one cares about, she concludes: "appearance
is only a trick of the nerves" and apparition "is only a lesser trick." To
her, ascension seems to be almost "a natural law," to which she adds "a
law of completion—that everything must finally be made comprehensi-
ble." But only desire is ruled by those laws, desire that, even broken,
grows as multiple and diffuse as light on water. When her mother's sorrow
was revealed by her death, Ruthie reflects, "we saw its wings and saw
it fly a thousand ways into the hills," and in its wake Helen was trans-
figured in Ruthie's memory. That, for Ruthie, is the meaning of resurrection. On the road to Emmaus, it was because Jesus "was so sharply
lacked and so powerfully remembered that his friends felt him beside
them as they walked along the road, and saw someone cooking fish on
the shore and knew it to be Him, and sat down to supper with Him, all
wounded as he was."[73] He is not restored, nor is Helen restored, but
desire, in their absence, finds its own fecundity.

"Memory is the sense of loss, and loss pulls us after it."[74] With the
loss of Lucille, Ruthie is unbound to the world of the living and feels
only the pull of the spirit world. Sylvie initiates her into that world,
bringing her at dawn across the lake to an isolated piece of land where,
Sylvie believes, ghost children live. "She could as well be my mother,"
Ruthie now thinks, and like a mother Sylvie leaves her alone to encounter
death. In the abandonment, Ruthie finds loneliness as an "absolute discovery," for "once alone, it is impossible to believe that one could ever
have been otherwise." "Let them come unhouse me of this flesh," she
prays, for even the body is "no shelter now," only a barrier against the
inrushing elements, a separation from the beloved dead.[75]

In the years after my brother's accident, my own fear of death was
the barrier between us, and it was flooded one night in a dream. He and
I were fish together, gliding along the ocean floor, and around us fish of
all colors drifted in fathomless silence. I felt my lungs breathe water, but
there was no struggle in my drowning. We were transmogrified into white
birds and he taught me to fly, over the roof of our childhood home. I
had never been able to fly in my dreams before but I learned it then, so
definitely that ever since I can fly at will and even teach others. I find

the current of the air and climb onto it, the way you would float on a current of water. It is an imperfect method, since I am subject to turbulence and cannot go in reverse. Still, to be carried by the elements is a great and heady power, and I may yet improve my skills. I had not expected this change. I had thought that in the vacuum of my loss every little pleasure and beauty would disintegrate, but against that open horizon they grew sharp and piercing instead. I was not prepared for the shock of joy in the spring when my eyes reopened on the world, which suddenly seemed like a vast and beautiful graveyard, where even every fallen bird is still beneath our feet.

But Fingerbone does not want the past that lies beneath its feet, and its narrow desires, too, exert force. When the town learns that Sylvie has taken the girl for a ride in a freight car, the women enter like a chorus, bearing casseroles and judgments. They react to Sylvie's housekeeping with what seemed "at first sight a moral reaction," since morality "is a check upon the strongest temptations" and Fingerbone, so "shallow rooted," is itself sorely tempted by death. Their need to judge, however, is a deflection of the judgment the townspeople feel against themselves. As Sylvie's house becomes more and more of an ark, overrun by the elements and undocked from its neighbors, they would notice that their own houses lacked "compass and keel" and would feel like Noah's neighbors, who must have "put their hands in their pockets and chewed their lips and strolled home to houses they now found wanting in ways they could not understand." They feel judged by Sylvie as by the transients who wander through town "like ghosts, terrifying as ghosts are because they are not very different from us."[76] Sylvie is a palpable invasion of the past, which no offering can satiate. In Fingerbone, it is the purpose of religion and of law to withstand such invasions, so law and religion conspire to separate Ruthie from Sylvie and attach Ruthie to the conventional world.

But what the townspeople see as social attachment is, for Sylvie and Ruthie, a violent disruption of family. Beyond death, family bonds grow even stronger; Helen, as Sylvie recalls, was never close to her father in life, yet followed him into the lake. Each of us, it seems, is drawn into the depths on a trail of particular footprints, and so is Ruthie. In order to avoid losing Ruthie, Sylvie tries to keep house as other women do, but her every gesture tears a wider opening to the other world. When Sylvie burns her accumulated newspapers and magazines, her housecleaning becomes, in Ruthie's eyes, a "fiery transfiguration" of images and words, for "words, too, must be salvaged." To be saved, for these two, is to be translated by fleeting light into lasting darkness. Through the inevitable accident of the sheriff's visit, that salvation becomes final.

Sylvie takes a burning broom and "makes an end of housekeeping," and the two escape across the railroad bridge to live the life of transients, leaving behind the impression of their deaths. Indeed, they are dead, for when Ruthie takes waitressing jobs, people become alarmed at her silence and her disinterest in food and "they begin to suspect me, and it is as if I put a chill on the coffee by serving it."[77]

Housekeeping ends as it began, on a note of sorrow and longing. Ruthie and Sylvie now ride through the present, seeing but not seen, felt in the world of the living only as an absence too subtle to name, a loss that itself has been lost. Ruthie imagines Lucille at a restaurant in Boston, and the scene is like a failed eschatological banquet. "Her water glass has left two-thirds of a ring on the table, and she works at completing the circle with her thumbnail." But "Sylvie and I do not flounce through the door" and "do not sit down at the table next to hers"; nor is Ruthie's mother there, nor her grandmother and grandfather:

> No one watching this woman smear her initials in the steam of her water glass with her first finger, or slip cellophane packets of oyster crackers into her handbag for the sea gulls, could know how her thoughts are thronged by our absence, or how she does not watch, does not listen, does not wait, does not hope, and always for me and Sylvie.[78]

Reproach is rarely the deepest of feelings, and a story about simple death does well to avoid it. *Housekeeping* presents a sorrow as old as the earth and challenges morality with perspective. Were morality nothing more than an effort to withstand the elements, and death no more than simple "nature," there would be nothing more to wonder about in this story than the depth and longevity of desire. But if moral life is the patching together of enough wholeness to keep us warm, then this story raises questions for those of us who have broken community with our families and our pasts. There is a danger of romanticizing such broken-ness, and this novel does not escape that danger. The past cannot be satiated, it is true, but it does appreciate gestures of feeding, and it is only recently that so many of us have forgotten those gestures. So we miscalculate the earth's gigantic memory, and the earth pays dearly for that. And we vampirize the histories of other cultures, and human beings pay dearly for that. It is time to pay something back, though to pay, as Robinson hints, is also to gain a blessing, priceless and insubstantial, like the kiss of a ghost.

Making the World Go On

Long ago, for the sake of right and reason, Christian theology made certain decisions about what and who could not be thought or cared about. "Evil" was that prohibited region. In the light of rationalism it was nothing to think about, and in the shadow of dualism nothing to mourn or salvage. In both cases, evil was an ontological question, and theology was to provide answers about its essence and existence, its origin and destiny. But just as the assumption of absolute intelligibility or goodness occludes the provisional extension of understanding and value, so ontological answers to evil do little to illuminate what we are doing when we make negative moral judgments. Today, at the end of modernity, when both the One and the Other are losing their ancient credibility, judgments of evil call for a ruddering interrogative, not the grounding legitimation of an appeal to absolutes.

With the theological emergence of those who have been cast by this tradition as demonic or inferior, "evil" begins to talk back. The Others narrate their own histories of suffering and struggle, their own memories, desires, and outrage. And they too set their faces against the causes of this suffering, causes no more accidental or inessential than any other part of the living world. As the historical victims of injustice identify their enemies and defend themselves, they too are seasoned and defiled by judgments of evil. Although the walls of paradise are being scaled from within and assaulted from without, it is still not possible to live without boundaries, not possible to avoid saying no. How shall those new boundaries be negotiated and defended? How shall new uprisings of difference within them be greeted? When enemies are frankly acknowledged as such, can the moral and intellectual costs of that be counted as honestly? To ask those uneasy questions is to treat all suffering and all judgments of evil as question-worthy; that is what a tragic heuristic requires.

Feminist theology, in its repudiation of metaphysical dualism and hierarchical social relations, disturbs the tomb in which patriarchal theology buried evil. Questioning both the "natural" and the "social" as they have been bequeathed to us, feminists of all backgrounds are radically redefining good and evil. There is a consensus that social injustices are to be changed, not hypostatized as the human condition, while embodiment and historicity are to be cherished despite the suffering that clings to them. Feminists have also brought good out of anti-tragic views of evil. For example, when Delores Williams, Susan Thistlethwaite, and Emilie Townes call upon a redemptive justice, it is to encourage and uphold the struggle of women against multiple oppressions. Rosemary

Radford Ruether deploys the notion of absolute transcendence mainly to ensure that within feminist or other communities of resistance the power of moral self-critique will not be lost. Carol P. Christ evokes the tradition of an essentially good eros or nature to reappropriate as thealogical resources the aesthetic and mystical sensibilities of women.

But if women scholars of religion had hoped to find in feminism a new One, they have since come to know differently. For if women are sisters, we are strangers too, and the differences between us cannot all be subsumed under a benign inclusivity. Neither "nature" nor "justice," neither "immanence" nor "transcendence" can adjudicate those differences; as long as these terms stand in for an absolute and invulnerable Good, they only serve to authorize moral positions that have already been reached by other paths. Moreover, I have suggested, the moral dualism that posits an absolute Good can never be fully severed from metaphysical dualism, because utter innocence, like pristine spirit, needs a cooler place than earth to live.

The central issue at stake in the treatment of evil, I have argued, is what theology can and should be for in a postmodern age. The question becomes especially pressing as theology draws more and more of its analyses of suffering and injustice from academic disciplines such as psychology, economics, and political theory, and when its authoritative sources reach beyond the traditional canons of scripture and theology to include, for example, feminist literature, political praxis, and ritual. Under those circumstances it can happen that the only distinctively theological part of the operation is also the part that has become least persuasive and perspicuous—the authorization of truth claims through appeal to an absolute referent. Fortunately, religion and spirituality have modes of meaning that are far more rich and subtle than that. It is in reflecting on these nonabsolute meanings, I propose, that theology can find its fullest role in the postmodern age. That, I believe, is what feminist scholars of religion are doing as they turn from idealized views of nature and the divine to the complex textures of mystical, aesthetic, and moral experience within particular historical communities.

Literature by women is one of those vital and nonideal modes of meaning. In meditating on four such pieces of literature I have hoped to highlight some of the colors that flood theology after the death of the One and the Other. In each story, meaning is a product of a community or family that is victimized or marginalized. But in none of the stories is community idealized; it is also the site of betrayal, loss, and division. In and with their people, women characters face elemental powers and make extreme choices, but without religious certitudes of the kind that theology often feels itself unable to live without. And in each case, traditional Christian language and imagery is woven into the narrative with ingenuity and insight, yet with magisterial disregard for doctrinal orthodoxy.

Meaning, like women's stories, is something both given and made up. It is bread and roses, without which we cannot even survive, but with which we know the scent of beauty and the color of blood. Meaning is never simply true or simply innocent, since it opens around the red shock of tragic contradiction and choice. In the stories I have discussed, purity is lost when power is found, and when connections come clear, mystery is just then apprehended. "Badness," for these characters, may be an injury and injustice, but a return to goodness is never the cure. And since it is impossible to do nothing in this world, creativity and desire are not the opposite of destructiveness and repression, but call for close discernment of what we are doing and to whom. Reading these stories beside my own, I find no answers to be believed in, but challenge and insight, delight and strength, that are fragile and finite but real. I leave them wondering and with work to do in an unfinished world. And while there is no perfect end in sight, there is the daily proliferation of difference and the limping jig of grace.

Theological wonder, I have suggested, is a practice of compassion. After the death of the metaphysical God, the demands of that practice become greater than ever. As feminists and others know, compassion does not allow us to feel that our moral duty has been discharged with the heaving of a sigh. As a practice, compassion is the hard, costly work of holding open boundaries of thought and care that are wider than the bounds of what we can choose and affirm. Compassion is opposition that is not benumbed to the enemy, negation that dares to understand. It cannot extract itself from the world of force, but within that world it counts the costs of violence to the seventh generation and beyond and chooses with open eyes.

To foster this practice in the colored world, feminists need religious aesthetics and mystical theologies that are as refined as our ethics. In bringing the aesthetics and mysticism of given communities to bear on our ethics, feminists might learn to do without the closure of absolutes. In the process, I believe, feminist ethics itself may learn to weave more artfully the multicolored threads of women's lives. Out here, beyond the walls of paradise, not only are the colors brighter and harder to match, but the fabric of our truths, beauties, and goods is always unraveling. Were our hopes to rely on perfect beginnings and ends, this would surely

be cause for despair. But if hope, instead, is our messy, multiform continuance, then what we need is rather to mourn and laugh and dance
until our flesh remembers how the world goes on.

NOTES

CHAPTER 1:
A MERMAID IN THE SHIP'S CABIN

1. Marilynne Robinson, *Housekeeping* (New York: Bantam Books, 1980), 99.

2. This image is inspired by Toni Morrison's *Beloved* (New York: New American Library, 1987), 275.

3. The classical Christian view of evil as privation can be found in Augustine, *Confessions* (7:13), "To You, then, evil utterly is not—and not only to You, but to your whole creation likewise, evil is not: because there is nothing over and above Your creation that could break in or derange the order that You imposed on it." [See *Confessions I—X*, trans. F. J. Sheed (New York: Sheed and Ward, 1942), 119.] In *De libero arbitrio*, Augustine sustains the same ontological position, but elaborates the origin of evil as sin and suffering from the defection of the free will from God. "All good is from God; therefore no kind of thing exists which is not from God. Hence that movement of turning away, which we agree to be sin, is a defective movement, and a defect comes from nothing." [See *De libero arbitrio*, trans. Dom Mark Pontifex (Westminster, Md.: the Newman Press, 1955), 20.54.] Citing Augustine as an authority, Thomas Aquinas repeated the privation view of evil and the definition of sin as a misuse of freedom; he went on to explicate the causes of evil (which could only be "accidental") in Aristotelean categories. [See *Summa Theologica* Part I: Question 49, articles 1—3, trans. Fathers of the English Dominican Province (Westminster, Md.: Christian Classics, 1981).]

An even more rationalistic strand of the Christian tradition on evil began with Irenaeus. [See *Against Heresies* in *The Ante-Nicene Fathers* vol. I, ed. Alexander Roberts and J. Donaldson (Grand Rapids: W. B. Eerdmans Co., 1974-75), 307-567.] Like Augustine's view, Irenaeus's was formulated against Gnostic metaphysical dualism and so is specificially designed to deny evil an ontic niche. Irenaeus saw suffering from an eschatological point of view, as the incompletion of creation, and sin as a disobedience rooted in human immaturity. Unlike Augustine, Irenaeus was prospectively oriented, concerned less with the origins of evil than with its function in the ongoing restoration of the *imago dei*. As Carter Heyward has suggested, that accounts for the enduring attractiveness of Irenaean theodicy to liberal-minded thinkers. Nonetheless, I would add, Irenaeus's optimism could not fully resolve the dualism to which all rationalistic theism remains subject; as Heyward also notes, Irenaeus's scheme still implies a gap between the best goodness that humanity can achieve and the perfect goodness of God. [See *The Redemption of God: A Theology of Mutual Relation* (Lanham, Md.: University Press of America, 1982), 114-15. For a contemporary Irenaean theodicy, see John Hick, "The World as a Vale of Soul-Making," in *The Problem of Evil: Selected Readings*, ed. Michael L. Peterson (Notre Dame, Ind.: Notre Dame University Press, 1992), 215-30.]

Contemporary process theology, because it alters the metaphysical premises of classical theism, is arguably the most significant revision of these two ancient strands of the Christian privation tradition. The process God includes change and relationality, and excludes coercive power. But there are still important moral and rational continuities with the God of classical theism; the process God is an inclusive goodness in which all occasions can find maximal harmony and intensity, and an intelligibility in whom all evident contradictions are resolvable. In this sense, process theodicy remains within the rationalist-privation tradition, and like that tradition is trailed by the dualism that must obtain between the finite world and any absolute perfection or intelligibility. For example, Lewis Ford argues that in the divine experience, but only in the divine experience, evil is fully overcome. Moreover, he suggests that this divine experience is "thoroughly truthful" even though the world, by virtue of its transience, can never be wholly conformed to it. [See "Divine Persuasion and the Triumph of God," in *The Problem of Evil*, ed. Michael Peterson, 247-265.] Marjorie Hewitt Suchocki extrapolates from process theology an eschatological theodicy; for her, the end of evil is found beyond history in God, who provides real but nonutopic possibilities for human moral progress. [See *The End of Evil: Process Eschatology in Historical Context* (Albany, N.Y.: State University of New York Press, 1988).]

Under the rubric of a "negative" and a "positive" view of evil, Mary Midgley describes interpretive patterns similar to those I call rationalism and dualism. See *Wickedness: A Philosophical Essay* (New York: Routledge, Chapman, and Hall, 1986).

On the Platonic chain of being and its modern survivals, see Arthur O. Lovejoy, *The Great Chain of Being: A Study of the History of an Idea* (Cambridge, Mass.: Harvard University Press, 1950).

4. Rosemary Radford Ruether has long observed this in regard to Romantic views of nature and women. See, for example, *Sexism and God-Talk: Toward a Feminist Theology* (Boston: Beacon Press, 1983), 104-9.

5. Martha C. Nussbaum, *The Fragility of Goodness: Luck and Ethics in Greek Tragedy and Philosophy* (Cambridge: Cambridge University Press, 1986).

6. Nell Noddings typologizes rather differently the treatment of women by Christian theology, distinguishing a classical view of women as demonized sexuality (Tertullian's "devil's gateway") from the romantic association of women with natural goodness (the "angel in the house"). See *Women and Evil* (Berkeley: University of California Press, 1989). In my view, these types both reflect dualistic patterns of thought and do not uncover the inner connection between the romanticization or demonization of women on the one hand and the rationalistic inferiorization of women on the other hand.

7. Aeschylus, "Agamemnon," trans. Richmond Lattimore, in *Greek Tragedies*, vol. 1, ed. David Greene and Richmond Lattimore (Chicago: University of Chicago Press, 1960), lines 621-22.

8. Audre Lorde, "The Master's Tools Will Never Dismantle the Master's House," in *Sister Outsider: Essays and Speeches* (Freedom, Calif.: Crossing Press, 1984), 110-13.

9. Nussbaum calls herself a "welfarist social democrat" who is liberal in the sense of adding to the concrete agenda of social welfare a notion of basic human rights. See "A Reply," in *Soundings* 72:4 (Winter 1989): 267.

10. On women in Greek tragedy, see Sarah Pomeroy, *Goddesses, Whores, Wives and Slaves: Women in Classical Antiquity* (New York: Schocken Books, 1975), 95-119.

Aristotle's influential definition of tragedy outlined what he saw as the formal features of tragic dramas (plot, character, diction, thought, spectacle, and music) and their emotional effects on viewers (pity and terror). [See *Poetics*, Ch. 6 in *The Basic Works of Aristotle*, ed. Richard McKeon (New York: Random House, 1941), 1460.]

Modern theories of tragedy often carry one or more of the following emphases: 1) canonical approaches, which circumscribe tragedy in terms of a specified body of dramatic literature (e.g., for Walter Kaufman, it is Sophocles, Aeschylus, Euripides, and Shakespeare); 2) moral or characterological approaches, which emphasize tragic heroes and their presumed flaws (e.g., Kaufman faults H. D. F. Kitto for this; Nussbaum mentions especially T. C. W. Stinton); 3) metaphysical approaches, which treat tragic conflict and resolution as a cosmic-historical process (e.g., G.W.F. Hegel); 4) historical or cultural materialist approaches, in which tragedy is an artistic process enabling the experience and resolution of social conflict (e.g., Raymond Williams); 5) approaches that promote a tragic vision or stance, for example resignation (Arthur Schopenhauer) or joy (Friederich Nietzsche); 6) aesthetic approaches, which treat tragedy as a dramatic form that elicits particular kinds of feelings (e.g., Suzanne Langer); 7) myth-ritual approaches, in which tragedy originates in the ritual year of ancient Greece and carries a perennial meaning about death as the condition for the new (Gilbert Murray, Jane Harrison, and the Cambridge School of classical philologists). [Cf. Walter Kaufman, *Tragedy and Philosophy* (Princeton, N.J.: Princeton University Press, 1968); Suzanne Langer, *Feeling and Form: A Theory of Art* (New York: Charles Scribner's Son, 1953), 351-68; Nussbaum, *The Fragility of Goodness*, 31-32, 63-66, and 501 n. 9; Raymond Williams, *Modern Tragedy* (Stanford, Calif.: Stanford University Press, 1966), 15-84.]

Theories of these types share in common an appreciation of tragedy as in some sense illuminating or compelling. Those who are less appreciative of tragedy employ definitions that are far more cursory and, by almost any measure, less adequate. For example, Peterson's introduction to the theistic problem of evil refers to tragedy simply as "gratuitious evil." [See Michael Peterson, *The Problem of Evil*, 18.] But all definitions of tragedy, whether appreciative or not, exert prescriptive force; they are meant to show what about tragedy is good or dangerous, illuminating or illogical, ennobling or demoralizing, transformative or complacent. For that reason, the definitions are appropriately assessed in terms of their socio-historical location and aims (that is, an assessment that is consciously relative to one's own location and aims) not in terms any presumed essence of tragedy, which would be subject to the same relativity.

My own definition is therefore frankly prescriptive. It does not aim to cover all actual usages of the terms *tragedy* or *tragic*, but only to highlight what I find crucial for theology in the postmodern moment and in the context of my own commitments. Like Kaufman and Nussbaum, I believe that theories of tragedies ought to attend to texts and stories, rather than defending preformulated philosophical positions. I see no necessary contradiction between defining tragedy in terms of social conflict and change, as does Raymond Williams, and reading tragedies as mythic-ritual disclosures of elemental powers and processes (though the dubious historical claims of the Cambridge school are to be avoided). Like Langer, I value the aesthetic aims of tragedies and do not want these aims to be swallowed up by metaphysical and moral concerns. But with Nussbaum, I believe that an integral moral philosophy (i.e., one not predicated on the Kantian distinction between moral and nonmoral goods) can and should draw wisdom from art and literature.

My approach is distinctive in focusing upon the *heuristic* functions of tragedy as a theatre for shared inquiry about conflict. This heuristic operates prior to distinctions between changeable and unchangeable suffering, social and personal fault, injustice and misfortune, guilt and innocence or defilement. Such judgments, I propose, ought to be outcomes of tragic discernment, rather than a priori criteria for deciding what is tragic and what is not. My definition is therefore able to address any and all narratives of profound suffering. It is this prereflective wonder about suffering as suffering and power as power that makes tragedy as I define it religious, and it is the translation of wonder into inquiry, discernment, and action that renders tragedy theological.

11. William Styron, *Sophie's Choice* (New York: Bantam Books, 1979). My reading of this text is indebted to my student, Megura Bell.

12. Philip Hallie, "Cruelty: The Empirical Evil," in *Facing Evil: Light at the Core of Darkness*, ed. Paul Woodruff and Harry Wilmer (La Salle, Ill.: Open Court Publishing Co., 1988), 119-37.

13. Catherine Keller, *From a Broken Web: Separation, Sexism and Self* (Boston: Beacon Press, 1986).

14. Luce Irigaray, *This Sex Which Is Not One*, trans. Catherine Porter (Ithaca, N.Y.: Cornell University Press, 1985), 26.

15. Alice Walker's dedication to *The Third Life of Grange Copeland* (New York: Pocket Books, 1976).

16. Morrison, *Beloved*, 6.

CHAPTER 2:
THE ONE AND THE OTHER

1. Augustine, *Confessions and Enchiridion*, trans. and ed. A. Outler, in *Library of Christian Classics*, vol. 7 (Philadelphia: Westminster Press, 1955), VII:iii.

2. Ibid., *Confessions*, II:vi; VII:xvi and V:x; VII:x-xi; VII:xvii; VII:iii.

3. Ibid., VIII:v.

4. Margaret R. Miles, *Fullness of Life: Historical Foundations for a New Asceticism* (Philadelphia: Westminster Press, 1981), 77. Miles also concurs that for Augustine, "The most characteristic feature of bodily life is a tendency to habituation" (73).

5. The distortions of desire are epitomized in sexuality and show up most vividly in adolescence; the effacement of reason is first evident in infancy, and in the *Confessions* is epitomized by inarticulateness and its attendant frustrations. Cf. Augustine, *City of God*, trans. H. Bettenson (New York: Penguin, 1984), XXII:22; *Confessions* I:vi.

6. Augustine, *Confessions*, I:vii.

7. On the anomie of the sinful will, see *Confessions*, VIII:ix-x. Miles observes that Augustine's postconversion problematization of pleasure has the effect of diminishing his appreciation of beauty, diversity, and the uniqueness of human personalities. In an analysis congruent with the one offered here, she links these losses to his sense of being "burned" by his own desires: "He insists now on loving only what he can love without fear of loss." See *Desire and Delight: A New Reading of Augustine's Confessions* (New York: Crossroad, 1992), 128.

8. Augustine, *City of God*, XIII and XIV.

9. Cf. Augustine, *City of God*, IV:27; VI:6; VIII:14. On Augustine's fear of derision, see Miles, *Desire and Delight*, 13.

10. Augustine, *Confessions*, IX:ix.

11. Martin Luther, "On the Bondage of the Will," in *Luther and Erasmus: Free Will and Salvation*, ed. E. Gordon Rupp and Philip Watson (Philadelphia: Westminster Press, 1969), 182-292.

12. John Calvin, *Institutes of the Christian Religion*, trans. H. Beveridge (Grand Rapids, Mich.: W.B. Eerdmans, 1979), Vol. I, Bk. II, Ch. II: S12-24.

13. G.W. von Leibniz, *Theodicy: Essays on the Goodness of God, the Freedom of Man and the Origin of Evil*, ed. Austin Farrer (London: Routledge and Kegan Paul, 1951).

14. Francis Schüssler Fiorenza, *Foundational Theology: Jesus and the Church* (New York: Crossroad, 1985), 256-64.

15. On Kant and theodicy, see A. L. Loades, *Kant and Job's Comforters* (Great Britain: Avero Publications, 1985).

16. On the freedom of the will, see Immanuel Kant, *Religion within the Limits of Reason Alone*, eds. T. Greene and H. Hudson (New York: Harper & Row, 1960), 36.

17. On morality in relation to happiness, see Kant, *Critique of Practical Reason*, trans. L. W. Beck (Indianapolis: Bobbs-Merrill, 1956), "Dialectic of Pure Practical Reason," II.i-v. Martha Nussbaum associates Kant with the Platonic anti-tragic tradition and thus with what I call rationalistic responses to evil. My own characterization of him is different, but this is not of great moment in terms of the anti-tragic implications of his position. Cf. Nussbaum, *The Fragility of Goodness: Luck and Ethics in Greek Tragedy and Philosophy* (Cambridge: Cambridge University Press, 1986), 4-5.

18. Kant, *Religion within the Limits*, 53. For the postulates of pure practical reason, see Kant, *Critique of Practical Reason*, "Dialectic," II.iv,v.

19. Cf. Jean-Jacques Rousseau's critique of Cartesian rational skepticism, in *The Creed of a Priest of Savoy*, trans. Arthur Beattie (New York: Frederick Ungar, 1978), 3-5.

20. G.W.F. Hegel, *Lectures on the Philosophy of World History; Introduction: Reason and Freedom in History*, trans. H. B. Nisbet (Cambridge: Cambridge University Press, 1975).

21. Arthur Schopenhauer, *Essay on the Freedom of the Will*, trans. K. Kolenda (Indianapolis: Bobbs-Merrill, 1960), 69, 85.

22. Friedrich Schleiermacher, *The Christian Faith*, ed. H. R. Mackintosh and J. S. Stewart (Philadelphia: Fortress Press, 1976), especially SS 66-69 and 75-78.

23. Schleiermacher, *Christian Faith*, S66.

24. Ernst Becker described the Enlightenment as effecting a shift to "secular theodicy" and argued that the driving concerns of nineteeth-century thought were moral. See his *The Structure of Evil* (New York: The Free Press, 1968).

25. Karl Barth, *Dogmatics in Outline*, trans. G. T. Thomson (New York: Harper & Row, 1959), 7.

26. Karl Barth, *Church Dogmatics*, trans. J. W. Edwards, O. Bussey, Harold Knight (Edinburgh: T. & T. Clark, 1958), 3/1: 406, 408, 411; 3/3:316-34.

27. Paul Tillich, *Systematic Theology* (Chicago: University of Chicago Press, 1951, 1957, 1963), esp. I:253-54; II: 132-34; III:38-39, 92-94, 244-45; Reinhold Niebuhr, *Beyond Tragedy: Essays on the Christian Interpretation of History* (New York: Charles Scribner's Sons, 1937); Edward

Farley, *Good and Evil: Interpreting a Human Condition* (Minneapolis: Fortress Press, 1990).

28. Tillich, *Systematic Theology*, III:93; Niebuhr, *Beyond Tragedy*, 164; Farley, *Good and Evil*, 29.

29. Tillich, *Systematic Theology*, III:93; Niebuhr, *Beyond Tragedy*, 161; Farley, *Good and Evil*, 123-24.

30. Tillich, *Systematic Theology*, I:253-54, 202; III:94; Niebuhr, *Beyond Tragedy*, 166, 167-68; Farley, *Good and Evil*, 124-38, 125.

31. Cf. Tillich's definition of essence, *Systematic Theology*, I:202.

32. Niebuhr, *Beyond Tragedy*, 289-306; Tillich, *Systematic Theology*, III.

33. Jürgen Moltmann, *The Way of Jesus Christ: Christology in Messianic Dimensions* (San Francisco: Harper & Row, 1990), 181; 170-196.

34. Moltmann, *The Way of Jesus Christ*, 172, 179.

35. José Míguez Bonino, *Toward a Christian Political Ethics* (Philadelphia: Fortress Press, 1983), 95-96.

36. James Cone, *A Black Theology of Liberation* (Maryknoll, N.Y.: Orbis Books, 1976), 102; 66; Míguez, *Toward a Christian Political Ethics*, 115.

37. James Cone, *My Soul Looks Back* (Maryknoll, N.Y.: Orbis Books, 1986), 63; William R. Jones, *Is God a White Racist? A Preamble to Black Theology* (Garden City, N.Y.: Doubleday, 1973), esp. 185-202.

38. Johannes B. Metz, *Faith in History and Society: Toward a Practical Fundamental Theology*, trans. David Smith (New York: Seabury Press, 1980), 162-63.

39. Gustavo Gutiérrez, *On Job: God-Talk and the Suffering of the Innocent*, trans. Matthew O'Connell (Maryknoll, N.Y.: Orbis Books, 1987), 102.

40. Gutiérrez, *On Job*, 103, 76.

41. Ibid., 54.

42. Ibid., 87-88.

43. Ibid., 79, 80, 100.

44. Cf. Mikhail Bahktin, *Rabelais and His World*, trans. H. Iswolsky (Bloomington: Indiana University Press, 1984); Harvey Cox, *Religion in the Secular City: Toward a Postmodern Theology* (New York: Simon and Schuster, 1984), esp. ch. 21.

45. Cf. David Parkin, ed., *The Anthropology of Evil* (New York: Basil Blackwell, 1985).

46. Míguez, *Toward a Christian Political Ethics*, 103-6.

47. George Lindbeck, *The Nature of Doctrine: Religion and Theology in a Postliberal Age* (Philadelphia: Westminister Press, 1984).

48. Mark C. Taylor, *Erring: A Postmodern A/theology* (Chicago: University of Chicago Press, 1984).

49. For an excellent critique of Taylor's and other deconstructive theologies as anti-tragic, see Robert Gall, "Of/From Theology and Deconstruction," *Journal of the American Academy of Religion* 58:3 (Fall 1990): 413-37.

50. For essays in constructive postmodern theology, see Leroy Rouner, ed., *On Community* (Notre Dame, Ind.: University of Notre Dame Press, 1991), and David Griffin, ed., *Sacred Interconnections: Postmodern Spirituality, Political Economy, and Art* (Albany, N.Y.: State University of New York Press, 1990). For an example of the conflict between popular Christian interpretations of evil and the Eurocentric theological tradition, see John S. Pobee, *Toward an African Theology* (Nashville: Abingdon Press, 1979), 99-119. Marc H. Ellis addresses the topics of guilt and evil in dialogue with Christian theologians in *Beyond Innocence and Redemption: Confronting the Holocaust and Israeli Power* (San Francisco: Harper & Row, 1990).

51. Cf. S. Davis, ed., *Encountering Evil: Live Options in Theodicy* (Atlanta: John Knox Press, 1980). In his "Postscript," John Cobb comments on the lack of interest among theologians in philosophical theodicy and suggests a pastorally oriented theological approach to the problem of evil.

CHAPTER 3:
ESCAPE FROM PARADISE

1. Judith Plaskow, with Karen Bloomquist, Margaret Early, and Elizabeth Farians, "The Coming of Lilith," in *Religion and Sexism: Images of Women in the Jewish and Christian Traditions*, ed. Rosemary Radford Ruether (New York: Simon and Schuster, 1974), 342-43.

2. Cf. Monica Sjöö and Barbara Mor, *The Great Cosmic Mother: Rediscovering the Religion of the Earth* (San Francisco: Harper & Row, 1987), 276-77.

3. Elaine Pagels, *Adam, Eve and the Serpent* (New York: Vintage Books, 1989), 130, 142.

4. Augustine, *City of God*, trans. H. Bettenson (New York: Penguin, 1984), XIII, 15-18.

5. Valerie Saiving, "The Human Situation: A Feminine View," in *Womanspirit Rising: A Feminist Reader in Religion*, ed. Carol Christ and Judith Plaskow (San Francisco: Harper & Row, 1979), 25-42.

6. Judith Plaskow, *Sex, Sin and Grace: Women's Experience and the Theologies of Reinhold Niebuhr and Paul Tillich* (Washington, D.C.: University Press of America, 1980), 2-3. Plaskow's modification of Saiving is also noted by Susan Brooks Thistlethwaite, *Sex, Race and God: Christian Feminism in Black and White* (New York: Crossroad, 1989), 78-79.

7. Letty Russell, *Human Liberation in a Feminist Perspective—A Theology* (Philadelphia: Westminster Press, 1974).

8. For an example of initial efforts to forge alliances among feminist and other liberation movements, see "The Feminist Theology Panel," in *Theology in the Americas*, ed. Sergio Torres and John Eagleson (Maryknoll, N.Y.: Orbis Books, 1976), 361-76.

9. Mary Hunt, *Feminist Liberation Theology: The Development of Method in Construction* (Dissertation: Graduate Theological Union, Berkeley, Calif., 1980), 45. On interstructured oppressions and the other points discussed here, see also Hunt's contribution to "Roundtable Discussion on Feminist Methodology," *Journal of Feminist Studies in Religion* 1:2 (Spring 1985): 83-87.

10. Carter Heyward, *The Redemption of God: A Theology of Mutual Relation* (Lanham, Md.: University Press of America, 1982).

11. Heyward, *Redemption of God*, 6.

12. Carter Heyward, *Touching Our Strength: The Erotic as Power and the Love of God* (San Francisco: Harper & Row, 1989); Rita Nakashima Brock, *Journeys by Heart: A Christology of Erotic Power* (New York: Crossroad, 1988); Judith Plaskow, *Standing Again at Sinai: Judaism from a Feminist Perspective* (San Francisco: Harper & Row, 1990), 197-210; Patricia Hunter, "Women's Power—Women's Passion: And God Said, 'That's Good,'" in *A Troubling in My Soul: Womanist Perspectives on Evil and Suffering*, ed. Emilie M. Townes (Maryknoll, N.Y.: Orbis Books, 1993), 189-98.

13. Audre Lorde, "Uses of the Erotic: The Erotic as Power," in *Sister Outsider: Essays and Speeches* (Freedom, Calif: Crossing Press, 1984), 53-59.

14. Rebecca Chopp, *The Power to Speak: Feminism, Language and God* (New York: Crossroad, 1989).

15. This is very clear in Plaskow's *Standing Again at Sinai*, where "inclusivity" refers to the historical reality of the Jewish people, which in fact has always included women. She rests her theological authority on the community of Jewish feminists, not on a notion of "true" Judaism (18-24). Nonetheless, she has long argued that the "right questions" about Judaism and feminism are theological rather than only legal or social, calling for less partial and more inclusive views of God, Israel, and Torah. For other examples, see Susannah Heschel, ed., *On Being a Jewish Feminist: A Reader* (New York: Schocken Books, 1983).

16. Cf. Brock, *Journeys by Heart*, and the discussion of Rosemary Radford Ruether in chapter 5 below.

17. For a fuller critical analysis of eros and tragedy in feminist theologies of sex, see my "Uses of the Thea(o)logian: Sex and Theodicy in Religious Feminism," *Journal of Feminist Studies in Religion* 8:1 (Spring 1992): 7-33.

18. See Christ and Plaskow's Introduction to *Womanspirit Rising*, 2-17.

19. The phrase "claiming the center" was popularized by Elisabeth Schüssler Fiorenza. See, for example, her article "The Will to Choose or Reject: Continuing Our Critical Work," in *Feminist Interpretation of the Bible*, ed. Letty Russell (Philadelphia: Westminster Press, 1985). Russell's anthology also contains many efforts to identify biblical traditions useful for feminists. The work of Rosemary Radford Ruether, as will be evident in chapters 4 and 5 below, contains many examples of the view of patriarchy and sexism as real but inauthentic expressions of biblical religion.

For the initial celebratory uses of terms such as "witch," "bitch," and "heretic," see "WITCH: Spooking the Patriarchy in the Late Sixties," in *The Politics of Women's Spirituality*, ed. Charlene Spretnak (New York: Anchor Books, 1982), 427-29; "The WITCH Manifesto" and Valerie Solanas, "The SCUM Manifesto," in *Masculine/Feminine: Readings in Sexual Mythology and the Liberation of Women*, ed. B. and T. Roszak (New York: Harper & Row, 1969), 259-69; Mary Daly, *Gyn/Ecology: The Metaethics of Radical Feminism* (Boston: Beacon Press, 1979). Carol Christ also began identifying herself as a heretic and a witch in the 1970s; see chapter 6 below and Christ's "Heretics and Outsiders: The Struggle over Female Power in Western Religion," originally published in 1978 and reprinted in *Laughter of Aphrodite: Reflections on a Journey to the Goddess* (San Francisco: Harper & Row, 1987), 35-56.

20. Spretnak, Introduction, *The Politics of Women's Spirituality*, xv.

21. Ibid., xvii.

22. Emily Erwin Culpepper, "Contemporary Goddess Thealogy: A Sympathetic Critique," in *Shaping New Visions: Gender and Values in American Culture*, vol. 2, The Harvard Women's Studies in Religion Series, ed. Clarissa Atkinson, Margaret Miles, and Constance Buchanan (Ann Arbor: University of Michigan Press, 1987).

Margot Adler criticizes some Goddess feminists in the same terms. See my interview with her, "From Evil to Ecstasy: Exploring the Goddess with Margot Adler," in *Sojourners* 18:9 (May 1993): 14-15.

23. Culpepper, "The Spiritual, Political Quest of a Feminist Freethinker," in *After Patriarchy*, ed. Paula Cooey, William Eakin, and Jay McDaniel (Maryknoll, N.Y.: Orbis Books, 1991), 146-65.

24. For Lust as a biophilic virtue, see Daly's *Pure Lust: Elemental Feminist Philosophy* (Boston: Beacon Press, 1984).

25. Mary Daly, *Beyond God the Father* (Boston: Beacon Press, 1982), 7-11, 96; and *Gyn/Ecology*, 7.

26. Daly, *Beyond God the Father*, 66; reiterated in *Pure Lust*, 164n.

27. Starhawk, *Dreaming the Dark: Magic, Sex and Politics* (Boston: Beacon Press, 1982), 141, 135-53. For more on sex in the culture of estrangement, see *Truth or Dare: Encounters with Power, Authority, Mystery* (San Francisco: Harper & Row, 1987), 203-6.

28. Michel Foucault, *The History of Sexuality*, vol. 1 (New York: Vintage Books, 1980), 36-49.

29. Audre Lorde, "Uses of the Erotic."

30. See, for example, the comments of Naomi Southard and Rita Nakashima Brock on the responses of Asian American women to cultural feminism. Southard and Brock, "The Other Half of the Basket: Asian American Women and the Search for a Theological Home," *Journal of Feminist Studies in Religion* 3:2 (Fall 1987): 149.

31. Cf. Cindy Patton, *Inventing AIDS* (New York: Routledge, 1990).

32. Kwok Pui-lan, "Claiming a Boundary Existence: A Parable from Hong Kong," *Journal of Feminist Studies in Religion* 3:2 (Fall 1987): 124. Elsewhere, Kwok makes a strong case that the feminist critique of Christian symbology and doctrine must also be historical and culturally contextualized. See *Chinese Women and Christianity: 1860–1927* (Atlanta,

Ga.: Scholars Press, 1992), 29-64. Ada-María Isasi-Díaz and Yolanda Tarango, *Hispanic Women: Prophetic Voice in the Church* (Minneapolis: Fortress Press, 1992), 70; Chung Hyun Kyung, *Struggle to Be the Sun Again: Introducing Asian Women's Theology* (Maryknoll, N.Y.: Orbis Books, 1990), 111-13.

33. Cheryl Townsend Gilkes, "The 'Loves' and 'Troubles' of African-American Women's Bodies," in *A Troubling in My Soul*, ed. Emilie M. Townes, 234; Susan Thistlethwaite, *Sex, Race and God: Christian Feminism in Black and White* (New York: Crossroad, 1989), 60-76; *Inheriting Our Mothers' Gardens: Feminist Theology in Third World Perspective*, ed. Katie Cannon, Ada-María Isasi-Díaz, Kwok Pui-lan, and Letty Russell (Philadelphia: Westminster, 1988). The image of the mother's garden is Alice Walker's.

34. Marta Benavides, "My Mother's Garden Is a New Creation," in *Inheriting Our Mothers' Gardens*, ed. Cannon et al., 123-41; Delores Williams, *Sisters in the Wilderness*, 185-86.

35. Emilie M. Townes, ed., *A Troubling in My Soul*.

36. Cf. William Jones, *Is God a White Racist? A Preamble to Black Theology* (Garden City, N.Y.: Doubleday, 1973). Jones's work on black theodicy is cited by Clarice Martin, Frances Wood, M. Shawn Copeland, Cheryl Kirk-Duggan, and Jacquelyn Grant. See *A Troubling in My Soul*, 22, 43, 160, 125 n. 5, 209-10.

37. Jamie T. Phelps, O.P., "Joy Came in the Morning Risking Death for Resurrection," and Clarice Martin, "Biblical Theodicy and Black Women's Spiritual Autobiography," in *A Troubling in My Soul*, ed. Townes, 48, 22.

38. Frances Wood, "Take My Yoke Upon You," 40; Cheryl Gilkes, "The 'Loves' and 'Troubles' of African-American Women's Bodies," 240; Jacquelyn Grant, "The Sin of Servanthood and the Deliverance of Discipleship," in *A Troubling in My Soul*, ed. Townes, 215.

39. Rosita deAnn Mathews, "Using Power from the Periphery: An Alternative Theological Model for Survival in Systems," 96; Marcia Y. Riggs, "A Clarion Call To Awake! Arise! Act!" 74; M. Shawn Copeland, " 'Wading Through Many Sorrows': Toward a Theology of Suffering in Womanist Perspective," in *A Troubling in My Soul*, ed. Townes, 109.

40. Riggs, "A Clarion Call," 74; Katie G. Cannon, " 'The Wounds of Jesus': Justification of Goodness in the Face of Manifold Evil," 225; Emilie Townes, "Living in the New Jerusalem: The Rhetoric and Movement of Liberation in the House of Evil," in *A Troubling in My Soul*, ed. Townes, 84-85.

41. Delores Williams, *Sisters in the Wilderness*, 60-83. On demonarchy, see Williams, "A Womanist Perspective on Sin," in *A Troubling in My Soul*, ed. Townes, 144 and 149 n. 45. In the latter article (147), Williams notes that this stress on black women's sexuality and self-esteem, together with an articulation of the link between the defilement of black women and the defilement of nature, are distinct contributions of womanist theology to black Christian thought.

42. Williams, *Sisters in the Wilderness*, 87, 161-67, 144, 198-99, 238.

43. See, for example, "Final Statements: Yaoundè, Cameroun, Women's Meeting of Francophone Africa" (August 3–9 and 19–23, 1986); "Final Statement: Asian Church Women Speak" (Manila, Philippines, November 21–30, 1985); "Final Statement: Latin American Conference on Theology from the Perspective of Women" (Buenos Aires, Argentina, Oct. 30–Nov. 3, 1985); "Final Document: Intercontinental Women's Conference" (Oaxtepec, Mexico, December 1–6, 1986) in *With Passion and Compassion: Reflections from the Women's Commission of the Ecumenical Association of Third World Theologians*, ed. Virginia Fabella, M.M. and Mercy Amba Oduyoye (Maryknoll, N.Y.: Orbis Books, 1989), 60-68, 118-24, 181-83, 184-90.

44. Isasi-Díaz and Tarango, *Hispanic Women*, 77; Chung, *Struggle to Be the Sun Again*, 47-52; Final Statements of African and Asian Church Women in *With Passion and Compassion*, ed. Fabella and Oduyoye, 60, 120.

45. "Conference Statement: Consultation on Asian Women's Theology" (Singapore, November 20–29, 1987), in *We Dare to Dream: Doing Theology as Asian Women*, ed. Virginia Fabella, M.M. and Sun Ai Lee Park (Hong Kong: Asian Women's Resource Center for Culture and Theology, 1989), 150.

46. Copeland, " 'Wading Through Many Sorrows,' " in *A Troubling in My Soul*, ed. Townes, 124.

47. Emilie Townes, "Introduction: On Creating Ruminations from the Soul," and "Living in the New Jerusalem," in *A Troubling in My Soul*, ed. Townes, 2, 78.

48. Jamie Phelps, "Joy Came in the Morning," in *A Troubling in My Soul*, ed. Townes, 49, 52-53; Isasi-Díaz and Tarango in *Hispanic Women*, 70; "Conference Statement: Consultation on Asian Women's Theology" in *We Dare to Dream*, ed. Fabella and Park, 153.

49. Wendy Farley, *Tragic Vision and Divine Compassion: A Contemporary Theodicy* (Louisville, Ky.: Westminster/John Knox Press, 1990).

50. Ibid., 27, 30-31, 116, 128, 130.

51. Ibid., 62, 29.

52. Thistlethwaite, *Sex, Race and God*, 74, 113.

53. Ibid., 73. Karen McCarthy Brown, "Why I Married the War God," in *Womanspirit Bonding*, ed. J. Kalven and M. Buckley (New York: Pilgrim Press, 1984).

54. Thistlethwaite, *Sex, Race and God*, 12-14.

55. Ibid., 112.

56. Sharon Welch, *Communities of Solidarity and Resistance: A Feminist Theology of Liberation* (Maryknoll, N.Y.: Orbis Books, 1985), 25.

57. Sharon Welch, *A Feminist Ethic of Risk* (Minneapolis: Fortress Press, 1990), 176, 173.

58. On the risk of nihilism, see Welch, *Communities of Solidarity and Resistance*, 14; on "the cultured despair of the middle class," see *A Feminist Ethic of Risk*, 14-15.

59. Welch, *Communities of Solidarity and Resistance*, 87-88.

60. Welch, *A Feminist Ethic of Risk*, 159, 167-72.

61. Spretnak, *States of Grace: The Recovery of Meaning in the Postmodern Age* (San Francisco: Harper & Row, 1991).

62. Cf. Judith Plaskow and Carol Christ, eds., *Weaving the Visions: New Patterns in Feminist Spirituality* (San Francisco: Harper & Row, 1989), 6-8.

63. Catherine Madsen, Starhawk, Emily Erwin Culpepper, Arthur Waskow, Anne Klein, Karen Baker-Fletcher, "If God Is God She Is Not Nice," *Journal of Feminist Studies in Religion* 5:1 (Spring 1989): 103-17. In other postbiblical feminists, one finds questions about the goodness of the divine—for example, in Christine Downing's encounters with the painful aspects of Goddesses, Margot Adler's critique of Goddess "monotheism," and Starhawk's reflections on "dreaming the dark." See Christine Downing, *The Goddess: Mythological Images of the Feminine* (New York: Crossroad, 1981), and notes 26 and 27 above.

64. Plaskow, *Standing Again at Sinai*, 151-52, and "Facing the Ambiguity of God," in *Tikkun* 6:5 (Sept./Oct. 1991): 70, 96.

65. Karen McCarthy Brown, *Mama Lola: A Vodou Priestess in Brooklyn* (Berkeley: University of California Press, 1991), 6. Brown's reference to

"knowing the dance" is a quote from John Miller Chernoff; see her "Women's Leadership in Haitian Vodou," in *Weaving the Visions*, ed. Plaskow and Christ, 228-29. Delores Williams, "Womanist Theology: Black Women's Voices," in *Weaving the Visions*, 184.

66. Katie G. Cannon, *Black Womanist Ethics* (Atlanta: Scholars Press, 1988); Sally McFague, *Models of God: Theology for an Ecological, Nuclear Age* (Philadelphia: Fortress Press, 1987), 137-55; Heyward, *Redemption of God*, esp. 73-100.

67. Brock and Southard, "The Other Half of the Basket," 145.

68. Chung, *Struggle to Be the Sun Again*, 154.

69. Soon-Hwa Sun, "Women, Work and Theology in Korea," *Journal of Feminist Studies in Religion* 3:2 (Fall 1987): 131. Shawn Copeland notes the questioning of God in the slave narrative of Harriet Jacobs and by Alice Walker's character Celie; she also traces the theodicy question as a strand within African American Christian thought. See her " 'Wading Through Many Sorrows,' " 120-21, 125 n. 5.

70. For example, Cheryl Kirk-Duggan notes a blend of humor and pathos in the spirituals and argues that "humor as ritual and comedy as myth become religious." See "African-American Spirituals: Confronting and Exorcising Evil Through Song," in *A Troubling in My Soul*, ed. Townes, 156-57.

71. Cf. Kathleen Sands, "Sacri-levity: Toward a Feminist Thealogy of Humor," unpublished paper presented at the American Academy of Religion, November 1993.

72. Sheila Greeve Davaney, "Problems with Feminist Theory: Historicity and the Search for Sure Foundations," in *Embodied Love: Sensuality and Relationship as Feminist Values*, ed. Paula Cooey, Sharon Farmer, and Mary Ellen Ross (San Francisco: Harper & Row, 1987), 79-95.

73. Frederick Jameson, *Postmodernism* (Durham, N.C.: Duke University Press, 1991).

74. Catherine Keller, "To Illuminate Your Trace: Self in Late Modern Feminist Theory," *Listening* 25:3 (Fall 1990): 212, 220. For other critical feminist responses to postmodernism, see *Feminism and Postmodernism*, ed. Linda Nicholson (New York: Routledge, 1990).

75. Chung, *Struggle to Be the Sun Again*, 43; " 'Han-pu-ri': Doing Theology from Korean Women's Perspective," in *We Dare to Dream: Doing Theology as Asian Women*, ed. Fabella and Park, 143.

CHAPTER 4
LILITH AND EVE: SISTERS IN STRUGGLE

1. Rosemary Radford Ruether, "Retrospective," *Religious Studies Review* 15:1 (January 1989): 2-3.

2. Carol P. Christ, "Rethinking Theology and Nature," in *Weaving the Visions: New Patterns in Feminist Spirituality*, ed. Judith Plaskow and Carol P. Christ (San Francisco: Harper & Row, 1989), 320-21.

3. Doris Lessing, *The Four-Gated City* (New York: New American Library, 1969), 419.

4. Interview of Carol Christ by Lene Sjørup in *A Time to Weep and a Time to Sing: Faith Journeys of Women Scholars of Religion*, ed. Mary Jo Meadows (Minneapolis: Winston Press, 1985), 109.

5. Carol P. Christ and Marilynn Collins, "Shattering the Idols of Men: Theology from the Perspective of Women," *Reflections* 69:4 (May 1972), 12-14; Christ, "Dialogues with God and Tradition," in *Laughter of Aphrodite: Reflections on a Journey to the Goddess* (San Francisco: Harper & Row, 1987), 7-8. For the characterization of herself among the feminist "revolutionaries" and Ruether as a radical among the "reformers," see Christ's "The New Feminist Theology: A Review of the Literature," *Religious Studies Review* 3:4 (October 1977): 203-11. In 1980 Christ referred to Rosemary Ruether as one of the feminists whose "brave and pioneering work" had made Christ's own work possible. See Christ's preface to the first edition of *Diving Deep and Surfacing: Women Writers on Spiritual Quest*, 2nd ed. (Boston: Beacon Press, 1986), xxxii.

For Ruether's theory of Christian anti-Semitism, see her *Faith and Fratricide* (New York: Seabury Press, 1974). Christ was also influenced by Gregory Baum's *Is the New Testament Anti-Semitic?* (Glen Rock: Paulist Press, 1965) and Richard Rubenstein's *After Auschwitz* (New York: Bobbs-Merrill, 1966).

6. Ruether, "A Religion for Women: Sources and Strategies," *Christianity and Crisis* 39:19 (December 1979), 307-11. Other postbiblical feminists Ruether has named in this and other critiques include Mary Daly, Naomi Goldenberg, Starhawk, and Z. Budapest.

7. Ruether, "Goddesses and Witches: Liberation and Countercultural Feminism," *Christian Century* 97:28 (September 1980), 842-47.

8. For example, Ruether has characterized self-absolutization or "the infallibility complex" as both "idolatry and demonic possession" ("Male

Chauvinist Theology and the Anger of Women," *Cross Currents* 21:2 [Spring 1971]: 183). Elsewhere, she referred to "the powers and principalities that are the perverse realizations of the stuff of our heavenly dreams" ("Paradoxes of Human Hope: The Messianic Horizon of Church and Society," *Theological Studies* 33:2 [June 1972]: 251). "The powers and principalities," she argues, "are still very much in control of most of the world" (*Sexism and God-Talk: Toward a Feminist Theology* [Boston: Beacon Press, 1983], 234). Feminism can say in Pauline language, "we 'do not struggle against flesh and blood but against powers and principalities' " ("Feminist Theology in the Academy," *Christianity and Crisis* 45:3 [March 1985]: 62). More recently, she has written that "appeal to ultimate dualisms of good and evil, God and Satan," exemplified by the Bush administration's rhetoric during the Gulf War, must be exposed as false. Still, she goes on to cite with apparent approval liberation theology's characterization of this kind of "state theology" as "idolatrous and demonic in nature" ("Witness to Hope in a Demonic World," *Sojourners* 20:7 [Aug.-Sept. 1991]: 22).

9. Ruether, "Goddesses and Witches," 846. Ruether deploys the same theological system as a critique of Goddess feminism in "Asking the Existential Questions," *Christian Century* 97:12 (April 1980), 374-78. See also her "Feminist Theology and Spirituality," in *Christian Feminism: Visions of a New Humanity,* ed. Judith Weidman (San Francisco: Harper & Row, 1984), 14. There she characterized biblical and Goddess feminism in terms of their respective "ethical" versus "aesthetic" orientations. For Goddess-aesthetic feminists, sin and evil are illusions, "foisted upon us by an antinatural civilization." Biblical-ethical feminists believe in natural harmony as a "symbol" for the ground and potential of human life, but see this harmony as broken in the world as we have it, "generating a massive historical counterreality, a system of evil relationships that divides all reality from its authentic potential." Her review of Starhawk's *Spiral Dance* was somewhat more positive; Ruether appreciated Starhawk's recommendation of social action in addition to changed consciousness. Nonetheless, she cited Starhawk's "inability to give an account of evil or alienation" as the book's main defect. See "The Way of Wicca," *Christian Century* 97:6 (February 1980): 208-9.

10. Christ's reply, which I cite here, appears in *Laughter of Aphrodite* under the title "A Spirituality for Women." Christ submitted this article to *Christianity and Crisis* as a reply to Ruether's two articles, "A Religion for Women" and "Goddesses and Witches." The journal first accepted the piece, she reports, but then refused to print it. Christ then published

the material in the form of two articles, "A Religion for Women," *Womanspirit* 7:25 (1980) and "Another Response to a Religion for Women," *Womanspirit* 6:24 (1980). See Christ, *Laughter of Aphrodite*, 14-15.

11. For further discussion of this point, see chapter 6 below, n. 70.

12. Christ, "Symbols of Goddess and God in Feminist Theology," reprinted in *Laughter of Aphrodite*, 135.

13. For Ruether's efforts to disentangle these two meanings of transcendence, see "Paradoxes."

14. Christ, "Symbols of Goddess and God," 148.

15. One exception to this tone was Ruether's 1972 article "Motherearth and the Megamachine: A Theology of Liberation in a Feminine, Somatic, and Ecological Perspective," *Christianity and Crisis* (April 1972): 267-72.

16. Christ, "Symbols of Goddess and God," 156-57.

17. Ruether, "Feminist Theology in the Academy," *Christianity and Crisis* 45:3 (March 1985), 57-62; also published as "The Future of Feminist Theology in the Academy," *Journal of the American Academy of Religion* 53:3 (Fall 1983), 703-13.

In fact, Ruether's construction of religious pluralism and religious exclusivism may contribute to the difficulty. In 1983 she wrote: "I have a great deal of sympathy with this option for Goddess feminism, as well as the communitarian and ecological values that are being expressed through it." However, she continued to object to those forms of Goddess feminism which become "a sectarian faith that declares that feminists must reject all biblical traditions and instead identify with a countermyth of the Goddess." See "Sexism, Religion and the Social and Spiritual Liberation of Women Today," in *Beyond Domination: New Perspectives on Women and Philosophy*, ed. Carol Gould (Totowa, N.J.: Rowman and Allanheld, 1983), 119-20; also Ruether and Daphne Hampson, "Is There a Place for Feminists in a Christian Church?" in *New Blackfriars* 68:801 (January 1987): 7-25.

A more nuanced discussion of the meaning of "rejecting" a religious tradition is in order. For although Ruether is certainly right in noting that simplistic and intolerant attitudes toward biblical religions exist in Goddess feminism, feminists ought not to be adjudged intolerant and exclusivist merely for rendering a considered judgment against the Bible or biblical religions. Otherwise the exit door from biblical religions is effectively shut. Moreover, the impression may be inadvertently created that Goddess themes and imagery can themselves be tolerated only as hitherto suppressed dimensions of biblical religion, not as parts of distinct traditions old and new.

18. For other references to Christa, see Ruether, "The Future of Feminist Theology in the Academy" (Fall 1985), which is a revised version of the article from the previous spring; also "Feminist Spirituality and Historical Religion: Renewal or New Creation?" *Harvard Divinity Bulletin* 16:3 (Feb.-March 1986), 5-7, 11 (which appeared as well in *Religion and Intellectual Life* 3:2 [Winter 1986], 7-20). Ruether's *Womanguides* includes a picture of the Christa with the caption, "The Crucified Woman: is she only a victim, or can women bring forth redemption from their sufferings on the cross of patriarchy?" (Boston: Beacon Press, 1985), 104.

Mary Hembrow Snyder finds the Christa image quite significant for Ruether's feminist Christology. For Ruether, "God continues to be revealed in 'other Christs,' particularly the 'Christa' or crucified woman." See Snyder, *The Christology of Rosemary Radford Ruether: A Critical Introduction* (Mystic, Conn.: Twenty-Third Publications, 1988), 108.

19. Christ, "Feminist Thealogy?" *Christianity and Crisis* 45:4 (April 1985), 161-62.

20. Ruether, "Female Symbols, Values and Context: Moving Beyond 'Who Killed the Goddess?' " *Christianity and Crisis* 46:19 (January 1987), 460-64. This article was a response to Christ's comments in a panel discussion at the Society of Biblical Literature in November 1985.

21. Ruether, "Female Symbols," 463.

22. Ibid., "Female Symbols," 463-64.

23. Christ and Ruether, Letters to the Editor, *Christianity and Crisis* 47:2 (Feb. 16, 1987): 55-56.

24. See Ruether, "Radical Victorians: The Quest for an Alternative Culture," in *Women and Religion in America: A Documentary History,* vol. 3, ed. R. Ruether and R. Keller (San Francisco: Harper & Row, 1986), 4-10.

25. Ruether, "Female Symbols," 460.

26. Christ, "Toward a Paradigm Shift in the Academy and in Religious Studies," in *The Impact of Feminist Research in the Academy,* ed. Christie Farnham (Bloomington: Indiana University Press, 1987), 71.

27. Christ, "Toward a Paradigm Shift," 72.

28. Ruether, *Gaia and God: An Ecofeminist Theology of Earth Healing* (San Francisco: Harper & Row, 1992), 143-72.

The theological polemic at work in this characterization is implicit in Ruether's choice of opponents; one would otherwise have expected more attention to the works of other Goddess feminists who have been deeply involved in Green politics and ecological activism, such as Charlene Spretnak, Margot Adler, or Starhawk.

29. Ruether, *Gaia and God*, 152-65.

30. Ibid., 163, 154.

31. Ibid., 154-55.

32. Christ, "Toward a Paradigm Shift," 62-63.

33. Vigorous debate on these questions has been going on for over a decade among Goddess feminists. See, for example, *The Politics of Women's Spirituality*, ed. Charlene Spretnak (Garden City, N.Y.: Anchor Books, 1982), 541-60.

34. See, for example, Mary Condren, *The Serpent and the Goddess: Women, Religion and Power in Celtic Ireland* (San Francisco: Harper & Row, 1989).

35. Ruether, *Gaia and God*, 165-72.

36. This was Ruether's reply to Charlene Spretnak's defense of Gimbutas at a session on *Gaia and God* at the American Academy of Religion, San Francisco, 1992. Spretnak had objected that Ruether had ignored major aspects of Gimbutas' and Sanday's theories, and that Ruether had failed to note the theoretical refinements that have placed most feminist theories of pre-patriarchal times well beyond the Romanticism Ruether continues to attribute to them.

CHAPTER 5:
RENATURING A FALLEN WORLD

1. Rosemary Radford Ruether, *Disputed Questions: On Being a Christian* (Nashville, Tenn.: Abingdon Press, 1982), 104-5.

2. Ruether, "Feminism and Religious Faith: Renewal or New Creation?" *Religion and Intellectual Life* 3:2 (Winter 1986): 16.

3. Ruether, *Sexism and God-Talk: Toward a Feminist Theology* (Boston: Beacon Press, 1983), 18.

4. Ruether, *Sexism and God-Talk*, 32.

5. Ruether, "Feminism and Religious Faith," 16.

6. Ruether, "What Is Shaping My Theology?" *Commonweal* 108:2 (January 1981): 46.

7. Ruether, "Sexism, Religion and the Social and Spiritual Liberation of Women Today," in *Beyond Domination: New Perspectives on Women and Philosophy*, ed. Carol Gould (Totowa, N.J.: Rowman and Allanheld, 1983), 108.

8. Ruether, *Gaia and God: An Ecofeminist Theology of Earth Healing* (San Francisco: Harper & Row, 1992), 141.

9. Ruether, *Gaia and God*, 255-56.

10. This association between evil and falsehood has spanned Ruether's theological career. See, for example, her description of the fall as an "alienation between humanity and God," concretized in "social alienation," which in turn "begins in self-alienation, experienced as an estrangement between the self and the body," in "Sexism and the Theology of Liberation: Nature, Fall and Salvation as Seen from the Experience of Women," *Christian Century* 90:45 (Dec. 12, 1973): 1224. She has characterized "evil" as "created being alienated from its relation to God," in "Christian Quest for Redemptive Community," *Cross Currents* 28:1 (Spring 1988): 10; injustice as a "false 'world'; an anti-society and anti-cosmos where man finds himself entrapped and alienated from his 'true home,'" in *Liberation Theology: Human Hope Confronts Christian History and American Power* (New York: Paulist Press, 1972), 8-9; patriarchal ideology as "the Big Lie," in *Sexism and God-Talk*, 264; patriarchal domination as founded on deceit, in *Gaia and God*, 115-201.

11. See, for example, Ruether, "Motherearth and the Megamachine: A Theology of Liberation in a Feminine, Somatic and Ecological Perspective," reprinted in *Womanspirit Rising*, eds. Carol P. Christ and Judith Plaskow (San Francisco: Harper & Row, 1979), 43-52; *Sexism and God-Talk*, 79-82; *Gaia and God*, 249-51.

12. "Ruether on Ruether" (Reply to Carter Heyward), *Christianity and Crisis* 39:8 (May 14, 1979): 126.

Ruether's critical focus on the problem of dualism, Heyward had suggested, seemed to presuppose that "In the beginning is the Idea." (See Heyward, "Ruether and Daly: Theologians Speaking and Sparking, Building and Burning," *Christianity and Crisis* 39:5 [April 1979]: 66-72.) Heyward was correct in a very important sense: consciousness for Ruether is clearly more than an epiphenomenon in relation to social structures. I would suggest, however, that it is consciousness as moral which for Ruether is more than epiphenomenal, while consciousness as ideological is not.

13. Ruether, *Liberation Theology*, 3.

14. Ruether, "Male Chauvinist Theology and the Anger of Women," *Cross Currents* 21:1 (Spring 1971): 181.

15. For example, these appear to be the grounds for Ruether's characterization of the ethic of competition as "false." See *Gaia and God*, 56.

16. Ruether, *The Church against Itself* (New York: Herder and Herder, 1968), 8.

17. Ruether, *Women-Church: Theology and Practice* (San Francisco: Harper & Row, 1985), 86-87.

18. For examples of this typology, see "Prophetic Tradition and the Liberation of Women: Promise and Betrayal," *Journal of Religion for Southern Africa* 73 (December 1990): 24-33; "Feminism and Patriarchal Religion: Principles of Ideological Critique of the Bible," *Journal for the Study of the Old Testament* 22 (1982): especially 55-56; "Feminist Interpretation: A Method of Correlation," in Letty Russell, ed., *Feminist Interpretation of the Bible* (Philadelphia: Westminster Press, 1985), 117-18. In the last cited article, she contends that there are in fact "two religions" in the Bible—that of the "sacred canopy" and that of the prophetic-messianic tradition.

19. Ruether has argued that "the great empires of classical society" all claimed to be founded on the cosmic order. Jewish and Christian messianism also believed that "God and the kingdom of man . . . should be in harmony and are intended to come together into an ultimate integration." In contrast to previous religious cultures, however, they "challenged the myth that this integration . . . already exists." See "Paradoxes of Human Hope: The Messianic Horizon of Church and Society," *Theological Studies* 33:2 (June 1972): 236. This has also been the drift of a number of her objections to Goddess feminism; see chapter 4 above.

20. Ruether, "Individual Repentance Is Not Enough," *Explor* 2:1 (Spring 1976): 47.

21. Ruether, "Feminism and Religious Faith," 9-10.

22. In "A Religion for Women: Sources and Strategies," *Christianity and Crisis* 39:19 (December 1979): 309, Ruether made this claim not only for religions but for "all significant works of culture." For reference to Marx in connection with her analysis of sacralism, see "Feminism and Religious Faith," 7.

23. Ruether, "Individual Repentance," 47.

24. Ruether, "Feminism and Religious Faith," 12; see also "The Development of My Theology," *Religious Studies Review* 15:1 (January 1989): 2, and "Recontextualizing Theology," *Theology Today* 43:1 (April 1986): 26.

25. Ruether, "Feminism and Patriarchal Religion," 62.

26. This is the thesis of *The Radical Kingdom: The Western Experience of Messianic Hope* (New York: Harper & Row, 1970). It has been repeated more recently. She has also suggested that feminism owes its historical lineage to biblical prophetism, though historically women have been betrayed by male-defined prophetic movements. See "Prophetic Tradition and the Liberation of Women," 24-33, "Recontextualizing Theology," 27, and "Feminism and Religious Faith," 13.

27. This dialectic also plays an important role in Ruether's definition of revelation; see *The Church against Itself*, 93.

28. Ruether, *The Church against Itself*, 3; *Contemporary Roman Catholicism: Crises and Challenges* (Kansas City, Mo.: Sheed and Ward, 1987), 64.

29. Ruether, *Sexism and God-Talk*, 161. For another statement supporting the feminist utility of "the biblical ideas of sin, the Fall and inherited evil," see "Sexism, Religion and the Social and Spiritual Liberation of Women Today," 121. Patriarchy, as she defined it in *Sexism and God-Talk*, includes "not only the subordination of females to males, but the whole structure of Father-ruled society: aristocracy over serfs, masters over slaves, king over subjects, racial overlords over colonized people" (61).

30. Ruether, "Sexism and Theology of Liberation," 1973.

31. Another problem bearing on the ontological status of evil is that of evil's systematicity. This shows up in Ruether's analysis of patriarchy, which she most often treats as an encompassing form of evil (see n. 29 above). For example, she has contended that "feminism attempts a comprehensive analysis of the systems of oppression that dehumanize us all and reaches for a comprehensive vision" of social change, and that patriarchy provides "the cultural, symbolic and psychological connections" among oppressions. See "Prophetic Tradition and the Liberation of Women," 31. From early on in her thought and continuing to the present, she has argued that sexism provides the symbolic template for every ideology of oppression, and that the oppression of women is "interstructured" within most other forms of domination. See *New Woman/New Earth:*

Sexist Ideologies and Human Liberation (New York: Seabury Press, 1983), 3-4.

On other occasions she has been more circumspect, calling patriarchy a "part of the systems of evil power." See "Christian Quest for Redemptive Community," 14. Although "the three alienations of race, sex and class" are interstructured, "I am not prepared to say that one is more basic than the others in any meaningful sociological sense"; therefore, "solving one alienation does not automatically solve the other two." See "Reply to Students at Union," *Christianity and Crisis* [June 24, 1974]: 142). She has also observed, as I have noted above, the many historical disjunctions among oppressions based on sex, race, and class. (See chapter 4, n. 20.)

Ruether's struggle with this conceptual problem reflects the dilemma of rationalistic and dualistic approaches to evil. The tendency to systematize, or even over-systematize, evil belongs to dualism and is echoed in the notion of the world as a fallen counterreality. Constructing various evils as part of a demonic system wins a strong theological warrant against them, but often at the cost of political and strategic intelligibility. No doubt this is partly why religious feminists for whom sexism is not the only or the worst oppression rarely share this encompassing view of patriarchy. This dualism, however, cannot be countered by a return to rationalism or its liberal progeny, because it is the assumption of a transcendent good which necessitates the hypothesis of a counterreality in the first place.

32. See, for example, Ruether, "Sexism and the Theology of Liberation," 1224, and n. 10 above; *New Woman/New Earth*, 4.

33. Ruether, "Paradoxes of Human Hope," 238-39.

34. Mostly, Ruether has used "nature" to refer to views of nature that are entangled with injustice. But prior to 1973, when she first sketched a feminist theology of the fall, this ideological suspicion had not matured into a full-blown critique of patriarchal "nature." On other occasions, the qualification around "nature" refers not to sin but to Ideal Being, reminding the reader that the meaning of Ideal Being cannot be fully known in a world of sin. See, for example, "Paradoxes of Human Hope," 249, where "man's unknown 'nature'" refers to human ideality. In *Gaia and God*, she is more explicit about her uses of "nature" and nature. "Nature" is now used to indicate that the term "is being used in a questionably static, unrelational or essentialist sense, or in contrast to 'grace'" (6). Interestingly, grace also appears in quotation marks here, implying perhaps that stasis and nonrelationality are not only inadequate notions of nature, but also inadequate notions of grace.

35. Ruether, "Male Chauvinist Theology," 184.

36. Ruether, "Paradoxes of Human Hope," 252.

37. Ruether, "Sexism and the Theology of Liberation," 1229.

38. Ruether, "Paradoxes of Human Hope," 249. More recently, in response to the dangers of sociobiological theories of the brain and gender, she has argued that only a nonpatriarchal culture "would give us a better sense of what our 'true' human nature and potential really is, as men and as women." See "Brain and Gender: The Missing Data," *Christian Century* 106:8 (March 8, 1989): 264.

39. Ruether, "The Biblical Vision of the Ecological Crisis," *Christian Century* 95:37 (November 1978): 1131-32.

40. Ruether, *To Change the World: Christology and Cultural Criticism* (New York: Crossroad, 1983), 68.

41. Ruether, "The Left Hand of God in the Theology of Karl Barth," *Journal of Religious Thought* 25:1 (1968-1969): 3-26. Other points of disagreement concerned Barth's paternalistic God, his disjunctive view of human works in relation to God's work, and his uncritical use of mythological language. This essay remains to date Ruether's most searching reflection on the problem of evil.

42. *To Change the World*; 66-70; *Sexism and God-Talk*, 85-86, 154.

43. *To Change the World*, 66-69; *Sexism and God-Talk*, 254.

44. *Sexism and God-Talk*, 266. In this work, Ruether singles out the fall as a dominant theological tradition that feminists can use (37-38) and returns to it often.

45. *Women-Church*, 102-4.

46. *Gaia and God*, 256, 31.

47. Ibid., 83. Both Platonism and Gnosticism are read this way in this book; Gnosticism is interpreted as exaggerated Platonism (122). Metaphysical dualism is also held responsible for the decline of Jewish prophetism into apocalypticism, which, "like Platonic eschatology, is based on the fantasy of escape from mortality" (83). I would suggest, on the contrary, that apocalypticism is primarily concerned with the escape from injustice, which when framed in absolutist terms becomes unimaginable under the conditions of finite existence. Taking Augustine at his word, Ruether assumes that he did indeed abandon Manichaean patterns of thought and attributes his sexual negativism to his Platonism rather than to his vestigial Manichaeanism (135). I have argued, on the contrary, that his worldview can be understood as a synthesis of Platonic and Manichaean themes.

48. Ibid., 83.

49. Ibid., 255-56, 4-5, 249.

50. "Is Feminism the End of Christianity? A Critique of Daphne Hampson's *Theology and Feminism*," *Scottish Journal of Theology* 43:3 (1990): 398-99.

51. For a description of Ruether's method as dialectical, see "Asking the Existential Questions," *Christian Century* 92:12 (April 1980): 377. The same method is described as historical in "The Development of My Theology," 2-3.

52. *Sexism and God-Talk*, 18-19; "Theology as Critique and Emancipation from Sexism," in *The Vocation of the Theologian*, ed. Theodore Jennings, Jr. (Philadelphia: Fortress Press, 1985), 28.

53. "Ruether on Ruether," 126.

54. Ruether's earliest explications of this dialectic were in the context of her critique of Christian theological anti-Semitism. Christianity, she argued, claimed for itself the messianic promise of the Hebrew Scriptures, while relegating to Jews God's wrathful judgment (*Faith and Fratricide: The Theological Roots of Anti-Semitism* [New York: Seabury, 1974]).

55. Ruether acknowledges that "there are indeed tribalistic triumphalism, sectarian rancour, justifications of slavery, and sexism in parts of scripture. The text then becomes a document of collective moral failure, rather than a prescriptive norm. These judgments are not foreign to scripture itself, because, at these points, one can also judge scripture by scripture." See *To Change the World*, 5.

56. Ruether, "Individual Repentance," 59, 61.

57. Ruether, "Recontextualizing Theology," 26.

58. Ruether, *Sexism and God-Talk*, 22. In an article of the same period she wrote: "The normative traditions of biblical faith are those which criticize patriarchy. Moreover, this norm for the critique of patriarchy is not an accidental or marginal principle found in a few scattered texts but rather derives from the central and critical norms biblical religion applies to itself within its own context." See "Feminism and Patriarchal Religion," 55.

59. Ruether, "Feminist Interpretation," 117-18.

60. Ibid., 117.

61. Ruether, "Feminism and Religious Faith," 13.

62. Tony Clarke-Sayer, "The Bible and the Religious Left: An Interview with Rosemary Radford Ruether," *The Witness* 66:3 (March 1983): 8, 10. See also "Feminism and Religious Faith," 13-14.

63. Ruether, "Recontextualizing Theology," 27.

64. Ruether, "Feminist Interpretation," 111-17.

65. Ruether, "Theology as Critique and Emancipation from Sexism," 28.

66. Ruether, *Womanguides: Readings Toward a Feminist Theology* (Boston: Beacon Press, 1985), ix-x. A year later she wrote: "Certainly, for me, the biblical liberation tradition is essential to my feminist (and not just my Christian) identity" ("Recontextualizing Theology," 26).

67. Ruether, *Women-Church*, 135-40; "Recontextualizing Theology," 22-27.

68. Ruether, "Recontextualizing Theology," 27.

69. Ruether, *Womanguides*, 105.

70. Ruether, "Christianity," in *Women and World Religions*, ed. Arvind Sharma (New York: SUNY Press, 1987) 214-15; *To Change the World*, 26, 39-42, 45-49.

71. Ruether, *Sexism and God-Talk*, 138.

72. Ruether, *Womanguides*; "The Liberation of Christology from Patriarchy," *Religion and Intellectual Life* 2:3 (Spring 1985): 116-28.

73. Ruether, *Womanguides*, 109.

74. Ruether, *Sexism and God-Talk*, 119-22, 134-38; *To Change the World*, 53-56.

75. Ruether, "An Invitation to Jewish-Christian Dialogue," *The Ecumenist* 10:2 (Jan.-Feb. 1972): 22.

76. Ruether, *Sexism and God-Talk*, 136-37, 152-56, 127-34.

77. Ibid., 127-34.

78. Ruether, "Lecture I: Sexism and God Talk," *Bethany Seminary Bulletin* (1977): 56.

79. Ruether, *To Change the World*, 35.

80. Ruether, *Sexism and God-Talk*, 1-11; "Sexism and God-Talk: Two Models of Relation," in *Process in Relationship: Issues in Theology, Philosophy and Religious Education*, ed. Iris Cully and Kendig Brubaker Cully (Birmingham, Ala.: Religious Education Press, Inc.: 1978), 75-81.

Kathryn Allen Rabuzzi also sees kenosis as a central theme in Ruether's theology. See "The Socialist Feminist Vision of Rosemary Radford Ruether: A Challenge to Liberal Feminism," in *Religious Studies Review* 15:1 (January 1989): 7.

81. Ruether, *To Change the World*, 54. In the same text she also argues that the imitation of Christ must avoid two temptations: to absolutize revolutionary victory so that the formerly oppressed become oppressors, and to "prefer failure and death rather than risk real efficacy" (30).

82. On at least one occasion, Ruether has strongly repudiated the ethic of the suffering servant when employed as an argument against legitimate self-defense or against the necessary violence of a just revolution. See Ruether, "Reader's Response: The Suffering Servant Myth," *Worldview* 17:3 (March 1974): 45-46.

83. Ruether, *Sexism and God-Talk*, 9.

84. Ruether, "The Development of My Theology," 4.

85. Ruether, "Robert Palmer: First the God, Then the Dance," *Christian Century* 107:5 (Feb. 7-14, 1990): 125-26. For another discussion of Palmer, and of Ruether's educational career, see *Disputed Questions*, 25-29.

86. Ruether, *Liberation Theology*, 3.

87. Besides Ruether's repudiation of romantic idealizations of women, perhaps the strongest example of this mixture of solidarity and moral realism are her treatments of Israel and of anti-Semitism. Despite her detailed analyses of the long historical and theological traditions of Christian anti-Semitism, and despite her refusal to apply the ideals of Christian pacifism to Israel, she has also been severely critical of Israel in its relation to the Palestinian people. For her analysis of Christian anti-Semitism, see *Faith and Fratricide*. For her objections to forcing Christian pacifism on Israel, see "The Suffering Servant Myth." For critical analyses of Christian "philo-Semitism" and Christian Zionism, see "Christian Zionism Is a Heresy," *Journal of Theology for Southern Africa* 69 (December 1989): 60-64, and "Jewish-Christian Relations in the Theology of Paul Van Buren," *Religious Studies Review* 16:4 (October 1990): 320-23. For critiques of Israeli policy toward Palestinians, see Ruether and Marc Ellis, *Beyond Occupation: American Jewish, Christian and Palestinian Voices for Peace* (Boston: Beacon Press, 1990); Rosemary Radford Ruether and Herman Ruether, *The Wrath of Jonah: The Crisis of Religious Nationalism in the Israeli-Palestinian Conflict* (San Francisco: Harper & Row, 1989).

88. Ruether, "Sexism and the Theology of Liberation," 1228. See also *To Change the World*, 22. In both cases, Ruether wanted to avoid both the

absolutizing of any particular social order as well as the relativizing of morally significant differences among social orders.

89. Ruether, "The Future of Feminist Theology in the Academy," *Journal of the American Academy of Religion* 53:3 (Fall 1985): 710. Rebecca S. Chopp also notes that Ruether's method relies on an ahistorical kind of truth, which Chopp perceives as a vestige of Enlightenment humanism. In Chopp's view, this represents a contradiction between Ruether's theological method and her religious vision. See Rebecca S. Chopp, "Seeing and Naming the World Anew: The Works of Rosemary Radford Ruether," *Religious Studies Review* 15:1 (January 1989): 8-11.

90. Ruether, "Feminist Theology in the Academy," *Christianity and Crisis* 45:3 (March 1985): 61 (also published as "The Future of Feminist Theology in the Academy"; see n. 88 above; *Sexism and God-Talk*, 19-20.

91. Beverly Wildung Harrison made a similar point in her justly famous piece "The Power of Anger in the Work of Love," reprinted in *Weaving the Visions: New Patterns in Feminist Spirituality*, ed. Judith Plaskow and Carol P. Christ (San Francisco: Harper & Row, 1989), 214-25.

92. Elie Wiesel has developed this type of reflective spirituality in the context of Jewish post-Holocaust thought. Some scholars have made strong arguments for the presence of a tragic sensibility in the Hebrew Scriptures. See, for example, W. Lee Humphreys, *The Tragic Vision and the Hebrew Tradition* (Philadelphia: Fortress Press, 1985), and J. Cheryl Exum, *Tragedy and the Biblical Narrative: Arrows of the Almighty* (Cambridge, England: Cambridge University Press, 1992).

CHAPTER 6:
A DESIRING NATURE

1. Elie Wiesel, *The Gates of the Forest*, trans. Frances Frenaye (New York: Schocken Books, 1989, 3.

2. Carol P. Christ, *Laughter of Aphrodite: Reflections on a Journey to the Goddess* (San Francisco: Harper & Row, 1987), 6.

3. Doris Lessing, *The Four-Gated City* (New York: New American Library, 1969), 395.

4. Ibid., 394-95, 484, 419, 471.

5. Ibid., 227.

6. Christ, *Diving Deep and Surfacing: Women Writers on Spiritual Quest* (Boston: Beacon Press, 1980; 2nd ed., 1986), 60, xxviii. Christ's earliest work on Lessing was "Explorations with Doris Lessing in Quest of the Four-Gated City," in *Women in Religion*, rev. ed., ed. Judith Plaskow and Joan Arnold Romero (Atlanta: AAR and Scholars' Press, 1974), 31-61.

7. Christ, "Spiritual Quest and Women's Experience," *Anima* 1:2 (Spring 1975): 4-5.

8. Christ, "Feminist Studies in Religion and Literature: A Methodological Reflection," *Journal of the American Academy of Religion* 44:2 (1976): 320.

9. This is best articulated in Christ's more recent work, for example, "Rethinking Theology and Nature," in *Weaving the Visions: New Patterns in Feminist Spirituality*, ed. Judith Plaskow and Carol Christ (San Francisco: Harper & Row, 1989), 314-25.

10. Christ, "Feminist Studies," 321-25.

11. Christ, *Diving Deep*, 15-18.

12. Ibid., 18.

13. Ibid., 20-23. The terms "unity" and "integration" were Christ's corrections of James's term "passivity," which seemed to her imprecise in relation to women's mysticism.

14. Christ, "Spiritual Quest," 5; *Diving Deep*, 23-26.

15. Christ, *Diving Deep*, xiii-xiv.

16. Lessing, *The Four-Gated City*, quoted by Christ in *Diving Deep*, 59.

17. Christ, "Explorations," 53-54; "Spiritual Quest," 15.

18. Christ, *Diving Deep*, 49, 51, 58, 65, 47, 43-44.

19. Christ, "Spiritual Quest," 15; "Explorations," 56.

20. Christ, *Diving Deep*, 73.

21. Ibid., 52, 51.

22. Christ, "Margaret Atwood: The Surfacing of Women's Spiritual Quest and Vision," *Signs* 2:2 (Winter 1976): 317.

23. Christ, "Spiritual Quest," 4.

24. Christ, *Diving Deep*, 97, 98, 99, 113, 117.

25. Ibid., 96, 76, 90, 86, 101, 89, 93, 94.

26. Ibid., xxxi, 92, 84.

27. Ibid., 61.

28. See Susan Thistlethwaite, *Sex, Race and God: Christian Feminism in Black and White* (New York: Crossroad, 1989), 44, 86. See also the exchange of letters between Christ and Thistlethwaite in *Christianity and Crisis* 47:13 (Sept. 28, 1987): 320.

29. Christ, *Diving Deep*, 28, 29, 35, 34, 33, 39.

30. Ibid., 47.

31. Sandra Gilbert and Susan Gubar also read this novel in an instructive way. They parallel Christ in casting Edna as a kind of failed Goddess. For them Edna is Aphrodite and the novel is an imaginative exploration of what would have happened to Aphrodite had she been incarnated in a nineteenth-century woman. In their view, *The Awakening* is not only a grafting of personalities but also of genres—social realism and mythic fantasy. The graft, however, cannot take, nor the myth become real, due to the limitations of the social context. See "The Second Coming of Aphrodite: Kate Chopin's Fantasy of Desire," in Gilbert and Gubar, *No Man's Land: The Place of the Woman Writer in the Twentieth Century*, vol. 2, *Sexchanges* (New Haven: Yale University Press, 1989), 83-122.

32. Chopin, *The Awakening* (New York: New American Library, 1976), 119, 90.

33. Christ, "Spiritual Quest," 6.

34. I am indebted on this point to Christ's response to an earlier draft of this work. Personal correspondence, September 5, 1990.

35. Ann-Janine Morey has observed the continued marginalization of Christ's *Diving Deep* and of women's literature generally within andro-centric religious studies. The reason for that marginalization, she argues, is that women's writings realize the ontological and linguistic challenges that androcentric postmodernism only feigns. At the same time, it should be noticed, in attending to the questions of difference as framed by postmodernism, Morey and others advance religious reflection on wom-en's literature in precisely the ways most necessary to the intellectual and political credibility of the field. See Morey, "Margaret Atwood and Toni Morrison: Reflections on Postmodernism and the Study of Religion and Literature," *Journal of the American Academy of Religion* 60:3 (Fall 1992): 493-513.

36. Christ, personal correspondence, September 1990.

37. Christ, *Laughter of Aphrodite*, 6, 11, 21.

38. Christ, "Yahweh as Holy Warrior," 73-92; "Heretics and Outsiders," 35-54; "A Spirituality for Women," 57-71, especially 62-63; all in *Laughter of Aphrodite.*

39. Christ, "Yahweh as Holy Warrior" and "A Spirituality for Women" in *Laughter of Aphrodite,* 75, 63.

40. Christ, "Symbols," in *Laughter of Aphrodite,* 135-60. In an earlier phase of her journey, however, Christ also conceived "the true God in her/his primordial nature both as male and female, neither female nor male" ("Women's Liberation and the Liberation of God," first published in 1976, reprinted in *Laughter of Aphrodite,* 22).

41. Christ, "Finitude, Death and Reverence for Life," in *Laughter of Aphrodite,* 216-26, and "Rethinking Theology and Nature."

42. Sarah B. Pomeroy, *Goddesses, Whores, Wives and Slaves: Women in Classical Antiquity* (New York: Schocken Books, 1975), 9.

43. Christ, "Reflections on the Initiation of an American Woman Scholar into the Symbols and Rituals of the Goddess," *Journal of Feminist Studies in Religion* 3:1 (Spring 1987): 59.

44. Christ, "Reclaiming Goddess History," in *Laughter of Aphrodite,* 161-82, especially 173; "In Praise of Aphrodite," in *Sacred Dimensions of Women's Experience,* ed. Elizabeth Dodson Gray (Wellesley, Mass.: Roundtable Press, 1988), 220-27; "Virgin Goddesses," in *The Encyclopedia of Religion,* vol. 15, ed. Mircea Eliade (New York: Macmillan, 1987), 276-79.

45. Christ, "Virgin Goddesses," 276; "Lady of Animals," in *The Encyclopedia of Religion,* vol. 8, 419-22; "Reclaiming Goddess History," 167.

46. Christ, "Toward a Paradigm Shift in the Academy and in Religious Studies," in *The Impact of Feminist Research in the Academy,* ed. Christie Farnham (Bloomington: Indiana University Press, 1987), 53-76; "Reclaiming Goddess History," 167.

47. Christ, *Laughter of Aphrodite,* xi.

48. Christ, "Rethinking Theology and Nature," 315; "Finitude, Death and Reverence for Life," 216.

49. On women's wills, see Christ, "Why Women Need the Goddess," in *Laughter of Aphrodite* 128; on confirmation, see "The Sources of My Thealogy," *Journal of Feminist Studies in Religion* 1:1 (Spring 1985): 122; on encounter with other viewpoints, see comments on empathy in "Toward a Paradigm Shift," 60.

50. Christ, "Rethinking Theology and Nature," 319.

51. Christ, "Journey to the Goddess," in *Laughter of Aphrodite*, 109.

52. Christ, "Why Women Need the Goddess," 122-23; "Journey to the Goddess," 110.

53. Wiesel, *The Gates of the Forest*; Christ, "Reflections on the Initiation," 57; "Laughter of Aphrodite," in *Laughter of Aphrodite*, 183.

54. Christ, "Reflections on the Initiation," 62. She also mentioned Rosemary Ruether as the popularizer of this view within religious studies.

55. Christ, "Mircea Eliade and the Feminist Paradigm Shift," in *Journal of Feminist Studies in Religion* 7:2 (Fall 1991): 75-94.

56. Christ, "Mircea Eliade," 75.

57. See Thomas Kuhn, *The Structure of Scientific Revolutions*, 2nd ed. (International Encyclopedia of Unified Science 2:2; Chicago: University of Chicago Press, 1970).

58. Christ, "Toward a Paradigm Shift," 57.

59. Cited in Christ, "Toward a Paradigm Shift," 58, 65.

60. Christ, "The Sources of My Thealogy," 123.

61. Christ, "Toward a Paradigm Shift," 61.

62. Christ, "Rethinking Theology and Nature," 319; "Finitude, Death, and Reverence for Life," 215.

63. Christ, "In Praise of Aphrodite," 220-23.

64. Christ, "Toward a Paradigm Shift," 72.

65. Christ, "Toward a Paradigm Shift," 59; "In Praise of Aphrodite," 221. Lorde's essay appears in *Sister Outsider: Essays and Speeches* (Freedom, Calif.: Crossing Press, 1984), 53-59.

66. Christ, "In Praise of Aphrodite," 224-25.

67. Christ, "Embodied Thinking," *Journal of Feminist Studies in Religion* 5:1 (Spring 1989): 13-14.

68. This interpretation, though widely accepted, is not beyond debate. Martha Nussbaum reads the *Symposium* as pointing to the disjunction between eros and philosophy and as urging a *tragic* choice in favor of philosophy; by the *Phaedrus*, she believes, Plato's position has grown into an *apologia* for eros as a divine and illuminating madness. See *The Fragility of Goodness: Luck and Ethics in Greek Tragedy and Philosophy* (Cambridge, England: Cambridge University Press, 1986), 165-233.

69. Christ, "Mircea Eliade," 76.

70. Christ argues that the Jungian feminine, derived from myths and literature produced by males, is at most "a secondary and compensatory aspect of the male psyche." Women's *self-experience*, on the other hand, can only be known by the study of women's own imaginations and lives. See "Some Comments on Jung, Jungians and the Study of Women," *Anima* 3:2 (Spring 1977): 66-69.

71. Cf. Linda Hutcheon, *The Politics of Postmodernism* (New York: Routledge, 1989), 13-14.

72. Christ, "Embodied Thinking," 15.

73. Christ, too, has been troubled by this, trying to distinguish the Goddess from "what patriarchal splitting has called 'the natural world' (as if there were any other)." See "Embodied Thinking," 14.

74. Christ, "Toward a Paradigm Shift," 71.

75. This is the title of an important paper presented by Christ in 1977, and reprinted in *Laughter of Aphrodite*, 117-34.

76. Cf. Christ, *Diving Deep*, preface to the first edition; Christ and Plaskow, *Womanspirit Rising: A Feminist Reader in Religion* (San Francisco: Harper & Row, 1979), Preface.

77. Christ, *Laughter of Aphrodite*, 193.

78. Judith Butler, *Gender Trouble: Feminism and the Subversion of Identity* (New York: Routledge, 1990).

79. Adrienne Rich, "Transcendental Etude," in *Dream of a Common Language* (New York: Norton and Company, 1978), 77.

CHAPTER 7:
A WORLD OF COLOR

1. Toni Morrison, *Beloved* (New York: New American Library, 1987), 201.

2. Linda Brown Bragg also comments on the significance of red in *Beloved*. See her review in *Religion and Intellectual Life* 5:3 (Spring 1988): 117-20.

3. Morrison, *Beloved*, 273.

4. Ibid., 180.

5. Ibid., 89, 179.

6. See Ann-Janine Morey, "Toni Morrison and the Color of Life," *Christian Century* 105:34 (Nov. 16, 1988) 1039-42.

7. Morrison, *Beloved*, 87, 104.

8. Delores S. Williams, *Sisters in the Wilderness: The Challenge of Womanist God-Talk* (Maryknoll, N.Y.: Orbis Books, 1993), 88.

9. Morrison herself provides an incisive analysis of the reflexive persona that white writers impose upon their black characters. See *Playing in the Dark* (Cambridge: Harvard University Press, 1993).

10. See, for example, Katie G. Cannon, *Black Womanist Ethics* (Atlanta: Scholars Press, 1988); Sharon D. Welch, *A Feminist Ethic of Risk* (Minneapolis: Fortress Press, 1990); Emily Erwin Culpepper, "New Tools for Theology: Writings by Women of Color," *Journal of Feminist Studies in Religion* 4:2 (Fall 1988): 39-50; Ann-Janine Morey, "Margaret Atwood and Toni Morrison: Reflections on Post-Modernism and the Study of Religion and Literature," *Journal of the American Academy of Religion* 60:3 (Fall 1992): 493-513; Trudy Bloser Bush, "Transforming Vision: Alice Walker and Zora Neale Hurston," *Christian Century* 105:34 (Nov. 16, 1988): 1035-39.

11. Morrison, *Beloved*, 177.

12. Ibid., 220.

13. See Welch, *A Feminist Ethic*, 116-22.

14. Morrison, *Beloved*, 79.

15. Ibid., 163.

16. Ibid., 188.

17. See Terri Otten, *The Crime of Innocence in the Fiction of Toni Morrison* (Columbia, Mo.: University of Missouri Press, 1989), 81-98.

18. Gerda Lerner, ed., *Black Women in White America: A Documentary History* (New York: Vintage Books, 1973), 60-63.

19. Morrison, *Beloved*, 108, 6, 112-13.

20. Ibid., 88.

21. Ibid., 164-65.

22. Ibid., 258-59.

23. Dorothy Allison, *Bastard Out of Carolina* (New York: Penguin Books, 1992), 293.

24. Ibid., 293, 203.

25. Ibid., 26.

26. Ibid., 1.

27. Ibid., 12, 23, 20-21.

28. Ibid., 37, 12, 123, 70.

29. Ibid., 51.

30. Ibid., 109.

31. Ibid., 234, 107, 114.

32. Ibid., 32, 104.

33. Ibid., 136.

34. Ibid., 166, 201.

35. Ibid., 93.

36. Ibid., 84, 91, 206.

37. Ibid., 273-74, 263.

38. Ibid., 63, 112, 253-54, 258.

39. Ibid., 276, 294, 301.

40. Ibid., 307.

41. Ibid., 309.

42. Louise Erdrich, *Love Medicine* (New York: Harper Collins, 1993), 195, 166. (First published in 1984 by Holt, Rinehart and Winston, New York).

43. Ibid., 272.

44. Ibid., 32.

45. Louise Erdrich, *The Beet Queen* (New York: Henry Holt, 1986); *Tracks* (New York: Henry Holt, 1988).

46. Sophocles, *The Trachinian Women* in *The Complete Plays of Sophocles*, ed. Moses Hadas (New York: Bantam Books, 1967); Aristophanes, *The Birds* and *The Frogs* in *The Complete Plays of Aristophanes*, ed. Moses Hadas (New York: Bantam Books, 1962).

47. Erdrich, *Love Medicine*, 89, 90.

48. Ibid., 91, 92, 104.

49. Ibid., 109.

50. Ibid., 53, 97, 58, 75.

51. Ibid., 45, 118.

52. Ibid., 14-15.

53. Cf. Luke 5:23; Mark 2:9; Matt. 9:6.

54. Erdrich, *Love Medicine*, 54, 128.

55. Ibid., 217.

56. Ibid., 220. In *Tracks*, the corpse is that of Marie's father.

57. Ibid., 217, 221.

58. Ibid., 222, 229, 231, 230.

59. Ibid., 235, 236.

60. Ibid., 241.

61. Sharon Manybeads Bowers suggests that the name Nanapush is a reference to Nanabozho, a Chippewa trickster hero. See her essay "Louise Erdrich as Nanapush," in *Women and Comedy*, ed. Regina Barreca, vol. 5 of *Studies in Gender and Culture* (Philadelphia: Gordon and Breach, 1992), 135-42.

62. Erdrich, *Love Medicine*, 203, 211.

63. Marilynne Robinson, *Housekeeping* (New York: Bantam Books, 1980), 153.

64. Ibid., 154.

65. Ibid., 51.

66. Ibid., 7.

67. Ibid., 193.

68. Ibid., 73, 192-93, 63, 5.

69. Ibid., 6, 12, 24.

70. Ibid., 156.

71. Ibid., 64, 48, 94, 49, 85, 82, 182, 185.

72. Ibid., 42, 192, 100, 196, 124, 140.

73. Ibid., 97, 122, 92, 198, 194.

74. Ibid., 194.

75. Ibid., 145, 157, 159.

76. Ibid., 178, 177, 184, 178.

77. Ibid., 185, 200, 214.

78. Ibid., 219.

INDEX